YEADON'S REGISTER

of

L N E R

LOCOMOTIVES

Volume Forty-Nine Part A

Classes N4, N5 & N6

ISBN 978-1-907094-55-2

YEADON'S REGISTER OF L.N.E.R. LOCOMOTIVES - VOLUME 49A

EDITORS NOTE AND ACKNOWLEDGEMENTS

Welcome to *Yeadon's Register of LNER Locomotives* Volume 49A which covers the three 0-6-2T classes originating from the Great Central Railway.
This volume reverts to the 96 page format to give everyone a break from the larger volumes which have prevailed of late. However, 49B will bring together all the rest of the N classes, some nine in all, of which there are some big classes involved. Therefore another large volume is promised.
As usual Eric Fry is to be thanked for his huge contribution both in his time and his knowledge of all things concerning LNER locomotives. Now that we are getting towards the end of the series a feeling of completeness is creeping upon us all but we are nevertheless keeping vigilant and on the look out for any minor blemishes which might spoil the finished product.
Judy Burg and her staff at the newly opened Hull History Centre are to be thanked for their continuing help and assistance in bringing this series to its inevitable conclusion. For anyone interested in railway, shipping or local history the HHC is worth a visit, its archive is rather grand and full of surprises.
Our photographic contributors have again provided a superb collection to illustrate this volume and we must thank them too, and although many are no longer with us, those that are realise the importance of their continued support. Our printers have not been mentioned of late but they know how much we appreciate the professionalism of their approach and dogged insistence to create each volume just right!
In Canada, Jean and Simon must realise that the postman will not be bearing those parcels from Nottingham for much longer but they hopefuly will have realised the waiting has been worth it.

Finally, thanks to all you readers for your patience and determination to stick with us to the end.

Volume 49B will cover classes N8, N9, N10, N11, N12, N13, N14, N15 & N18.

The catalogue reference for the locomotives featured in this volume are as follows:
DYE 1/58; DYE 1/108; DYE 2/7; DYE 2/17; DYE 2/19.

The Yeadon Collection is available for inspection and anyone who wishes to inspect it should contact -
Hull History Centre
Worship Street
Freetown Way
Hull
HU2 8BG
A catalogue of the Yeadon Collection is available.

First published in the United Kingdom by
BOOK LAW PUBLICATIONS 2010 in association with Challenger
382 Carlton Hill, Nottingham, NG4 1JA
Printed and bound by The Amadeus Press, Cleckheaton, West Yorkshire.

INTRODUCTION

Class N4

At the close of 1889 Thomas Parker introduced the first three engines of what was to become his standard 0-6-2 tank design on the Manchester, Sheffield & Lincolnshire Railway. Classified 9A they had the same size chassis as his initial six 0-6-0 tender engines (LNER Class J13) built earlier in the year, except for having 5ft 1in. instead of 4ft 10in. diameter coupled wheels. Joy valve gear was employed and the boiler, common to both classes, had a round top firebox. During 1890-92 fifty-two more of these 0-6-2Ts were built, three more by Gorton and the remainder by Neilson & Co., the final fourteen of which differed in having a 6in. longer bunker.

The design was updated in 1891 to reflect Parker's current thinking in that a change to Stephenson link motion was made together with the experimental adoption of a Belpaire firebox, the first such use in the United Kingdom. Following extended trials with the initial engine; one hundred and thirty more were turned out, the last of them in 1901. The updated design became Class N5 on the LNER.

Incidentally, LNER Class J9 was the 0-6-0 tender version of Class N4 and J10 of Class N5, all having 5ft 1in. coupled wheels.

The 0-6-2Ts proved to be very useful for both shunting and short distance goods work. In later days Class N5 also became prominent on passenger duties.

When the boilers on the N4 engines wore out they were replaced with the Belpaire firebox version, known at Gorton as the No.1 Standard and used on many other engine classes. On Class N4 fitting of these began in November 1908 and the final three engines were not done until after Grouping, the last (No.5610) in December 1928. The valve gear was left unchanged.

As was Gorton practice at the time of building, the whole class were equipped with vacuum ejectors for both engine and train braking.

At Grouping the class was divided into two class parts, 1 with short bunkers and 2 with the longer type. Fitting of shorter chimneys, which brought the class within the Composite Load Gauge, commenced in October 1925 and in December 1927 this was recognised by altering the sub classification as follows:-

N4/1 Short bunker. Outside LNER gauge.
N4/2 Short bunker. Within LNER gauge.
N4/3 Long bunker. Outside LNER gauge.
N4/4 long bunker. Within LNER gauge.

Eight N4/1 engines never became N4/2 because they still retained their Robinson chimneys when withdrawn during 1932-33. The last N4 to receive a short chimney was No.5623 in August 1936, but the class parts 2 and 4 continued in use up to the extinction of the class.

An unusual feature was the open well in the top of the right hand side tank immediately in front of the cab. This is plainly evident if you look at the run of the rivets (compare this with the left hand tank side where no well exists). The purpose of this well was to accommodate the forward extension of the linkage from the screw reverse mounted on top of the water tank within the cab. Classes F1, F2 and N5 had a similar arrangement.

The first three engines (built 1889/90) were numbered 161, 165 and 173 but became 512, 513 and 514 in 1893. Numbers 601, 602 and 603 followed from Gorton in 1891 and 604 to 638 from Neilson & Co. during 1890-91. The final fourteen, Nos.712 to 725, which were 6 inches longer at the rear end, were built by Neilson's in 1892.

Under the Thompson 1943 renumbering scheme the twenty-four surviving N4s were allotted numbers 9225 to 9248 and all except No.5725 (due to become 9248) received their new numbers when the scheme was put into effect three years later.

As mentioned earlier, the N4 class engines became very useful shunting engines and also excelled in short trip working between industrial premises and concentration yards. Perhaps for this reason the majority of the class spent all of their lives working amongst the collieries and steel works in the areas surrounding Sheffield. Just before Grouping they were allocated to three sheds in the Sheffield area Neepsend, Mexborough and Staveley. Barnsley had previously housed a number of them and was to do so again when the LNER came into being. However, from 1921 to 1936 various comings and goings saw single members of the class spending time at numerous other sheds mainly on the eastern side of the Pennines although No.5513 had time at Gorton before moving back east over Woodhead. One engine got as far south as Leicester whilst another went to Immingham. Before the outbreak of hostilities in September 1939, the class was once again concentrated in and around Sheffield with Barnsley gaining a dozen of them at the expense of Mexborough. In April 1943 the cramped depot at Neepsend was closed and its entire allocation transferred to a brand new shed at Darnall. The post-war allocations changed slightly in that Mexborough got four of the class but by 1950 the survivors were all at Darnall from which depot they worked to withdrawal.

Although withdrawals started in 1932, wartime requirements curtailed this and there were still twenty-two of the class in service at nationalisation in 1948. Class N4 became extinct at the end of 1954.

Class N5

Class N5 was developed by Parker from his earlier 1889 design which became N4 on the LNER. The first one, No.7 (later 515), was turned out from Gorton in September 1891 and differed principally in having Stephenson in place of Joy valve gear and a boiler, although of the same size, which had a Belpaire firebox. This latter feature was adopted on the recommendation of the Chief Draughtsman at Gorton who had been employed previously by the neighbouring firm of Beyer, Peacock. It was the first use of a Belpaire firebox by a British railway company despite the fact that Beyer, Peacock had built engines incorporating this design of boiler for overseas railways for nearly twenty years.

Parker took nearly a year to evaluate his new design before further construction took place and the other two engines of the initial order were built. Large scale production of the class began in 1893 and, by 1901, some one hundred and thirty-one had been built. The production series had a slight modification made to the layout of the valve gear. They were separately classified 9F, the original three being 9C. All were constructed at either Gorton or by Beyer, Peacock and the later engines were delivered under the regimes of Parker's successors, Pollitt and Robinson.

Two of the class, Nos.754 and 755 built by Beyer Peacock in 1894, were sold during the following year to the West Lancashire Railway where they became Nos.8 and 9 and were repainted in purple livery! The WLR was absorbed by the Lancashire & Yorkshire Railway in July 1897 whereupon they were renumbered again to 1368 and 1369, and were scrapped in January 1914. The original numbers 754 and 755 were re-used in 1896 by the MS&LR for engines of the same class.

Another two 9F engines had been delivered direct in 1896 to the Wrexham, Mold & Connahs Quay Railway and took their numbers 17 and 18. When that railway was taken over by the GCR in 1905 they became numbers 409 and 410, thus making up the total to 129 members of the class passed to the LNER in 1923.

It may be mentioned that at the same time that the WM&CQR purchased Nos.17 and 18, they hired three more of the class from the MS&LR and renumbered them 19, 20 and 21. They were returned to the GCR (as the MS&LR had become) in 1901, and took back their old numbers 754, 755 and 756. It will be seen that, confusingly, the first two of these numbers had been borne earlier by the pair of engines sold to the WLR mentioned above.

Under LNER ownership only eight were withdrawn, starting in 1936, so that 121 were taken over by British Railways. Most of these remained in service until 1955 and the last survivors were condemned in 1960.

As already mentioned, the initial three engines had a valve gear arrangement that differed from all those built subsequently, the latter also having larger coupled axlebox journals. Engines built prior to December 1895 had bunkers in which the top of the backs curved outwards. Starting with No.756 the curve was eliminated, except that curiously on Nos.51, 173 and 189 – built in 1898 at Gorton – reversion was made to the original pattern, although No.251 built at the same time had a straight back bunker.

Modifications were made to the tube arrangement of the boilers down the years. The 1910 version was adopted as the Standard No.1 type and, as already mentioned, was used on many other GCR classes. The reboilering of Class N5 with this type had largely been completed by 1924 although No.5904 carried the earlier version until December 1932 and is believed to have been the last N5 to do so.

Several No.1 boilers were fitted with superheaters and ten of them found use on N5 class, Nos.127, 200, 410, 521, 530, 539, 544 and 771 in 1915-16, followed by Nos.518 and 763 early in 1923. No.5410 went to the scrap yard in 1936 still with superheater, but the other nine reverted to saturated boilers from 1925 onwards, the last to be superheated being No.5518 to June 1943.

Only one engine was rebuilt. This was No.771 in November 1915 in order to increase its coal and water capacity. The side tanks were enlarged and extended forward, level with the front of the smokebox, itself extended to carry the superheater fitted at this time. The cab and bunker were also made bigger. The trailing radial axle was changed to a pony truck and screw couplings along with carriage warming apparatus were fitted. No.771 was reclassified 9O by the GCR. Its superheater, though not the longer smokebox, was removed in October 1930. It was withdrawn as No.69311 by BR in February 1952.

All, including the initial three engines, were classified N5 by the LNER at first, there being no class parts. No.771 had a separate engine diagram marked 'Engine 771 only'.

Fitting of the short lived Gorton 'one-piece' chimneys to a few engines, followed by the universal adoption of the flowerpot type chimney after Grouping brought the class within the LNER Composite Load gauge. In 1927 the unmodified engines still with their Robinson chimneys, were made Class N5 Part 1 whilst those with shorter chimneys (and domes) became N5/2. The process was completed in 1938 but the part number 2 was not dropped until 1949. The rebuilt engine, No.5771, was given class Part 3 in 1938 and this was retained through to withdrawal in 1952.

The standard braking system for the whole class was vacuum for both engine and train, however, the two built for the WM&CQR had steam brake for the engines along with vacuum ejectors for train working. At some time between the latter company being absorbed into the GCR and Grouping these two locomotives apparently had their steam brakes changed to vacuum.

Twelve members of the class were renumbered by the MSLR or GCR before Grouping. These were:-

7	to	515	10/1893
47	to	516	10/1893
171	to	517	12/1893
200A	to	200	1/1896
201A	to	54	8/1900
202A	to	21	10/1900
203A	to	25	8/1900
204A	to	51	10/1900
205A	to	173	8/1900
206A	to	189	8/1900
207A	to	251	8/1900
538	to	127	-/1903

The numbers suffixed A resulted from the original method of running a duplicate list on the MSLR. Unusually it was the engines in the Capital List that carried the suffix instead of the older engines still kept running for a few more years. It was GCR practice to fill gaps in the engine number register as quickly as possible, hence the renumberings in 1900. The renumbering of 538 to 127 was connected with the decision to put an old 0-6-0ST 538B back into Capital Stock as number 538.

When the 1946 renumbering took place on the LNER, the 121 surviving N5s took the series 9250 to 9370. There were several minor deviations from the normal order, that of construction. One major anomaly was the renumbering of the surviving WMCQ N5 No.5409 as 9270 right in the middle of the 1893-94 Beyer, Peacock batch although it was not built until October 1896. This was due to an error in the Gorton records which gave its building date as March 1894.

In view of the rather mixed pre 1946 numbers borne by the class, a numerical table is included.

Unlike the N4, the N5 class was not concentrated into one area of the railway and by Grouping could be found at a dozen or so GCR depots, mainly west of the Pennines but also in the south Midlands and at Neasden where nine of the class resided. Mexborough shedded the largest number at forty engines but this number was very much reduced by the early-30s when J11 0-6-0s took over their duties after the tender engines had been displaced by the large influx of former ROD 2-8-0s. By then, no less than twenty-five LNER sheds had one or more of the N5 class allocated. It was much the same on the eve of

The first engines of LNER Class N4 were built at Gorton during December 1889 and January 1890. They were numbered 161, 165 and 173 on the MS&LR, but became 512, 513 and 514 in 1893. Nos.601, 602 and 603 followed from Gorton in May and July 1891. Only No.601 had not got a Belpaire firebox by the Grouping.

The first three engines of what became LNER Class N5, MS&LR Nos.9, 47 and 171 were built at Gorton in September 1891, and August and November 1892 respectively. They were renumbered 515, 516 and 517 respectively in 1893. They were fitted with Stephenson link motion and Belpaire firebox which was its first application on locomotives working in the United Kingdom.

Eight engines, numbered 1 to 8, were built by Kitson & Co., Leeds during the period September to December 1895 for the Lancashire, Derbyshire & East Coast railway. They were taken over by the GCR on 1st January 1907 and renumbered 1145B to 1147B and 1154 to 1158. From 1903 replacement boilers changed the firebox type from round-top to Belpaire and those done prior to 1907 had washout plugs in the sides just above the side tanks. The Ramsbottom safety valves were mounted on a circular base, and the vacuum ejector exhaust pipe was outside the boiler. The LNER classified them N6.

nationalisation and remained so until serious withdrawals began in BR days. Sheffield Neepsend and its successor Darnall did not have an appreciable allocation of the class until BR days whereas Gorton always had a couple of dozen up to WW2 and thereafter could still boast nearly a dozen or so. Like the N4, Class N5 was intended for shunting and short trip working but also got involved with passenger working at various periods during LNER and BR days, mainly from Barnsley, Bradford, Chester, Colwick, Copley Hill, Gorton, Neasden, Newark, New England, Northwich, Trafford Park, and Wrexham. No.5523 (later 69257) was fitted with auto-gear in 1942 for use a spare engine to Class c13 that normally worked the Chesham branch service. From 1951 No.69257 also saw periods of use from King's Cross on the Alexandra Palace branch and from Stratford on the Epping-Ongar line. By the late 1950s most of the survivors were in store and the last of the class, No.69307 was withdrawn at Gorton shed in December 1960.

Class N6

The initial eight engines of Class A were delivered in 1895 in advance of the opening of the first section of the Lancashire, Derbyshire & East Coast Railway in November 1896. Numbered 1 to 8, these were the company's first engines. Like all subsequent LDECR engines they were designed and constructed by Kitson & Co. of Leeds.

Ten more, Nos.19 to 28, were built in 1899 but the second five were not actually delivered until a year later due to the financial difficulties of the railway company. The order had been for fifteen and the LDECR was forced to cancel the final five because of ever worsening finances. The first of these was actually delivered to Tuxford, numbered 29, but was quickly returned to the makers. However, a buyer for the five was soon found in the shape of the Hull & Barnsley Railway and they were duly also acquired by the LNER in 1923 but were separately classified N11 by their new owners as by then there were appreciable differences.

The water supply on the LDECR system was extremely hard and was soon causing problems with the locomotive boilers, compounded by inadequate repair facilities at Tuxford works. The Locomotive Superintendent shouldered the blame for engines being out of traffic under repair, and they came and went with some frequency. It was not until R.A.Thom was appointed in 1902 that he was able to get to grips with the problem. Water softening plants were installed and Thom began the reboilering of Class A in 1903 with new boilers with a Belpaire firebox instead of the round top type originally provided.

Records of reboilering before the Great Central takeover in 1907 are scanty, but it is known that the first Belpaire boiler was ordered from Kitsons in 1903 and put on No.21. Soon afterwards two more such boilers were ordered, one of which was for No.19. Between October 1904 and April 1906 Yorkshire Engine Co. received orders for nine Belpaire boilers. Records are incomplete but it is known that Nos.7, 22 and 26 were converted before 1907.

From 1907 onwards replacement Belpaire boilers for the class were constructed at Gorton works. These were to a slightly altered design conforming more closely to the Parker and Pollitt 0-6-2Ts (LNER classes N4 and N5). The main change was a reduction in the diameter of the barrel from 4ft 6in. to 4ft 4in.

It is also known that in the period 1907-9 some boilers were fitted with new fireboxes at Gorton and some of the Class A boilers may have been among them.

Nos.1154 and 1156 (ex 4 and 6) were reboilered in February and June 1910. All the class had been given Belpaire boilers by Grouping.

In contrast to Class N6, the five N11s were still running with their original round top firebox boilers when the LNER was formed.

The first two members of the class delivered to the LDECR, Nos.1 and 2, had steam brakes only whilst subsequent engines were supplied with both steam brakes and vacuum ejectors for passenger train working. Nos.1 and 2 were altered at Tuxford to enable them to work passenger trains also.

Although intended to work the coal traffic on the parent system, with running powers over the GCR from Pyewipe Junction to Grimsby docks from 1902, it was clear that the traffic was proving to be too heavy for the engines and in 1904 they were relegated to working solely on LDECR lines. When the GCR took over in 1907 the N6 class was further relegated to shunting duties and trip working between collieries and concentration yards, duties to which they were then entrusted to withdrawal. The whole class – with one exception hardly worth recalling but necessary for completeness – worked the whole of their existence from the two LD&ECR sheds, Langwith Junction and Tuxford. The exception was No.6412 which spent twelve days at the former GC shed in Leicester during January 1935.

The renumbering history of this class saw the Great Central give them new and unrelated numbers to their former LDECR numbers. Further renumbering by the GCR saw three of the class join the Duplicate list by gaining a B suffix. Five others, Nos.1164 to 1168 became Nos.40 to 43 and 66. The LNER simply added 5000 to the existing numbers except in the case of the three duplicate engines which changed from 1145B, 1146B and 1147B to 6414, 6413 and 6412 in that order!

Withdrawals started in September 1933 with No.6163 being condemned. The following year four of the class were condemned. In 1935 no less than seven of the class were withdrawn, a sign of the economic times and the ages of the engines. The condemnations continued up to 1938 when the last two members of the class, Nos.5042 and 6414 finally succumbed.

Class N5 Numerical Index

No.	1946 no.	Page
5021	9294	47
5025	9295	47
5051	9315	56
5054	9296	50
5127	9269	35
5173	9316	57
5189	9317	57
5200	9292	47
5251	-	57
5409	9270	38
5410	-	38
5515	9250	27
5516	9251	27
5517	9252	27
5518	9253	27
5519	9254	30
5520	9255	30
5521	-	30
5522	9256	30
5523	9257	30
5524	9258	33
5525	9259	33
5526	9260	33
5527	9261	33
5528	9262	34
5529	9263	34
5530	9264	34
5531	-	34
5532	9265	34
5533	9266	35
5534	9267	35
5535	9268	35
5536	9293	47
5537	9271	38
5539	9272	38
5540	9273	38
5541	9274	39
5542	9275	39
5543	9276	39
5544	9277	39
5545	9278	39
5546	9279	42
5547	9280	42
5548	9281	42
5744	9282	42
5745	9283	43
5746	9284	43
5747	9285	43
5748	9286	43
5749	9287	43
5750	9288	46
5751	9289	46
5752	9290	46
5753	9291	46
5754	-	51
5755	9302	51
5756	-	47
5757	9297	50
5758	-	50
5759	9298	50
5760	9299	51
5761	9300	51
5762	9301	51
5763	9303	52
5764	9304	52
5765	9305	52
5766	9306	52
5767	9307	52
5768	9308	55
5769	9309	55
5770	9310	55
5771	9311	55
5772	9312	56
5773	9313	56
5774	-	56
5775	9314	56
5894	9318	57
5895	9319	60
5896	9320	60
5897	9321	60
5898	9322	60
5899	9323	62
5900	9324	62
5901	9325	62
5902	9326	62
5903	9327	62
5904	9328	63
5905	9329	63
5906	9330	63
5907	9331	63
5908	9332	66
5909	9333	66
5910	9334	66
5911	9335	66
5912	9336	66
5913	9337	67
5914	9338	67
5915	9339	67
5916	9340	67
5917	9341	69
5918	9342	69
5919	9343	69
5920	9344	69
5921	9345	69
5922	9346	70
5923	9347	70
5924	9348	70
5925	9349	70
5926	9350	71
5927	9351	71
5928	9352	71
5929	9353	71
5930	9354	74
5931	9355	74
5932	9356	74
5933	9357	74
5934	9358	74
5935	9359	77
5936	9360	77
5937	9361	77
5938	9362	77
5939	9363	77
5940	9364	78
5941	9365	78
5942	9366	78
5943	9367	78
5944	9368	79
5945	9369	79
5946	9370	79

1946 Numbers

1946 no.	Orig.no.
9250	5515
9251	5516
9252	5517
9253	5518
9254	5519
9255	5520
9256	5522
9257	5523
9258	5524
9259	5525
9260	5526
9261	5527
9262	5528
9263	5529
9264	5530
9265	5532
9266	5533
9267	5534
9268	5535
9269	5127
9270	5409
9271	5537
9272	5539
9273	5540
9274	5541
9275	5542
9276	5543
9277	5544
9278	5545
9279	5546
9280	5547
9281	5548
9282	5744
9283	5745
9284	5746
9285	5747
9286	5748
9287	5749
9288	5750
9289	5751
9290	5752
9291	5753
9292	5200
9293	5536
9294	5021
9295	5025
9296	5054
9297	5757
9298	5759
9299	5760
9300	5761
9301	5762
9302	5755
9303	5763
9304	5764
9305	5765
9306	5766
9307	5767
9308	5768
9309	5769
9310	5770
9311	5771
9312	5772
9313	5773
9314	5775
9315	5051
9316	5173
9317	5189
9318	5894
9319	5895
9320	5896
9321	5897
9322	5898
9323	5899
9324	5900
9325	5901
9326	5902
9327	5903
9328	5904
9329	5905
9330	5906
9331	5907
9332	5908
9333	5909
9334	5910
9335	5911
9336	5912
9337	5913
9338	5914
9339	5915
9340	5916
9341	5917
9342	5918
9343	5919
9344	5920
9345	5921
9346	5922
9347	5923
9348	5924
9349	5925
9350	5926
9351	5927
9352	5928
9353	5929
9354	5930
9355	5931
9356	5932
9357	5933
9358	5934
9359	5935
9360	5936
9361	5937
9362	5938
9363	5939
9364	5940
9365	5941
9366	5942
9367	5943
9368	5944
9369	5945
9370	5946

Thirty-five engines, Nos.604 to 638, were built by Neilson & Co., Glasgow from July 1890 to May 1891. All except No.610 (*see* page 8, top) had been rebuilt with a Belpaire firebox before grouping.

Neilson & Co., Glasgow supplied fourteen more engines, Nos.712 to 725, between February and April 1892. These had six inch longer frames and bunkers. All except No.721 had a Belpaire firebox fitted by Grouping.

CLASS N 4

5512

Gorton.

To traffic 12/1889.

REPAIRS:
Gor. 6/1—11/2/11.**G**.
Gor. 15/6—10/8/12.**G**.
Gor. 23/9/16—27/1/17.**G**.
Belpaire boiler fitted.
Gor. 16/12/22—10/2/23.**G**.
Gor. 15/8—24/10/25.**G**.
Altered to LNE gauge.
Gor. 25/8—13/10/28.**G**.
Gor. 23/8—27/9/30.**G**.
Gor. 11/11—2/12/33.**G**.
Gor. 15—29/2/36.**G**.
Gor. 20/1/38. *Not repaired.*

BOILERS:
540 11/2/11.
461 *(exJ13 568)* 10/8/12.
1660 *(new)* 27/1/17.
559 *(exJ9 5658)* 24/10/25.
584 *(exJ8 5551)* 27/9/30.
377 *(exN5 5535)* 2/12/33.
454 *(ex 5713)* 29/2/36.

SHED:
Staveley.

RENUMBERED:
5512 24/10/25.

CONDEMNED: 20/1/38.
Cut up at Doncaster 5/3/38.

5513

Gorton.

To traffic 12/1889.

REPAIRS:
Gor. ?/?—6/5/11.**G**.
Belpaire boiler fitted.
Gor. 29/6—7/12/18.**G**.
New cylinders.
Gor. 30/7 –1/10/21.**G**.
Gor. 12/4 –21/6/24.**G**.
Gor. 4/12/26—22/1/27.**G**.
Gor. 16/2—13/4/29.**G**.
Altered to LNE gauge.
Gor. 18—25/2/33.**G**.
Gor. 10—24/8/35.**G**.
Gor. 16—30/10/37.**G**.
Gor. 21/10—28/8/10/39.**G**.
Gor. 2—27/12/41.**G**.
Gor. 9—23/1/43.**L**.
After collision.
Gor. 24/6—22/7/44.**G**.
Gor. 5/4—3/5/47.**G**.
New cylinders.
Gor. 27/8—3/9/49.**C/H**.
Gor. 23/2—8/3/52.**G**.

BOILERS:
998 *(exN5 938)* 6/5/11.
1765 *(new)* 7/12/18.
12 *(exN5 5942)* 22/1/27.
82 *(exN5 5051)* 13/4/29.
173 *(exJ9 5650)* 25/2/33.
4186 *(new)* 24/8/35.
4226 *(new)* 30/10/37.
1667 *(exN5 5054)* 28/10/39.
568 *(exN5 5920)* 27/12/41.
737 *(ex 5713)* 22/7/44.
1897 *(exN5 9330)* 3/5/47.
4201 *(exJ10 5173)* 3/9/49.
22744 *(exN5 69311)* 8/3/52.

SHEDS:
Staveley 17/11/22.
Lincoln 12/1/23.
Langwith Junction ?/?
Barnsley 16/5/29.
Sheffield 16/4/32.
Staveley 26/11/37.
Sheffield 30/9/43.
Barnsley 16/2/44.
Mexborough 7/4/46.
Sheffield 18/12/49.

RENUMBERED:
5513 21/6/24.
9225 3/11/46.
69225 3/9/49.

CONDEMNED: 31/12/54.
Cut up at Gorton 19/3/55.

5514

Gorton.

To traffic 1/1890.

REPAIRS:
Gor. ?/?—27/7/12.**G**.
Gor. 2/4—13/8/21.**G**.
Belpaire boiler fitted.
Gor. 24/5—12/7/24.**G**.
Gor. 5/2—9/4/27.**G**.
Gor. 13/7—10/8/29.**G**.
Gor. 9—23/7/32.**G**.
Altered to LNE gauge.
Gor. 26/1—2/2/35.**G**.
Gor. 10—31/7/37.**G**.
Gor. 18—25/11/39.**G**.
Gor. 25/9—3/10/42.**G**.
New cylinders.
Don. 26/5—5/6/43.**L**.
Gor. 27/1—17/2/45.**G**.
Gor. 30/8—20/9/47.**G**.

BOILERS:
1041 27/7/12.
1713 *(exJ9 666)* 13/8/21.
490 *(ex 5614)* 10/8/29.
209 *(ex 5622)* 23/7/32.
758 *(exN5 5517)* 2/2/35.
1044 *(N5 5021)* 31/7/37.
4 *(exJ10 5839)* 25/11/39.
4269 *(exN5 5906)* 17/2/45.

SHEDS:
Barnsley.
Sheffield 23/7/32.
Retford 21/1/33.
Sheffield 25/9/36.
Barnsley 27/9/36.
Sheffield 5/10/36.
Retford 13/9/37.
Sheffield 29/8/43.

RENUMBERED:
5514 12/7/24.
9226 12/5/46.

CONDEMNED: 31/10/49.
Cut up at Gorton 10/12/49.

5601

Gorton.

To traffic 5/1891.

REPAIRS:
Gor. ?/?—20/5/05.**G**.
Gor. 22/7—14/10/22.**G**.
Gor. 27/9—22/11/24.**G**.
Belpaire boiler fitted.
Gor. 9/4—21/5/27.**G**.
Gor. 4/5—1/6/29.**G**.
Altered to LNE gauge.
Gor. 25/4—16/5/31.**G**.
Reverted to GC gauge.
Gor. 6/10/33. *Not repaired.*

BOILERS:
1125.
564 *(new)* 22/11/24.

SHED:
Sheffield.

RENUMBERED:
5601 22/11/24.

CONDEMNED: 6/10/33.
Cut up at Doncaster 24/3/34.

5602

Gorton.

To traffic 5/1891.

REPAIRS:
Gor. ?/?—13/2/09.**G**.
Belpaire boiler fitted.
Gor. 18/12/20—24/9/21.**G**.
Gor. 1/9—3/11/23.**G**.
Gor. 10/10—5/12/25.**G**.
Gor. 21/4—2/6/28.**G**.
Gor. 10/5—7/6/30.**G**.
Gor. 24/2—17/3/34.**G**.
Altered to LNE gauge.
Gor. 23/5—6/6/36.**G**.

BOILERS:
113 *(new)* 13/2/09.
153 *(new)* 24/9/21.
917 *(exN5 5753)* 7/6/30.
1586 *(exN5 5771)* 17/3/34.
4204 *(new)* 6/6/36.

SHED:
Sheffield 28/2/11.

RENUMBERED:
602c 3/11/23.
5602 5/12/25.

CONDEMNED: 1/8/39.
Cut up at Gorton 23/9/39.

WORKS CODES:- Dar - Darlington. Don - Doncaster. Gor - Gorton. Mex - Mexborough. RSH - Robert, Stephenson & Hawthorn. Str - Stratford. Wrx - Wrexham. YECo - Yorkshire Engine Co.
REPAIR CODES:- **C/H** - Casual Heavy. **C/L** - Casual Light. **G** - General. **H**- Heavy. **H/I** - Heavy Intermediate. **L** - Light. **L/I** - Light Intermediate. **N/C** - Non-Classified.

The three still with round-top fireboxes were rebuilt to Belpaire by the LNER as follows: No.721c (15th September 1923), 5601 (22nd November 1924) and 5610 (1st December 1928), the latter being the only one with round-top to get LNER livery. It was also odd in having Ross 'pop' safety valves put onto a Ramsbottom mounting.

(above) **Although all originally had a stovepipe chimney, the GCR had replaced them with this Robinson cast type, which had a height from rail of 13ft 3in. Eight, Nos. 5603, 5612, 5613, 5619, 5626, 5627, 5631 and 5638, withdrawn January 1932 to October 1933, retained this style.**

(left) **Beginning with No.5512 (24th October 1925) and 5629 (5th December 1925), change was made to a 2ft 9in. flowerpot type chimney from the 3ft 3⅝in. cast type to bring such engines within the 13ft 0in. composite load gauge. When No.5623 was cut down, ex works 22nd August 1936, the forty which survived were all then less than 13ft 0in. height.**

By Grouping, the normal safety valves were Ramsbottom on a low seating and in a rectangular enclosure. In the 1930-45 period most lost the enclosure and the last to carry one was No.9246 (ex 5721) until August 1949.

Without the enclosure this is how Ramsbottom safety valves appeared. No.9228 still had them to 28th January 1950 but they finally went out of use on No.69232 (26th April 1952) and 69230 (7th June 1952).

(below) **Replacement boilers built from 1935 had Ross 'pop' safety valves and the first N4 to get them were Nos.5513 and 5618, both ex works 24th August 1935. Ultimately twenty-seven of the class had boilers with Ross 'pops' plus No.5610 during the years 1924-28.**

5603

Gorton.

To traffic 7/1891.

REPAIRS:
Gor. ?/?—?/5/12.**G**.
Belpaire boiler fitted.
Gor. 16/1—10/4/15.**G**.
Gor. 12/6—31/7/20.**G**.
Gor. 14/4—16/6/23.**G**.
Gor. 30/4—13/8/27.**G**.
Gor. 22/3—19/4/30.**G**.
Gor. 28/8/33. *Not repaired.*

BOILERS:
??? *(?)* ?/5/12.
534 10/4/15.
452 *(new)* 16/6/23.
427 *(exJ10 5126)* 19/4/30.

SHED:
Staveley.

RENUMBERED:
5603 13/8/27.

CONDEMNED: 28/8/33.
Cut up at Doncaster 14/10/33.

5604

Neilson 4091.

To traffic 7/1890.

REPAIRS:
Gor. 21/3—19/9/08.**G**.
Gor. 29/1/20—3/12/21.**G**.
Belpaire boiler fitted.
Gor. 20/10—15/12/23.**G**.
Gor. 7/11—26/12/25.**G**.
Gor. 13/1—2/3/29.**G**.
Altered to LNE gauge.
Gor. 4—25/4/31.**G**.
Gor. 6—20/4/35.**G**.
Gor. 21/8—4/9/37.**G**.
Gor. 15/8/39. *Not repaired.*

BOILERS:
653 *(new)* 19/9/08.
1594 *(J10 804)* 3/12/21.
22 *(new)* 2/3/29.
482 *(new)* 25/4/31.
465 *(exJ10 5084)* 20/4/35.
4222 *(new)* 4/9/37.

SHED:
Sheffield 2/3/10.

RENUMBERED:
604c 15/12/23.
5604 26/12/25.

CONDEMNED: 15/8/39.
Cut up at Gorton 11/11/39.

5605

Neilson 4092.

To traffic 7/1890.

REPAIRS:
Gor. ?/?—19/4/02.**G**.
Gor. 28/2—1/5/20.**G**.
Belpaire boiler fitted.
Gor. 20/5—24/6/22.**G**.
Gor. 26/7—6/9/24.**G**.
Gor. 4/6—16/7/27.**G**.
Gor. 12/10—9/11/29.**G**.
Gor. 20/2—5/3/32.**G**.
Altered to LNE gauge.
Gor. 3—24/3/34.**G**.
Gor. 17/4—1/5/37.**G**.
Gor. 17/6—1/7/39.**G**.
Gor. 21/7—9/8/41.**G**.
Gor. 21/7—7/8/43.**G**.
New cylinders.
Gor. 16/3—6/4/46.**G**.
Heat app. (B&F) fitted.
Gor. 15/5—5/6/48.**G**.
Gor. 18/11—9/12/50.**G**.

BOILERS:
385 *(new)* 19/4/02.
1055 *(N5 755)* 1/5/20.
516 *(N5 5895)* 5/3/32.
400 *(N5 5897)* 24/3/34.
387 *(N5 5928)* 1/5/37.
4193 *(ex 5718)* 1/7/39.
669 *(exJ10 5811)* 9/8/41.
387 *(exN5 5519)* 7/8/43.
4271 *(exJ10 5120)* 6/4/46.
4293 *(exJ10 5144)* 5/6/48.
22671 *(exN5 69302)* 9/12/50.

SHEDS:
Sheffield 19/3/06.
Staveley 21/5/37.
Sheffield 26/8/43.

RENUMBERED:
5605 6/9/24.
9227 12/5/46.
69227 5/6/48.

CONDEMNED: 9/11/53.
Into Gor. for cut up 14/11/53.
To Dar. for c/u.C/u 22/11/53.

5606

Neilson 4093.

To traffic 7/1890.

REPAIRS:
Gor. ?/?—12/4/02.**G**.
Gor. 20/5—22/7/16.**G**.
Belpaire boiler fitted.
Gor. 31/1—28/2/20.**G**.
Gor. 29/8/21—5/1/22.**H**.
Gor. 2/6—14/7/23.**G**.
Gor. 13/6—15/8/25.**G**.
Gor. 5/11—17/12/27.**G**.
Gor. 25/1—22/2/30.**G**.
Gor. 4—25/6/32.**G**.
Altered to LNE gauge.
Gor. 20/10—10/11/34.**G**.
New cylinders.
Gor. 13—20/2/37.**G**.
Gor. 9—23/12/39.**G**.
Gor. 23/6—25/7/42.**G**.
Gor. 12—26/8/44.**G**.
Gor. 1—22/11/47.**G**.
Gor. 28/1—18/2/50.**G**.
Gor. 9—23/8/52.**L/I**.

BOILERS:
383 *(new)* 12/4/02.
1629 *(new)* 22/7/16.
1653 *(ex 5611)* 25/6/32.
426 *(exN5 5923)* 10/11/34.
46 *(ex 5635)* 20/2/37.
415 *(exJ10 5124)* 23/12/39.
142 *(exN5 5528)* 25/7/42.
188 *(exN5 5753)* 26/8/44.
53 *(exN5 9250)* 22/11/47.
4311 *(exN5 9274)* 18/2/50.
4311 reno.22775 23/8/52.

SHED:
Sheffield.

RENUMBERED:
5606 15/8/25.
9228 7/4/46.
69228 18/2/50.

CONDEMNED: 31/12/54.
Cut up at Gorton 28/5/55.

5607

Neilson 4094.

To traffic 7/1890.

REPAIRS:
Gor. ?/?—28/3/03.**G**.
Gor. 5/4—9/8/19.**G**.
Belpaire boiler fitted.
Gor. 4/11/22—24/3/23.**G**.
Gor. 31/1—28/3/25.**G**.
Gor. 15/10—19/11/27.**G**.
Gor. 2—30/11/29.**G**.
Gor. 28/5—11/6/32.**G**.
Altered to LNE gauge.
Gor. 3—24/11/34.**G**.

BOILERS:
679 28/3/03.
126 *(exN5 760)* 9/8/19.
151 *(ex 724)* 24/3/23.
1625 *(exJ12 6417)* 19/11/27.
1648 *(exJ10 5846)* 11/6/32.
56 *(exN5 5515)* 24/11/34.

SHED:
Sheffield.

RENUMBERED:
5607 28/3/25.

CONDEMNED: 10/4/37.
Into Gor. for cut up 17/4/37.
To Don. for c/u. C/u 12/6/37.

5608

Neilson 4095.

To traffic 7/1890.

REPAIRS:
Gor. ?/?—18/10/02.**G**.
Gor. 22/1—29/4/16.**G**.
Belpaire boiler fitted.
Gor. 25/9—30/10/20.**G**.
Gor. 16/9—28/10/22.**G**.
Gor. 11/10—22/11/24.**G**.
Gor. 18/6—30/7/27.**G**.
Gor. 30/11—21/12/29.**G**.
Gor. 9—30/4/32.**G**.
Altered to LNE gauge.
Gor. 10/11—1/12/34.**G**.

BOILERS:
522 *(new)* 18/10/02.
1611 *(new)* 29/4/16.
15 *(new)* 30/10/20.
1919 *(exJ10 5640)* 21/12/29.
1657 *(exN5 5919)* 30/4/32.
99 *(exJ9 5666)* 1/12/34.

SHEDS:
Sheffield.
Retford 12/5/25.
Barnsley 19/9/36.
Sheffield 27/9/36.

RENUMBERED:
5608 22/11/24.

CONDEMNED: 29/4/37.
Into Gor. for cut up 1/5/37.
To Don. for c/u.C/u 19/6/37.

From the mid-1890s al carried three open coal rails, and on only four was alteration made, and then not until 1944.

(above) **On four of the class, Nos.5614 (10th June 1944), 5625 (12th August 1944), 5718 (30th December 1944) and 5635 (30th June 1945) the open rails were replaced by steel sheet, with the back plate in line with the rear of the bunker and not the edge of the flare top as the rails had been. From 1946 these four became Nos.9230, 9234, 9244 and 9239 respectively.**

Until after 1945 the upper lamp iron was fastened on the front plate of the smokebox, at the top.

(above) **For easier access and to reduce proximity to the overhead electric wires being erected around the Sheffield/ Barnsley area, the upper lamp iron was moved lower and fixed on the smokebox door.**

The original sanding arrangement was steam applied ahead of the middle, and behind the rear coupled wheels. Some retained it through to withdrawal.

Even before Grouping a change to gravity applied sanding started, but was never pushed vigorously.

5609

Neilson 4096.

To traffic 7/1890.

REPAIRS:
Gor. 29/2—4/4/08**G**.
Gor. 5/9—21/11/14.**G**.
Belpaire boiler fitted.
Gor. 12/2—2/4/21.**G**.
Gor. 17/11/23—8/3/24.**G**.
Gor. 26/11—31/12/27.**G**.
Gor. 5/7—9/8/30.**G**.
Gor. 18—25/11/33.**G**.
Altered to LNE gauge.
Gor. 15/9/36. *Not repaired.*

BOILERS:
106A 4/4/08.
644 *(exN5 515)* 21/11/14.
98 *(new)* 2/4/21.
1895 *(exN5 5755)* 31/12/27.
105 *(exJ10 5676)* 25/11/33.

SHEDS:
Staveley.
Sheffield 13/10/30.
Barnsley 20/10/30.

RENUMBERED:
5609 8/3/24.

CONDEMNED: 15/9/36.
Cut up at Doncaster 30/1/37.

5610

Neilson 4097.

To traffic 7/1890.

REPAIRS:
Gor. ?/?—19/3/02.**G**.
Gor. 22/11/19—24/1/20.**G**.
Gor. 3/11/23—1/3/24.**G**.
Gor. 13/3—22/5/26.**G**.
Gor. 27/10—1/12/28.**G**.
Belpaire boiler fitted.
Gor. 20/12/30—24/1/31.**G**.
Altered to LNE gauge.
Gor. 18/11—2/12/33.**G**.
Gor. 8—22/8/36.**G**.

BOILERS:
380 *(new)* 19/3/02.
1062 *(ex 618)* 24/1/20.
795 *(ex 5612)* 1/12/28.
1917 *(exN5 5051)* 24/1/31.
104 *(exD7 5689)* 2/12/33.
1689 *(exN5 5909)* 22/8/36.

SHEDS:
Staveley.
Barnsley 4/10/35.
Staveley 19/2/36.

RENUMBERED:
5610 1/3/24.

CONDEMNED: 30/11/38.
Into Gor. for cut up 3/12/38.
To Don. for c/u. C/u 18/2/39.

5611

Neilson 4098.

To traffic 8/1890.

REPAIRS:
Gor. ?/?—7/11/08.**G**.
Belpaire boiler fitted.
Gor. 29/1—2/4/21.**G**.
Gor. 2/6—21/7/23.**G**.
Gor. 13/6—8/8/25.**G**.
Gor. 22/10—3/12/27.**G**.
Gor. 19/10—16/11/29.**G**.
Gor. 14/5—4/6/32.**G**.
Altered to LNE gauge.
Gor. 7—28/7/34.**G**.
Gor. 18—25/7/36.**G**.
Gor. 21—28/10/39.**G**.
Gor. 9—30/3/40.**L**.
Second hand cyls ex 5634.
Gor. 5—26/12/42.**G**.
Gor. 10—21/10/44.**G**.
Gor. 18/1—15/2/47.**G**.
Gor. 25/3—8/4/50.**G**.

BOILERS:
779 *(new)* 7/11/08.
1653 *(exN5 5547)* 3/12/27.
380 *(exN5 5025)* 4/6/32.
106 *(exN5 5173)* 28/7/34.
286 *(ex 5624)* 25/7/36.
4212 *(exJ10 5118)* 28/10/39.
1897 *(exN5 5902)* 26/12/42.
393 *(exN5 5940)* 21/10/44.
4194 *(exN5 9299)* 15/2/47.
4206 *(exN5 69361)* 8/4/50.

SHED:
Sheffield 5/11/06.

RENUMBERED:
5611 8/8/25.
9229 17/11/46.
69229 8/4/50.

CONDEMNED: 23/6/52.
Into Don. for cut up 3/7/52.

5612

Neilson 4099.

To traffic 8/1890.

REPAIRS:
Gor. 28/4—23/6/17.**G**.
Gor. 20/11/20—7/5/21.**G**.
Belpaire boiler fitted.
Gor. 31/3—21/4/23.**G**.
Gor. 8/8—10/10/25.**G**.
Gor. 21/4—26/5/28.**G**.
Gor. 15/3—5/4/30.**G**.

BOILERS:
381 23/6/17.
795 *(exD7 704)* 7/5/21.
1799 *(ex 5634)* 26/5/28.

SHEDS:
Sheffield.
Barnsley 20/10/30.
Sheffield 13/4/32.

RENUMBERED:
5612 10/10/25.

CONDEMNED: 1/8/33.
Cut up at Doncaster 23/9/33.

5613

Neilson 4100.

To traffic 8/1890.

REPAIRS:
Gor. ?/?—?/8/14.**G**.
Belpaire boiler fitted.
Gor. 16/6—18/8/17.**G**.
Gor. 16/4—23/7/21.**G**.
Gor. 16/8—11/10/24.**G**.
Gor. 8/10—19/11/27.**G**.
Gor. 4/1—1/2/30.**G**.

BOILERS:
??? *(ex?)* ?/8/14.
467 *(new)* 18/8/17.
1689 *(exJ9 662)* 23/7/21.
1767 *(exD7 5687)* 19/11/27.

SHEDS:
Barnsley.
Sheffield 16/4/32.

RENUMBERED:
5613 11/10/24.

CONDEMNED: 3/4/33.
Cut up at Doncaster 10/6/33.

5614

Neilson 4101.

To traffic 11/1890.

REPAIRS:
Gor. ?/?—8/3/02.**G**.
Gor. 8/4—12/8/11.**G**.
Belpaire boiler & new cylinders fitted.
Gor. 26/1—8/6/18.**G**.
Gor. 8/1—19/2/21.**G**.
Gor. 6/10/23—26/1/24.**G**.
Gor. 11/12/26—12/2/27.**G**.
Gor. 29/6—27/7/29.**G**.
New cylinders.
Gor. 4—18/2/33.**G**.
Altered to LNE gauge.
Gor. 27/6—11/7/36.**G**.
Gor. 17/6—1/7/39.**G**.
Gor. 1—24/1/42.**G**.
Gor. 27/5—10/6/44.**G**.
Gor. 10/5—7/6/47.**G**.
Gor. 3—24/12/49.**G**.
Gor. 7—28/6/52.**G**.

BOILERS:
379 *(new)* 8/3/02.
1128 *(new)* 12/8/11.
714 *(exN5 759)* 8/6/18.
490 *(exJ12 5493)* 12/2/27.
1782 *(exN5 5905)* 27/7/29.
950 *(exJ10 5811)* 18/2/33.
101 *(exJ10 5079)* 11/7/36.
140 *(exN5 5536)* 1/7/39.
326 *(ex 5623)* 10/6/44.
4210 *(exJ10 5173)* 7/6/47.
737 *(ex 9241)* 24/12/49.
22765 *(exN5 69282)* 28/6/52.

SHEDS:
Staveley 25/9/08.
Immingham 17/2/33.
Tuxford 18/7/35.
Lincoln 10/2/36.
Barnsley 16/3/36.
Sheffield 20/7/37.

RENUMBERED:
5614 26/1/24.
9230 10/11/46.
69230 24/12/49.

CONDEMNED: 31/12/54.
Cut up at Gorton 3/9/55.

5615

Neilson 4102.

To traffic 11/1890.

REPAIRS:
Gor. 28/8—7/11/08.**G**.
Gor. 2—30/7/10.**G**.
Gor. 26/8/16—10/2/17.**G**.
Belpaire boiler fitted.
Gor. 6/11/20—26/3/21.**G**.
Gor. 9/2—26/4/24.**G**.
Gor. 24/12/27—28/1/28.**G**.
Altered to LNE gauge.
Gor. 8/2—8/3/30.**G**.
Gor. 20/2—5/3/32.**G**.
Gor. 7—21/12/35.**G**.
Gor. 21/12/37. *Not repaired.*

BOILERS:
243 7/11/08.
532 *(ex 715)* 30/7/10.
1656 *(new)* 10/2/17.
1386 *(exD7 682)* 26/3/21.
204 *(exJ13 5570)* 28/1/28.
314 *(exD7 5707)* 8/3/30.
1715 *(exN5 5764)* 5/3/32.
793 *(exJ10 5812)* 21/12/35.

SHED:
Staveley.

RENUMBERED:
5615 26/4/24.

CONDEMNED: 21/12/37.
Cut up at Doncaster 29/1/38.

5616

Neilson 4103.

To traffic 11/1890.

REPAIRS:
Gor. 30/12/16—14/7/17.**G**.
Belpaire boiler fitted.
Gor. 9/10/20—22/1/21.**G**.
Gor. 12/1—29/3/24.**G**.
Gor. 8/10—19/11/27.**G**.
Gor. 14/12/29—11/1/30.**G**.
Altered to LNE gauge.
Gor. 22/4/33. *Not repaired.*

BOILERS:
551 *(ex 621)* 14/7/17.
52 *(new)* 22/1/21.
1768 *(exN5 5765)* 19/11/27.
304 *(new)* 11/1/30.

SHED:
Staveley.

RENUMBERED:
5616 29/3/24.

CONDEMNED: 22/4/33.
Cut up at Doncaster 10/6/33.

5617

Neilson 4104.

To traffic 11/1890.

REPAIRS:
Gor. 17/6—1/8/08.**G**.
Gor. 2/3—29/6/18.**G**.
Belpaire boiler fitted.
Gor. 26/8—14/10/22.**G**.
Gor. 27/9—8/11/24.**G**.
Gor. 14/5—25/6/27.**G**.
Gor. 15/6—13/7/29.**G**.
Gor. 1—29/8/31.**G**.
Altered to LNE gauge.
Gor. 19/8—2/9/33.**G**.
Gor. 8/8/36. *Not repaired.*

BOILERS:
933 1/8/08.
1128 *(ex 614)* 29/6/18.
735 *(new)* 29/8/31.
425 *(exN5 5544)* 2/9/33.

SHED:
Sheffield.

RENUMBERED:
5617 8/11/24.

CONDEMNED: 25/8/36.
Cut up at Gorton 26/9/36.

5618

Neilson 4105.

To traffic 11/1890.

REPAIRS:
Gor. 15/7—24/10/08.**G**.
Gor. 14/10/16—10/3/17.**G**.
Gor. 1/11/19—3/4/20.**G**.
Belpaire boiler fitted.
Gor. 6/1—3/3/23.**G**.
Gor. 28/11/25—30/1/26.**G**.
Gor. 6/10—3/11/28.**G**.
Altered to LNE gauge.
Gor. 14/3—4/4/31.**G**.
Gor. 10—24/8/35.**G**.
Gor. 28/9/37. *Not repaired.*

BOILERS:
224 24/10/08.
1062 *(ex 629)* 10/3/17.
1700 *(exD7 683* 3/4/20.
106 *(ex 5620)* 30/1/26.
1681 *(ex 5637)* 3/11/28.
1643 *(N5 5897)* 4/4/31.
4187 *(new)* 24/8/35.

SHED:
Staveley.

RENUMBERED:
5618 30/1/26.

CONDEMNED: 28/9/37.
Cut up at Doncaster 27/11/37.

5619

Neilson 4106.

To traffic 11/1890.

REPAIRS:
Gor. 20/2—3/4/15.**G**.
Gor. 19/3—13/8/21.**G**.
Belpaire boiler fitted.
Gor. 4/8—6/10/23.**G**.
Gor. 7/11—31/12/25.**G**.
Gor. 7/1—11/2/28.**G**.
Gor. 1—22/2/30.**G**.
Gor. 13/10/33. *Not repaired.*

BOILERS:
129 3/4/15.
678 *(exD7 690)* 13/8/21.

SHED:
Sheffield.

RENUMBERED:
619c 6/10/23.
5619 31/12/25.

CONDEMNED: 13/10/33.
Cut up at Doncaster 2/12/33.

5620

Neilson 4107.

To traffic 11/1890.

REPAIRS:
Gor. ?/?—11/10/02.**G**.
Gor. 22/8—24/10/14.**G**.
Belpaire boiler fitted.
Gor. 25/12/20—11/6/21.**G**.
Tux. 21/5—15/7/24.**H**.
Gor. 31/10—31/12/25.**G**.
Altered to LNE gauge.
Gor. 14/7—15/9/28.**G**.
Gor. 24/1—14/2/31.**G**.
Gor. 28/3—18/4/36.**G**.
Gor. 23/4—7/5/38.**G**.
Gor. 4—25/1/41.**G**.
Gor. 26/6—3/7/43.**G**.
Gor. 30/11—21/12/46.**G**.
Gor. 7/1—4/2/50.**G**.
Secondhand cyls. Ex.9243.
Gor. 22/9—13/10/51.**C/L**.
After collision.
Gor. 3—24/5/52.**G**.
New cylinders.

BOILERS:
514 *(new)* 11/10/02.
477 *(exN5 907)* 24/10/14.
106 *(new)* 11/6/21.
1121 *(exJ10 5798)* 31/12/25.
449 *(exN5 5754)* 14/2/31.
1710 *(N5 5543)* 7/5/38.
105 *(N5 5944)* 3/7/43.
4301 *(new)* 21/12/46.
4331 *(new)* 4/2/50.
4331 reno.22710 13/10/51.
22760 *(exN5 69341)* 24/5/52.

SHEDS:
Lincoln 26/5/22.
Langwith Junction ?/?
Annesley 14/2/29.
Sheffield 26/2/31.
Barnsley 17/4/31.
Sheffield 7/11/34.
Barnsley 12/2/45.
Mexborough 7/4/46.
Sheffield 18/12/49.

RENUMBERED:
5620 15/7/24.
9231 21/7/46.
69231 4/2/50.

CONDEMNED: 1/10/54.
Into Gor. for c/u 2/10/54.
Sent to Don. for c/u 16/10/54.

5621

Neilson 4108.

To traffic 12/1890.

REPAIRS:
Gor. 11/8/08—9/1/09.**G**.
Gor. 12/8—24/12/10.**G**.
Belpaire boiler fitted.
Gor. 22/7—23/12/16.**G**.
Gor. 22/1—2/4/21.**G**.
Tux. 18/1—14/3/24.**H**.
Gor. 11/6—30/7/27.**G**.
Gor. 20/12/30—17/1/31.**G**.
Gor. 28/7—18/8/34.**G**.
Altered to LNE gauge.

BOILERS:
184 9/1/09.
551 24/12/10.
1653 *(new)* 23/12/16.

5621 cont./
94 *(new)* 2/4/21.
1765 *(ex 5513)* 30/7/27.
52 *(exN5 5746)* 17/1/31.
1896 *(exN5 5946)* 18/8/34.

SHEDS:
Langwith Junction.
Leicester 17/3/28.
Sheffield 3/2/31.
Barnsley 3/3/31.
Sheffield 23/7/37.

RENUMBERED:
5621 14/3/24.

CONDEMNED: 2/10/37.
Cut up at Doncaster 13/11/37.

5622

Neilson 4109.

To traffic 12/1890.

REPAIRS:
Gor. ?/? -6/2/04.**G**.
Gor. 28/3—23/5/14.**G**.
Belpaire boiler fitted.
Gor. 16/9—18/11/22.**G**.
Gor. 20/12/24—7/2/25.**G**.
Gor. 2/7—13/8/27.**G**.
Gor. 10/8—21/9/29.**G**.
Gor. 7—21/5/32.**G**.
Altered to LNE gauge.
Gor. 21—28/4/34.**G**.
Gor. 28/8—25/9/37.**G**.
Gor. 27/4—18/5/40.**G**.
Gor. 6—23/1/43.**G**.
Gor. 2—30/6/45.**G**.
Gor. 11/10—8/11/47.**G**.
Gor. 12/11—3/12/49.**G**.
Gor. 26/4—17/5/52.**G**.

BOILERS:
106 6/2/04.
209 *(new)* 23/5/14.
1919 *(ex 5608)* 21/5/32.
1898 *(ex 5714)* 28/4/34.
4223 *(new)* 25/9/37.
428 *(exN5 5765)* 23/1/43.
451 *(exN5 5927)* 30/6/45.
167 *(exN5 9367)* 3/12/49.
22756 *(exN5 69333)* 17/5/52.

SHEDS:
Sheffield. 14/7/11.
Barnsley 29/11/34.
Sheffield. 27/7/37.

RENUMBERED:
5622 7/2/25.
9232 14/7/46.
69232 3/12/49.

CONDEMNED: 31/12/54.
Cut up at Gorton 10/9/55.

5623

Neilson 4110.

To traffic 12/1890.

REPAIRS:
Gor. 7/7—21/8/09.**G**.
Gor. ?/?—?/7/19.**G**.
Belpaire boiler fitted.
Gor. 1/10—10/12/21.**G**.
Gor. 27/9—8/11/24.**G**.
Gor. 30/6—28/7/28.**G**.
Gor. 8—29/8/31.**G**.
Gor. 8—22/8/36.**G**.
Altered to LNE gauge.
Gor. 20/5—3/6/39.**G**.
Gor. 28/6—12/7/41.**G**.
Gor. 29/4—13/5/44.**G**.
Gor. 16/11—14/12/46.**G**.
Gor. 31/1—14/2/48.**G**.
Gor. 24/12/49—21/1/50.**G**.
Gor. 29/9—13/10/51.**C/L**.
After collision.
Gor. 6—20/9/52.**G**.

BOILERS:
1387 *(new)* 21/8/09.
??? *(ex?)* ?/7/19.
87 *(exN5 5758)* 28/7/28.
4206 *(new)* 22/8/36.
326 *(exN5 5546)* 3/6/39.
4191 *(exN5 5896)* 13/5/44.
1642 *(exN5 9251)* 14/12/46.
4242 *(exN5 69352)* 21/1/50.
4242 reno.22714 13/10/51.
22782 *(exN5 69367)* 20/9/52.

SHEDS:
Barnsley.
Sheffield 30/7/37.

RENUMBERED:
5623 8/11/24.
9233 14/7/46.
E9233 14/2/48.
69233 21/1/50.

CONDEMNED: 3/12/54.
Into Gor. for cut up 4/12/54.
To Don. for c/u. C/u 31/12/54.

5624

Neilson 4111.

To traffic 1/1891.

REPAIRS:
Gor. ?/?—2/11/07.**G**.
Gor. 13/2—10/4/15.**G**.
Belpaire boiler fitted.
Gor. 28/4—14/7/23.**G**.
Gor. 26/3—14/5/27.**G**.
Gor. 26/10—30/11/29.**G**.
Gor. 29/10—12/11/32.**G**.
Altered to LNE gauge.
Gor. 20/6—11/7/36.**G**.

BOILERS:
314 *(new)* 2/11/07.
1105 *(new)* 10/4/15.
469 *(new)* 14/7/23.
480 *(exJ10 5796)* 30/11/29.
286 *(exN5 5545)* 12/11/32.
289 *(exN5 5924)* 11/7/36.

SHED:
Staveley.

RENUMBERED:
5624 14/5/27.

CONDEMNED: 13/7/38.
Cut up at Doncaster 27/8/38.

5625

Neilson 4112.

To traffic 1/1891.

REPAIRS:
Gor. 26/2—9/4/10.**G**.
New cylinders.
Gor. 10/4—26/6/15.**G**.
Gor. 6/12/19—3/4/20.**G**.
Belpaire boiler fitted.
Gor. 12/5—21/7/23.**G**.
Tux. 24/8/25—6/2/26.**G**.
Gor. 23/7—3/9/27.**G**.
New cylinders.
Gor. 3—24/10/31.**G**.
Altered to LNE gauge.
Gor. 14—28/3/36.**G**.
Gor. 24/9—15/10/38.**G**.
Gor. 15—22/2/41.**G**.
Gor. 2—31/7/43.**G**.
Gor. 12/8/44.**L**.
Gor. 13/4—11/5/46.**G**.
Heat app. (B&F) fitted.
Gor. 3/7—7/8/48.**G**.
Gor. 16—30/12/50.**H/I**.
Gor. 12/1/53. *Not repaired.*

BOILERS:
958 9/4/10.
314 *(ex624)* 26/6/15.
968 *(exD8 511B)* 3/4/20.
1709 *(exJ12 6443)* 3/9/27.
175 *(exJ10 5828)* 24/10/31.
551 *(exJ10 5097)* 28/3/36.
735 *(exN5 5907)* 22/2/41.
196 *(exN5 5945)* 31/7/43.
4228 *(exJ10 5098)* 11/5/46.
4317 *(new)* 7/8/48.
4317 reno.22676 30/12/50.

SHEDS:
Staveley 22/10/04.
Langwith Junction ?/?
Leicester 2/6/28.
Sheffield 10/10/31.
Staveley 31/12/32.
Sheffield 29/1/34.

RENUMBERED:
5625 6/2/26.
9234 27/1/46.
69234 7/8/48.

CONDEMNED: 12/1/53.
Into Don. for cut up 27/1/53.

5626

Neilson 4113.

To traffic 1/1891.

REPAIRS:
Gor. 28/11/14—9/1/15.**G**.
Belpaire boiler fitted.
Gor. 2/10/20—22/1/21.**G**.
Gor. 10/2—17/3/23.**G**.
Gor. 31/1—7/3/25.**G**.
Gor. 14/5—30/6/27.**G**.
Gor. 20/7—17/8/29.**G**.

BOILERS:
994 *(new)* 9/1/15.
46 *(new)* 22/1/21.

SHED:
Sheffield.

RENUMBERED:
5626 7/3/25.

CONDEMNED: 16/1/32.
Cut up at Doncaster 24/9/32.

5627

Neilson 4114.

To traffic 1/1891.

REPAIRS:
Gor. 4/12/15—22/1/16.**G**.
Gor. 1/6—9/11/18.**G**.
Belpaire boiler fitted.
Gor. 6/1—3/2/23.**G**.
Gor. 27/12/24—21/2/25.**G**.
Gor. 4/6—16/7/27.**G**.
Gor. 3—31/8/29.**G**.

(above) **Mainly employed for goods shunting, 3-link couplings were the standard fitment. As built, all had buffers with taper shank and end collar.** *(left)* **After Grouping there was a very gradual change to screw couplings. Many were also changed to GC buffers with parallel shank and hollow spindle. Only one, No.69240 –** *see* **page25, bottom – has been found fitted with buffers of Group Standard type.** *(below)* **For use as passenger pilots at Sheffield (Victoria) station, four of the class, Nos.5720 (22nd January 1944), 5633 (1st April 1944), 5605 (6th April 1946), and 9234[ex5625] (11th May 1946) were fitted at both ends with connection for carriage heating.**

Although the smokebox door was at first fastened by two handles, by Grouping they had the Robinson style of wheel and handle, in most cases.

Odd ones kept two handle fastening, and from 1945, those with a wheel, had it replaced by a second handle (*see* page 24).

(below) **All had vacuum brake, both on engine and for train working. Note 1924 LNER load class 2 collar on front standpipe.**

5627 cont./
BOILERS:
118 22/1/16.
1763 *(new)* 9/11/18.

SHED:
Sheffield.

RENUMBERED:
5627 21/2/25.

CONDEMNED: 1/4/32.
Cut up at Doncaster 4/6/32.

5628

Neilson 4115.

To traffic 1/1891.

REPAIRS:
Gor. ?/?—28/6/02.**G**.
Gor. 15/1—30/4/21.**G**.
Belpaire boiler fitted.
Gor. 21/7—25/8/23.**G**.
Gor. 8/8—26/9/25.**G**.
Gor. 3/3—14/4/28.**G**.
New cylinders.
Gor. 8/2—8/3/30.**G**.
Gor. 1—15/10/32.**G**.
Altered to LNE gauge.
Gor. 21/9—5/10/35.**G**.
Gor. 7—21/1/39.**G**.
Gor. 12/12/42—2/1/43.**G**.
Gor. 10/2—3/3/45.**G**.
Gor. 10/5—7/6/47.**G**.
Gor. 24/9—15/10/49.**G**.
Gor. 1—22/3/52.**G**.

BOILERS:
438 *(new)* 28/6/02.
767 *(exD7 5706)* 30/4/21.
158 *(exJ13 5570)* 15/10/32.
193 *(exN5 5534)* 5/10/35.
4185 *(exN5 5760)* 21/1/39.
541 *(exN5 5532)* 2/1/43.
4201 *(exN5 5923)* 3/3/45.
455 *(exJ10 5183)* 7/6/47.
4255 *(ex 9244)* 15/10/49.
22747 *(exN5 69301)* 22/3/52.

SHEDS:
Sheffield.
Staveley 30/12/32.
Sheffield 26/9/33.
Barnsley 5/10/36.
Sheffield 2/3/43.

RENUMBERED:
628c 15/9/23.
5628 26/9/25.
9235 24/3/46.
69235 15/10/49.

CONDEMNED: 2/8/54.
Cut up at Gorton 1/12/54.

5629

Neilson 4116.

To traffic 4/1891.

REPAIRS:
Gor. ?/?—28/10/11.**G**.
Gor. 8/7—23/12/16.**G**.
Belpaire boiler fitted.
Gor. 4/12/20—29/1/21.**G**.
Gor. 24/3—28/4/23.**G**.
Gor. 3/10—5/12/25.**G**.
Altered to LNE gauge.
Gor. 13/10—17/11/28.**G**.
Gor. 23/4—7/5/32.**G**.
Gor. 9—23/2/35.**G**.
Gor. 7—21/5/38.**G**.
Gor. 9—16/11/40.**G**.
Gor. 26/6—3/7/43.**G**.
Gor. 5—26/1/46.**G**.
Gor. 3—10/5/47.**L**.
Firebox fractured.
Gor. 6—27/3/48.**G**.
Gor. 21/1—4/2/50.**G**.
Secondhand cyls. ex 9226.
Gor. 24/5—14/6/52.**G**.

BOILERS:
1062 *(new)* 28/10/11.
1652 *(new)* 23/12/16.
228 *(exJ9 5645)* 5/12/25.
1705 *(exN5 5543)* 7/5/32.
567 *(new)* 23/2/35.
378 *(exJ10 5828)* 16/11/40.
4274 *(new)* 3/7/43.
4249 *(exJ10 5815)* 26/1/46.
4316 *(new)* 27/3/48.
4332 *(new)* 4/2/50.
22670 *(exJ10 65199)* 14/6/52.

SHEDS:
Barnsley.
Sheffield 26/1/34.

RENUMBERED:
5629 5/12/25.
9236 7/4/46.
69236 27/3/48.

CONDEMNED: 8/11/54.
Cut up at Gorton 19/2/55.

5630

Neilson 4117.

To traffic 4/1891.

REPAIRS:
Gor. 8/8—26/9/14.**G**.
Belpaire boiler fitted.
Gor. 11/6—20/8/21.**G**.
Gor. 26/4—14/6/24.**G**.
Gor. 5/3—30/4/27.**G**.
Gor. 17/8—21/9/29.**G**.
Altered to LNE gauge.

BOILERS:
475 *(exN5 769)* 26/9/14.
653 *(ex 604)* 20/8/21.
619 *(exN5 5534)* 21/9/29.

SHED:
Barnsley.

RENUMBERED:
5630 14/6/24.

CONDEMNED: 25/3/33.
Cut up at Doncaster 18/11/33.

5631

Neilson 4118.

To traffic 4/1891.

REPAIRS:
Gor. ?/?—?/6/11.**G**.
Belpaire boiler fitted.
Gor. 23/6—13/10/17.**G**.
Gor. 1/1—9/4/21.**G**.
Gor. 11/8—6/10/23.**G**.
Gor. 11/8—6/10/23.**G**.
Gor. 28/11/25—16/1/26.**G**.
Gor. 3/12/27—21/1/28.**G**.
Gor. 11/1—8/2/30.**G**.

BOILERS:
??? *(ex?)* ?/6/11.
1183 13/10/17.
147 *(exD7 700)* 9/4/21.

SHED:
Sheffield.

RENUMBERED:
631c 6/10/23.
5631 16/1/26.

CONDEMNED: 6/6/32.
Cut up at Doncaster 16/7/32.

5632

Neilson 4119.

To traffic 4/1891.

REPAIRS:
Gor. ?/?—3/6/05.**G**.
Gor. 19/2—25/6/21.**G**.
Belpaire boiler fitted.
Gor. 28/7—29/9/23.**G**.
Gor. 19/9—7/11/25.**G**.
Gor. 19/11—31/12/27.**G**.
Gor. 18/1—15/2/30.**G**.
Gor. 20/8—3/9/32.**G**.
Altered to LNE gauge.
Gor. 16—30/11/35.**G**.
Gor. 5—19/2/38.**G**.
New cylinders.
Gor. 28/9—12/10/40.**G**.
Gor. 8—19/6/43.**G**.
Gor. 23/10—6/11/43.**G**.
After collision.
Gor. 17/6/44.**L**.
Gor. 25/5—22/6/46.**G**.
Gor. 10/4—8/5/48.**G**.

BOILERS:
1130 *(new)* 3/6/05.
1226 *(exJ10 103)* 25/6/21.
1609 *(exJ10 5824)* 3/9/32.
158 *(ex 5628)* 30/11/35.
4233 *(ex N5 5542)* 12/10/40.
4272 *(new)* 19/6/43.
4200 *(ex N5 5520)* 22/6/46.
4283 *(ex N5 9361)* 8/5/48.

SHEDS:
Sheffield 6/10/03.
Staveley 30/12/32.
Sheffield 26/9/33.

RENUMBERED:
632c 29/9/23.
5632 7/11/25.
9237 22/6/46.
69237 8/5/48.

CONDEMNED: 7/7/50.
Cut up at Gorton 19/8/50.

5633

Neilson 4120.

To traffic 4/1891.

REPAIRS:
Gor. 16/9—15/10/10.**G**.
Gor. 26/10/12—15/2/13.**G**.
Belpaire boiler fitted.
Gor. 29/1—5/3/21.**G**.
New cylinders.
Gor. 28/4—11/8/23.**G**.
Gor. 11/7—19/9/25.**G**.
Gor. 22/10—3/12/27.**G**.
Gor. 12/10—16/11/29.**G**.
Altered to LNE gauge.
Gor. 9—23/4/32.**G**.
Gor. 17/3—7/4/34.**G**.
Gor. 5—19/2/38.**G**.
Gor. 28/10—11/11/39.**G**.

5633 cont./
Gor. 10/5—28/6/41.**G**.
Gor. 15/3—1/4/44.**G**.
Heating app. (b&f) fitted.

BOILERS:
579 15/10/10.
376 *(ex 636)* 15/2/13.
1751 *(exJ12 5491)* 3/12/27.
1605 *(exN5 5935)* 23/4/32.
1625 *(exN5 5772)* 19/2/38.
303 *(exN5 5929)* 11/11/39.
4186 *(exN5 5189)* 1/4/44.

SHEDS:
Sheffield 6/2/11.
Barnsley 29/11/34.
Sheffield 10/5/44.

RENUMBERED:
633c 1/9/23.
5633 19/9/25.
9238 14/7/46.

CONDEMNED: 25/7/47.
Cut up at Gorton 13/9/47.

5634

Neilson 4121.

To traffic 5/1891.

REPAIRS:
Gor. 18/4 -30/5/08.G.
Gor. 18/1—20/9/19.**G**.
Belpaire boiler fitted.
Gor. 14/1—18/3/22.**G**.
Gor. 1/11/24—10/1/25.**G**.
Gor. 3/12/27—14/1/28.**G**.
Gor. 4/10—1/11/30.**G**.
Gor. 16/12—30/12/33.**G**.
Altered to LNE gauge.
Gor. 10/4—1/5/37.**G**.

BOILERS:
518 30/5/08.
1799 *(new)* 20/9/19.
94 *(ex 5621)* 14/1/28.
83 *(exD7 5691)* 30/12/33.
4217 *(new)* 1/5/37.

SHEDS:
Barnsley.
Sheffield 17/5/37.
Mexborough 9/1/39.

RENUMBERED:
5634 10/1/25.

CONDEMNED: 16/3/40.
Cut up at Gorton 29/6/40.

5635

Neilson 4122.

To traffic 5/1891.

REPAIRS:
Gor. ?/?—17/2/12.**G**.
Belpaire boiler fitted.
Gor. 11/11/16—17/3/17.**G**.
Gor. 1/1—26/2/21.**G**.
Gor. 1/3—7/6/24.**G**.
New cylinders.
Gor. 8/10—19/11/27.**G**.
Gor. 9/11—7/12/29.**G**.
Gor. 23/7—6/8/32.**G**.
Altered to LNE gauge.
Gor. 31/12/36—23/1/37.**G**.
Gor. 30/9—14/10/39.**G**.
Gor. 4/7—1/8/42.**G**.
Gor. 10/2—13/3/43.**L**.
After collision.
Gor. 9—30/6/45.**G**.
Gor. 10/4—1/5/48.**G**.
Gor. 29/12/51—26/1/52.**G**.

BOILERS:
151 *(new)* 17/2/12.
1670 *(new)* 17/3/17.
511 *(new)* 7/6/24.
46 *(ex 5626)* 6/8/32.
727 *(exN5 5946)* 23/1/37.
4215 *(exN5 5522)* 14/10/39.
415 *(ex 5606)* 1/8/42.
4239 *(exN5 5529)* 30/6/45.
428 *(exN5 9304)* 1/5/48.
22732 *(exN5 69340)* 26/1/52.

SHEDS:
Staveley.
Lincoln 9/10/25.
Sheffield 10/12/27.
Staveley 31/12/32.
Sheffield 26/9/33.
Barnsley 7/12/34.
Sheffield 14/9/37.
Barnsley 10/5/44.
Sheffield 23/6/44
Barnsley 12/7/44.
Mexborough 7/4/46.
Sheffield 18/12/49.

RENUMBERED:
5635 7/6/24.
9239 21/7/46.
69239 1/5/48.

CONDEMNED: 23/3/54.
Cut up at Gorton 3/7/54.

5636

Neilson 4123.

To traffic 5/1891.

REPAIRS:
Gor. ?/?—1/3/02.**G**.
Gor. 19/10—30/11/12.**G**.
Belpaire boiler fitted.
Gor. 13/11/20—12/3/21.**G**.
Gor. 29/12/23—5/4/24.**G**.
Gor. 3/9—15/10/27.**G**.
Gor. 18/1—22/2/30.**G**.
Gor. 20/5—27/6/33.**G**.
Altered to LNE gauge.
Gor. 9—23/5/36.**G**.
Gor. 25/6—2/7/38.**G**.
Gor. 7—21/12/40.**G**.
Gor. 20/2—13/3/43.**G**.
New cylinders.
Gor. 6—20/10/45.**G**.
Gor. 17/1—14/2/48.**G**.
Gor. 20/5—10/6/50.**G**.

BOILERS:
376 *(new)* 1/3/02.
645 *(exN5 763)* 30/11/12.
1384 *(ex 715)* 12/3/21.
1123 *(exN5 5939)* 15/10/27.
1768 *(ex 5616)* 22/2/30.
1722 *(exN5 5768)* 27/6/33.
153 *(exJ10 5819)* 23/5/36.
538 *(exN5 5526)* 2/7/38.
1230 *(ex ?)* 21/12/40.
289 *(exN5 5937)* 13/3/43.
505 *(exN5 5914)* 20/10/45.
4209 *(exN5 9289)* 14/2/48.
4282 *(exN5 69363)* 10/6/50.

SHEDS:
Staveley 4/3/11.
Sheffield 31/8/43.

RENUMBERED:
5636 5/4/24.
9240 28/11/46.
E9240 14/2/48.
69240 10/6/50.

CONDEMNED: 10/11/52.
Cut up at Gorton 17/1/53.

5637

Neilson 4124.

To traffic 5/1891.

REPAIRS:
Gor. ?/?—5/11/04/.**G**.
Gor. 4/4—4/7/14.**G**.
Gor. 20/3—8/5/20.**G**.
Belpaire boiler fitted.
Gor. 8/7—21/10/22.**G**.
Gor. 27/12/24—7/3/25.**G**.
New cylinders.
Gor. 7/4—12/5/28.**G**.
Gor. 19/4—17/5/30.**G**.
Altered to LNE gauge.
Gor. 4—18/3/33.**G**.
Gor. 12/10—2/11/35.**G**.
Gor. 18—31/12/37.**G**.
Gor. 16/3—6/4/40.**G**.
Gor. 11—25/4/42.**G**.
Gor. 26/8—9/9/44.**G**.
New cylinders.
Gor. 17—24/3/45.**L**.
After collision.
Gor. 12/4—10/5/47.**G**.

BOILERS:
1071 5/11/04.
390 4/7/14.
1655 *(exN5 517)* 8/5/20.
1681 *(exN5 545)* 21/10/22.
1810 *(exN5 5914)* 12/5/28.
324 *(new)* 17/5/30.
120 *(exN5 5930)* 18/3/33.
443 *(exJ10 5670)* 2/11/35.
428 *(exN5 5922)* 31/12/37.
4227 *(exJ10 5131)* 6/4/40.
324 *(exN5 5894)* 25/4/42.
4275 *(new)* 9/9/44.
737 *(ex 9225)* 10/5/47.

SHEDS:
Staveley
Sheffield 29/10/43.

RENUMBERED:
5637 7/3/25.
9241 14/7/46.

CONDEMNED: 26/9/49.
Cut up at Gorton 29/10/49.

5638

Neilson 4125.

To traffic 5/1891.

REPAIRS:
Gor. ?/?—?/6/14.**G**.
Belpaire boiler fitted.
Gor. 22/7—19/8/16.**G**.
Gor. 26/8—30/9/22.**G**.
Gor. 18/10—6/12/24.**G**.
Gor. 9/4—4/6/27.**G**.
Gor. 29/6—17/8/29.**G**.
Gor. 15/1/32. *Not repaired.*

BOILERS:
??? *(ex?)* ?/6/14.
1187 *(new)* 19/8/16.
1771 *(exN5 5764)* 17/8/29.

(above) **Being only goods shunters, after Grouping they only got one coat of black paint and no lining was applied. Until June 1923, initials were shown as L.&N.E.R. and eleven got this style: February – 627 (3rd), 512 (10th); March – 618 and 724 (3rd), 626 (17th), 607 and 722 (24th); April – 612 (21st), 629 (28th); May – 723 (5th); June – 603 (16th). During July the ampersand and full points were then discarded for Nos.606 and 624 (14th), 611 and 625 (21st).**

(left) **To avoid duplication with numbers in other areas, a C suffix was added during the remaining months of 1923 to: September – 633 and 719 (1st), 628 and 721 (15th), 632 (29th); October – 619 and 631 (6th), 715 (13th), 717 (20th), 725 (27th); November – 602 (3rd); December – 604 (15th). These are ex paint shop at Gorton.**

From the beginning of February 1924 the suffix was replaced by a prefix 5 and this style was unchanged to July 1942

Labour and material shortages due to war caused only NE to be put on from July 1942 but Gorton changed to 12 inch transfers for it.

(above) **Although LNER was restored at repaintings from January 1946, many were re-numbered whilst still with NE. Those done at sheds got 8 inch stencilled figures. No.5721 changed to 9246 on Sunday 12th May 1946 at Mexborough shed.**

Although restoring LNER, Gorton continued using 12 inch shaded transfers for some months, No.9237 being ex works 22nd June 1946 in this style.

5638 cont./
SHED:
Sheffield.

RENUMBERED:
5638 6/12/24.

CONDEMNED: 15/1/32.
Cut up at Doncaster 26/3/32.

5712

Neilson 4356.

To traffic 2/1892.

REPAIRS:
Gor. ?/?—?/10/13.**G**.
Belpaire boiler fitted.
Gor. 26/5—28/7/17.**G**.
Gor. 25/12/20—9/7/21.**G**.
Gor. 28/6—23/8/24.**G**.
Gor. 21/1—3/3/28.**G**.
Altered to LNE gauge.
Gor. 12/4—10/5/30.**G**.

BOILERS:
??? *(ex?)* ?/10/13.
262 28/7/17.
142 *(new)* 9/7/21.
177 *(exN5 5770)* 3/3/28.

SHED:
Staveley.

RENUMBERED:
5712 23/8/24.

CONDEMNED: 12/10/33.
Cut up at Doncaster 2/12/33.

5713

Neilson 4357.

To traffic 2/1892.

REPAIRS:
Gor. 20/4—19/6/09.**G**.
Gor. 9/8/19—17/1/20.**G**.
Belpaire boiler fitted.
Gor. 7/10—4/11/22.**G**.
Gor. 20/12/24—14/2/25.**G**.
Gor. 16/6—14/7/28.**G**.
Altered to LNE gauge.
Gor. 16/8—20/9/30.**G**.
Gor. 11—25/11/33.**G**.
Gor. 1—22/2/36.**G**.
Gor. 23/10—13/11/37.**G**.
New cylinders.
Gor. 12—19/8/39.**G**.
Gor. 7—25/10/41.**G**.
Gor. 8—22/4/44.**G**.
Gor. 21/12/46—18/1/47.**G**.
Gor. 5—26/2/49.**G**.

BOILERS:
503 19/6/09.
692 *(exJ12 38B)* 17/1/20.
148 *(exJ8 5560)* 14/7/28.
93 *(exD7 5685)* 20/9/30.
454 *(exJ10 5130)* 25/11/33.
458 *(exN5 5939)* 22/2/36.
502 *(ex?)* 13/11/37.
4204 *(ex 5602)* 19/8/39.
737 *(exJ10 5798)* 25/10/41.
727 *(exN5 5903)* 22/4/44.
4229 *(exN5 9347)* 18/1/47.
4236 *(exJ10 5208)* 26/2/49.

SHEDS:
Staveley.
Sheffield 20/9/43.

RENUMBERED:
5713 14/2/25.
9242 26/5/46.
69242 26/2/49.

CONDEMNED: 14/1/52.
Into Gor. for cut up 19/1/52.
Sent to Don. for cut up 6/2/52.

5714

Neilson 4358.

To traffic 2/1892.

REPAIRS:
Gor. 4/1—29/2/08.**G**.
Gor. 5/2—13/5/16.**G**.
Belpaire boiler fitted.
Shf. 6/3—25/7/22.**H**.
Gor. 15/3—17/5/24.**G**.
Gor. 17/4—3/7/26.**G**.
Gor. 20/10—1/12/28.**G**.
Gor. 23/8—27/9/30.**G**.
Altered to LNE gauge.
Gor. 19/7/33. *Not repaired.*

BOILERS:
549 29/2/08.
1614 *(new)* 13/5/16.
1898 *(new)* 27/9/30.

SHEDS:
Barnsley.
Sheffield 3/2/28.

RENUMBERED:
5714 17/5/24.

CONDEMNED: 19/7/33.
Cut up at Doncaster 24/2/34.

5715

Neilson 4359.

To traffic 2/1892.

REPAIRS:
Gor. ?/?—8/11/02.**G**.
Gor. 6/2—17/4/09.**G**.
Belpaire boiler fitted.
Gor. 13/11—4/12/20.**G**.
Gor. 28/7—13/10/23.**G**.
Gor. 9/7—27/8/27.**G**.
Gor. 31/8—5/10/29.**G**.
Gor. 12—31/12/31.**G**.
Altered to LNE gauge.
Gor. 23/2—9/3/35.**G**.

BOILERS:
532 *(new)* 8/11/02.
1384 *(new)* 17/4/09.
994 *(ex 626)* 4/12/20.
1661 *(exN5 5516)* 13/10/23.
1688 *(exN5 5775)* 5/10/29.
144 *(exD7 5567)* 31/12/31.
1705 *(ex 5629)* 9/3/35.

SHED:
Staveley.

RENUMBERED:
715c 13/10/23.
5715 27/8/27.

CONDEMNED: 6/5/37.
Into Gor. for cut up 8/5/37.
Sent to Don. Cut up 4/9/37.

5716

Neilson 4360.

To traffic 2/1892.

REPAIRS:
Shf. 13/3—1/9/08.**H**.
Gor. ?/?—?/5/20.**G**.
Belpaire boiler fitted.
Gor. 29/4—27/5/22.**G**.
Gor. 17/5—12/7/24.**G**.
Gor. 14/8—23/10/26.**G**.
Gor. 6/10—10/11/28.**G**.
Gor. 6/9—11/10/30.**G**.
Gor. 29/9—13/10/34.**G**.
Altered to LNE gauge.
Gor. 18—31/12/37.**G**.
Gor. 10/2—9/3/40.**G**.
Gor. 4—16/5/42.**G**.
Gor. 27/9—7/10/44.**G**.
Gor. 5/4—17/5/47.**G**.

BOILERS:
1163 *(new)* 1/9/08.
??? *(ex?)* ?/5/20.
408 *(new)* 13/10/34.
510 *(exN5 5517)* 31/12/37.
4217 *(ex 5634)* 9/3/40.
426 *(exN5 5930)* 16/5/42.
324 *(ex 5637)* 7/10/44.
4275 *(ex 9241)* 17/5/47.

SHEDS:
Sheffield 26/5/05.
Barnsley 25/5/35.
Staveley 1/4/38.
Sheffield 30/9/43.

RENUMBERED:
5716 12/7/24.
9243 14/7/46.

CONDEMNED: 31/10/49.
Cut up at Gorton 10/12/49.

5717

Neilson 4361.

To traffic 2/1892.

REPAIRS:
Gor. 12/6—25/9/09.**G**.
Belpaire boiler fitted.
Gor. 1—29/1/21.**G**.
Gor. 28/7—20/10/23.**G**.
Gor. 10/4—17/7/26.**G**.
Gor. 15/12/28—9/2/29.**G**.
Altered to LNE gauge.
Gor. 13/12/30—10/1/31.**G**.
Reverted to GC gauge.
Gor. 24/2/34. *Not repaired.*

BOILERS:
771 *(new)* 25/9/09.
113 *(ex 602)* 29/1/21.
105 *(new)* 20/10/23.
460 *(exJ13 5571)* 9/2/29.
151 *(exN5 5200)* 10/1/31.

SHED:
Staveley.

RENUMBERED:
717c 20/10/23.
5717 17/7/26.

CONDEMNED: 24/2/34.
Cut up at Doncaster 28/4/34.

5718

Neilson 4362.

To traffic 2/1892.

REPAIRS:
Gor. ?/?—2/12/11.**G**.

5718 cont./
Belpaire boiler fitted.
Gor. 24/4—25/9/20.**G.**
Gor. 18/11—23/12/22.**G.**
Gor. 25/4—20/6/25.**G.**
Gor. 12/5—16/6/28.**G.**
Altered to LNE gauge.
Gor. 4—18/2/33.**G.**
Gor. 21/12/35—18/1/36.**G.**
New cylinders.
Gor. 29/4—13/5/39.**G.**
Gor. 29/8—11/10/41.**G.**
Gor. 22/4—6/5/44.**G.**
Gor. 23—30/12/44.**L.**
Gor. 4/1—1/2/47.**G.**
Gor. 30/7—20/8/49.**G.**
Gor. 1/3/52. *Not repaired.*

BOILERS:
974 *(exD7 689)* 2/12/11.
1382 *(exN5 251)* 25/9/20.
211 *(exD7 5683)* 16/6/28.
265 *(exN5 5767)* 18/2/33.
4193 *(new)* 18/1/36.
609 *(exJ10 5792)* 13/5/39.
4194 *(exN5 5763)* 11/10/41.
574 *(exJ10 5174)* 6/5/44.
4255 *(exN5 9323)* 1/2/47.
4233 *(exN5 9337)* 20/8/49.

SHEDS:
Barnsley.
Sheffield 30/5/38.

RENUMBERED:
5718 20/6/25.
9244 29/11/46.
69244 20/8/49.

CONDEMNED: 25/2/52.
Sent to Don. for cut up 24/3/52.

5719

Neilson 4363.

To traffic 3/1892.

REPAIRS:
Gor. ?/?—2/9/11.**G.**
Belpaire boiler fitted.
Gor. 15/1—12/2/21.**G.**
Gor. 23/6—18/8/23.**G.**
Gor. 10/7—18/9/26.**G.**
Gor. 19/1—16/3/29.**G.**
Gor. 17—24/6/33.**G.**
Altered to LNE gauge.
Gor. 5/9/36. *Not repaired.*

BOILERS:
1038 *(new)* 2/9/11.
17 *(exN5 5930)* 18/9/26.
587 *(exN5 5516)* 16/3/29.
15 *(exN5 5944)* 24/6/33.

SHED:
Barnsley.

RENUMBERED:
719c 1/9/23.
5719 18/9/26.

CONDEMNED: 7/9/36.
Cut up at Gorton 3/10/36.

5720

Neilson 4364.

To traffic 3/1892.

REPAIRS:
Gor. ?/?—5/8/11.**G.**
Belpaire boiler fitted.
Gor. 27/8—3/12/21.**G.**
Gor. 20/9—15/11/24.**G.**
Gor. 22/10—10/12/27.**G.**
Gor. 8—29/3/30.**G.**
Gor. 19/8—2/9/33.**G.**
Altered to LNE gauge.
Gor. 21/3—4/4/36.**G.**
New cylinders.
Gor. 17—31/12/38.**G.**
Gor. 24/5—14/6/41.**G.**
Gor. 23/11—4/12/43.**G.**
Gor. 21—22/1/44.**L.**
Heating app. (b&f) fitted.
Gor. 27/4—25/5/46.**G.**
Gor. 29/5—12/6/48.**G.**

BOILERS:
615 5/8/11.
221 *(new)* 3/12/21.
240 *(exJ10 5075)* 10/12/27.
1123 *(ex 5636)* 29/3/30.
1703 *(exN5 5519)* 2/9/33.
82 *(exD7 5689)* 4/4/36.
347 *(exJ10 5789)* 31/12/38.
449 *(exN5 5547)* 14/6/41.
4257 *(exJ10 5640)* 4/12/43.
4227 *(exN5 9253)* 12/6/48.

SHEDS:
Staveley 13/2/05.
Retford 28/11/37.
Barnsley 29/8/43.
Sheffield 4/2/44.

RENUMBERED:
5720 15/11/24.
9245 25/5/46.
69245 12/6/48.

CONDEMNED: 30/10/50.
Cut up at Gorton 30/12/50.

5721

Neilson 4365.

To traffic 3/1892.

REPAIRS:
Gor. ?/?—15/1/10.**G.**
Gor. 23/4—28/5/21.**G.**
Gor. 9/6—15/9/23.**G.**
Belpaire boiler fitted.
Gor. 11/7—5/9/25.**G.**
Gor. 31/3—5/5/28.**G.**
Gor. 1—29/3/30.**G.**
Gor. 10—24/2/34.**G.**
Altered to LNE gauge.
Gor. 15—29/8/36.**G.**
Gor. 8—29/7/39.**G.**
Gor. 10—24/4/43.**G.**
Gor. 10/11—1/12/45.**G.**
New cylinders.
Gor. 13/8—3/9/49.**G.**

BOILERS:
377 15/1/10.
25 *(exJ10 799 & sp.)* 15/9/23.
1614 *(exN5 5922)* 24/2/34.
4209 *(new)* 29/8/36.
523 *(exJ10 5119)* 29/7/39.
275 *(exN5 5772)* 24/4/43.
4202 *(exN5 5539)* 1/12/45.
4328 *(new)* 3/9/49.

SHEDS:
Sheffield 1/3/10.
Barnsley 13/12/30.
Sheffield 11/12/37.
Barnsley 8/3/40.
Sheffield 25/6/44.
Barnsley 12/7/44.
Mexborough 7/4/46.
Sheffield 18/12/49.

RENUMBERED:
721c 15/9/23.
5721 5/9/25.
9246 12/5/46.
69246 3/9/49.

CONDEMNED: 28/4/52.
Cut up at Gorton 31/5/52.

5722

Neilson 4366.

To traffic 3/1892.

REPAIRS:
Gor. ?/?—?/5/13.**G.**
Belpaire boiler fitted.
Gor. 8/7—16/9/16.**G.**
Gor. 30/4—4/6/21.**G.**
Gor. 24/2—24/3/23.**G.**
Gor. 14/2—11/4/25.**G.**
Gor. 16/7—27/8/27.**G.**
Gor. 21/9—19/10/29.**G.**
Altered to LNE gauge.
Gor. 20/5/32. *Not repaired.*

BOILERS:
??? *(ex?)* ?/5/13.
152 *(new)* 16/9/16.
1693 *(exJ10 5815)* 19/10/29.

SHEDS:
Sheffield.
Barnsley 13/12/30.

RENUMBERED:
5722 11/4/25.

CONDEMNED: 20/5/32.
Cut up at Doncaster 25/6/32.

5723

Neilson 4367.

To traffic 3/1892.

REPAIRS:
Gor. ?/?—11/10/02.**G.**
Gor. 6/7—23/11/18.**G.**
Belpaire boiler fitted.
Gor. 19/2—19/3/21.**G.**
Gor. 14/4—5/5/23.**G.**
Gor. 31/1—9/5/25.**G.**
Gor. 5/5—9/6/28.**G.**
Gor. 19/4—24/5/30.**G.**
Gor. 18—25/11/33.**G.**
Altered to LNE gauge.
Gor. 29/8—26/9/36.**G.**

BOILERS:
515 *(new)* 11/10/02.
1766 *(new)* 23/11/18.
1893 *(exJ13 5570)* 9/5/25.
98 *(ex 5609)* 9/6/28.
1799 *(ex 5612)* 25/11/33.
87 *(ex 5623)* 26/9/36.

SHEDS:
Mexborough.
Barnsley 19/1/29.
Sheffield 27/6/33.

RENUMBERED:
5723 9/5/25.

CONDEMNED: 24/8/39.
Cut up at Doncaster 2/3/40.

5724

Neilson 4368.

To traffic 3/1892.

REPAIRS:
Gor. ?/?—11/3/11.**G**.
Belpaire boiler fitted.
Gor. 23/12/16—16/6/17.**G**.
Gor. 30/12/22—3/3/23.**G**.
Gor. 10/7—25/9/26.**G**.
Gor. 2/3—13/4/29.**G**.
Gor. 19/3—2/4/32.**G**.
Altered to LNE gauge.
Gor. 16—30/3/35.**G**.
Gor. 15/10—12/11/38.**G**.
Gor. 13—20/5/39.**L**.
Gor. 5—19/4/41.**G**.
Gor. 8—17/4/43.**G**.
Gor. 24/11—15/12/45.**G**.
Gor. 20/12/47—10/1/48.**G**.

BOILERS:
427 11/3/11.
151 *(ex 635)* 16/6/17.
126 *(ex 5607)* 3/3/23.
373 *(exN5 5900)* 2/4/32.
1695 *(exJ10 5835)* 30/3/35.
4234 *(new)* 12/11/38.
1695 *(exN5 5908)* 17/4/43.
448 *(exN5 5938)* 15/12/45.
4265 *(exN5 9302)* 10/1/48.

SHEDS:
Barnsley.
Sheffield 5/2/38.

RENUMBERED:
5724 25/9/26.
9247 13/10/46.

CONDEMNED: 1/5/50.
Cut up at Gorton 24/6/50.

5725

Neilson 4369.

To traffic 4/1892.

REPAIRS:
Gor. 4/11—26/12/08.**G**.
Gor. 20/5—11/11/11.**G**.
Gor. 15/1—30/4/21.**G**.
Belpaire boiler fitted.
Gor. 11/8—27/10/23.**G**.
Gor. 5/12/25—30/1/26.**G**.
Gor. 28/7—1/9/28.**G**.
Altered to LNE gauge.
Gor. 23/5—13/6/31.**G**.
Gor. 2—16/5/36.**G**.
Gor. 7—21/10/39.**G**.
Gor. 30/4—8/5/43.**G**.
Gor. 5/1/46. *Not repaired.*

BOILERS:
767 *(new)* 26/12/08.
379 *(ex 614)* 11/11/11.
101 *(new)* 30/4/21.
174 *(exN5 5746)* 1/9/28.
523 *(new ?)* 13/6/31.
313 *(exJ10 5811)* 16/5/36.
490 *(exJ10 5076)* 21/10/39.
523 *(ex 5721)* 8/5/43.

SHEDS:
Barnsley.
Sheffield 7/11/34.

RENUMBERED:
725c 27/10/23.
5725 30/1/26.
9248 *allocated.*

CONDEMNED: 1/2/46.
Cut up at Gorton 15/6/46.

(below) **By May 1947 on No.9241 Gorton had gone back to standard 7½ in. letters and No.9226, ex works 20th September 1947, also 9232 ex works 8th November 1947 and 9228 ex works 22nd November 1947, got shaded transfers so no N4 was turned out with LNER in Gill sans lettering.**

New ownership caused the number to be moved to the bunker, and the end of shaded transfers. First ex works were Nos.E9233 and E9240 on 14th February 1948 with 12 inch painted and unshaded figures and similar 7in. letters, and with full BR number No.69236 was out 27th March 1948. No.69227 (5th June 1948) was the first N4 fitted with a smokebox numberplate, and those with the 7½in. letters were Nos.69227, 69236, 69237, 69239, 69245, and possibly No.69234 on 7th August 1948.

By 1949 Gorton had changed to standard Gill sans letters and figures in matching 10 inch size; in 1949 four were in this style: 69242 (26th February), 69244 (20th August), 69225 and 69246 (3rd September).
(below) **Eight of the class survived to get the BR emblem: 69235 (15th October 1949), 69232 (3rd December 1949), 69230 (24th December 1949), 69233 (21st January 1950), 69231 (4th February 1950), 69228 (18th February 1950), 69229 (8th April 1950), 69240 (10th June 1950). Last of class were Nos.69228, 69230, and 69232, all withdrawn on 31st December 1954.**

Between August 1893 and March 1894 a further thirty engines, numbered 518 to 535, and 537 to 548, were built by Beyer, Peacock & Co.. No.538 of this batch was renumbered 127 in 1903. Their valve motion differed from the three originals by having indirect drive via a valve spindle link, and they had 8in. journals instead of 7½in. used for Nos.515-517. These two items were then made standard for the rest of the class.

Twelve more engines, numbered 744 to 755 were built by Beyer, Peacock & Co. between August and November 1894. Of these, Nos.754 and 755 were sold in 1895 to the West Lancashire Railway ultimately becoming Lancashire & Yorkshire Railway Nos.1368 and 1369. The numbers 754 and 755 were used again for two new N5s in January 1896, built by Beyer, Peacock – *see* page 28, bottom.

CLASS N 5

5515

Gorton.

To traffic 9/1891.

REPAIRS:
Gor. 14/10—4/12/09.**G**.
Gor. 31/5—6/9/13.**G**.
Mex. 1/6—8/8/21.**G**.
Gor. 6/10—24/11/23.**G**.
Gor. 13/2—10/4/26.**G**.
Altered to LNE gauge.
Gor. 10/11—8/12/28.**G**.
Gor. 29/8—26/9/31.**G**.
Reverted to GC gauge.
Gor. 27/10—10/11/34.**G**.
Altered back to LNE gauge.
Gor. 13—27/11/37.**G**.
Gor. 14—28/12/40.**G**.
New cylinders.
Gor. 11/2—4/3/44.**G**.
Gor. 25/10—8/11/47.**G**.
Gor. 10—24/2/51.**G**.
Gor. 9—23/1/54.**C/L**.
After collision.

BOILERS:
644 4/12/09.
240 *(new)* 6/9/13.
272 *(ex spare)* 24/11/23.
1199 *(ex spare)* 10/4/26.
56 *(ex 5751)* 26/9/31.
1893 *(ex 5918)* 10/11/34.
92 *(ex 5925)* 27/11/37.
53 *(ex 5525)* 4/3/44.
4196 *(ex 9283)* 8/11/47.
22683 *(ex 9358)* 24/2/51.

SHEDS:
Barnsley.
Doncaster 22/12/28.
Mexborough 22/1/29.
Trafford Park 25/7/32.
Gorton 9/2/40
Northwich 9/4/40
Brunswick 9/5/43.
Gorton 21/11/48.

RENUMBERED:
7 24/10/93.
515c 8/12/23.
5515 10/4/26.
9250 15/9/46.
69250 24/2/51.

CONDEMNED: 13/8/56.
Into Gor. for cut up 18/8/56.
Sent to Dar. 25/8/56 for c/u.

5516

Gorton.

To traffic 8/1892.

REPAIRS:
Gor. ?/?—21/11/08.**G**.
Gor. 29/9—11/11/11.**G**.
Gor. 23/9/16—27/1/17.**G**.
Gor. 30/12/22—17/3/23.**G**.
Gor. 28/2—4/4/25.**G**.
Gor. 14/7—11/8/28.**G**.
Altered to LNE gauge.
Gor. 25/4—16/5/31.**G**.
Gor. 16—30/3/35.**G**.
Gor. 13—27/11/37.**G**.
Gor. 10—24/8/40.**G**.
Gor. 10—25/12/43.**G**.
Gor. 9/11—7/12/46.**G**.
New cylinders.

BOILERS:
620 21/11/08.
131 *(new?)* 11/11/11.
1661 *(new)* 27/1/17.
587 *(ex 5763)* 17/3/23.
296 *(exJ12 6422)* 11/8/28.
1654 *(exD7 5686)* 16/5/31.
1688 *(ex 5919)* 30/3/35.
98 *(ex 5771)* 27/11/37.
272 *(exJ10 5122)* 24/8/40.
1642 *(ex 5536)* 25/12/43.
479 *(ex 5895)* 7/12/46.

SHEDS:
Mexborough 6/2/06.
Barnsley 7/1/39.
Doncaster 4/3/41.
Bidston 7/11/42.
Northwich 13/11/42.
Heaton Mersey 16/12/45.

RENUMBERED:
47 10/10/93.
5516 4/4/25.
9251 2/6/46.
69251 12/2/49.

CONDEMNED: 18/7/49.
Cut up at Gorton 6/8/49.

5517

Gorton.

To traffic 11/1892.

REPAIRS:
Gor. 1/2—28/3/08.**G**.
Gor. 16/9/10—21/1/11.**G**.
Gor. 19/8—30/12/16.**G**.
Gor. 28/2/20—16/7/21.**G**.
Gor. 15/12/23—8/3/24.**G**.
Gor. 23/10—31/12/26.**G**.
Gor. 5/1—16/2/29.**G**.
Gor. 26/9—17/10/31.**G**.
Altered to LNE gauge.
Gor. 12—26/1/35.**G**.
Gor. 13—27/11/37.**G**.
Gor. 7—21/12/40.**G**.
Gor. 23/12/43—8/1/44.**G**.
Gor. 15/3—12/4/47.**G**.
Gor. 18/6—23/7/49.**G**.
Gor. 4/8/51. *Not repaired.*

BOILERS:
544 28/3/08.
483 *(new)* 21/1/11.
1655 *(new)* 30/12/16.
120 *(new)* 16/7/21.
1579 *(exJ12 6424)* 16/2/29.
758 *(new)* 17/10/31.
510 *(exJ10 5675)* 26/1/35.
405 *(ex 5200)* 27/11/37.
564 *(ex 5745)* 8/1/44.
735 *(ex 9346)* 12/4/47.
4235 *(ex 9287)* 23/7/49.

SHEDS:
Mexborough 22/4/08.
Trafford Park 25/7/32.
Wigan 7/7/33.
Gorton 21/8/33.
Heaton Mersey 15/1/34.
Gorton 3/6/45.
Walton-on-the-Hill 7/10/45.
Gorton 25/11/45.
Trafford Park 6/1/46.

RENUMBERED:
171 14/12/93.
5517 8/3/24.
9252 12/5/46.
69252 29/1/49.

CONDEMNED: 20/8/51.
Cut up at Gorton 8/9/51.

5518

Beyer, Peacock 3552.

To traffic 8/1893.

REPAIRS:
Gor. ?/?—3/6/05.**G**.
Gor. 3/3—27/5/11.**G**.
Gor. 14/10/16—10/3/17.**G**.
Gor. 30/12/22—10/3/23.**G**.
Wrx. 3/12/24—25/4/25.**G**.
Gor. 29/9—3/11/28.**G**.
Gor. 19/12/31—9/1/32.**G**.
Gor. 8/2—7/3/36.**G**.
Altered to LNE gauge.
Gor. 5—19/3/38.**G**.
Gor. 2—23/11/40.**G**.
Gor. 20/5—5/6/43.**G**.
Gor. 1—29/9/45.**G**.
Gor. 28/2—20/3/48.**G**.
Gor. 6/11/48.**L**.
Gor. 25/2—11/3/50.**G**.
Gor. 22/11—6/12/52.**G**.

BOILERS:
1127 *(new)* 3/6/05.
745 *(ex 771)* 27/5/11.
131 *(ex 516)* 10/3/17.
402 *(new)* 10/3/23 *(sup.)*.
382 *(exJ10 5083)* 5/6/43 *(sat.)*.
4227 *(ex 5548)* 29/9/45.
4315 *(new)* 20/3/48.
451 *(exN4 9232)* 11/3/50.
22714 *(exN4 69233)* 6/12/52.

SHEDS:
Gorton.
Wrexham 1/3/24.
Northwich (*by* 3/32).
Gorton 22/1/36.
Ardsley 7/3/36.
Bradford 29/4/36.
Lincoln 21/5/50.
Immingham 3/2/52.
Lincoln 10/2/52.
Sheffield 4/4/54.

RENUMBERED:
5518 25/4/25.
9253 20/10/46.
69253 20/3/48.

CONDEMNED: 5/11/55.
Cut up at Darlington.

WORKS CODES:- Dar - Darlington. Don - Doncaster. Gor - Gorton. Mex - Mexborough. RSH - Robert, Stephenson & Hawthorn. Str - Stratford. Wrx - Wrexham. YECo - Yorkshire Engine Co.
REPAIR CODES:- **C/H** - Casual Heavy. **C/L** - Casual Light. **G** - General. **H**- Heavy. **H/I** - Heavy Intermediate. **L** - Light. **L/I** - Light Intermediate. **N/C** - Non-Classified.

As part of an order for twelve, Gorton built another five engines, Nos.536, 200, 54, 21 and 25 between May 1895 and December 1896. They were similar to the preceding engines in having the bunker back curved outwards at the top. Nos.200, 54, 21 and 25 had run as 200A to 203A until 1896 (No.200) and 1900 (Nos54, 21, 25).

The other seven engines of the Gorton order, Nos.756 to 762, built December 1895 to June 1896, had bunkers with straight back plates, which from 1896 became standard.

The replacement Nos.754 and 755, from Beyer, Peacock in January 1896, had curved tops to the bunker back plate.

(above) **In March 1896, two engines of the same design, except for straight back plates, were built by Beyer, Peacock & Co. as Wrexham, Mold & Connah's Quay Railway Nos.17 and 18. When that line was taken over by the GCR in 1905, they were renumbered 409 and 410. No.410 got a superheater in April 1916.**

Between March and August 1898, Beyer, Peacock & Co. supplied the MS&LR with thirteen more of the class. They were numbered 763 to 775.

Gorton too built four more, Nos.189, 251, 51 and 173, from February to May 1898. Curiously, only No.251 had a straight back plate, the other having the curved top discarded from 1896. These four engines had run as Nos.206A, 207A, 204A and 205A respectively until 1900.

5519

Beyer, Peacock 3553.

To traffic 9/1893.

REPAIRS:
Gor. 22/4—22/5/09.**L.**
Gor. 18/10—29/11/13.**G.**
Gor. 26/3—7/5/21.**G.**
Gor. 12/4—21/6/24.**G.**
New cylinders.
Gor. 5/2—2/4/27.**G.**
Gor. 15/11—13/12/30.**G.**
Gor. 29/7—5/8/33.**G.**
Altered to LNE gauge.
Gor. 5—26/9/36.**G.**
Gor. 15—29/7/39.**G.**
Gor. 15—26/6/43.**G.**
Gor. 26/1—16/2/46.**G.**
Gor. 18/9—9/10/48.**G.**
Gor. 3—17/2/51.**H/I.**
Gor. 11/4—2/5/53.**G.**

BOILERS:
603 22/5/09.
1356 *(ex 745)* 29/11/13.
1703 *(ex 5750)* 2/4/27.
460 *(ex 5757)* 5/8/33.
1614 *(exN4 5721)* 26/9/36.
387 *(exN4 5605)* 29/7/39.
951 *(ex 5928)* 26/6/43.
4232 *(ex 5750)* 16/2/46.
4264 *(ex 9311)* 9/10/48.
4264 reno.22682 17/2/51.
22814 *(ex 69303)* 2/5/53.

SHEDS:
Gorton 27/5/07.
Chester 20/11/33.
Wrexham 3/3/34.
Gorton 26/6/39.
Northwich 1/11/39.
Gorton 10/5/40.
Sheffield 22/11/43.
Barnsley 4/2/44.
Gorton 16/2/44.
Wrexham 17/1/45.
Gorton 2/11/47.
Brunswick 2/1/49.
Wrexham 22/10/55.

RENUMBERED:
5519 21/6/24.
9254 20/9/46.
69254 9/10/48.

CONDEMNED: 2/4/56.
Cut up at Gorton 16/6/56.

5520

Beyer, Peacock 3554.

To traffic 9/1893.

REPAIRS:
Gor. ?/?—14/3/02.**G.**
Gor. 20/3—19/6/15.**G.**
Gor. 23/4—28/5/21.**G.**
New cylinders.
Gor. 5/7—30/8/24.**G.**
Gor. 31/8—28/9/29.**G.**
Gor. 27/8—17/9/32.**G.**
Altered to LNE gauge.
Gor. 21/12/35—4/1/36.**G.**
Gor. 23/7—6/8/38.**G.**
Gor. 27/7—3/8/40.**G.**
Gor. 26/6—10/7/43.**G.**
Gor. 4—25/5/46.**G.**
Furness lubricator fitted.
Gor. 26/6—31/7/48.**G.**
Gor. 21/10—11/11/50.**H/I.**
Gor. 1—15/3/52.**C/H.**
Gor. 9—23/5/53.**G.**
Gor. 8/8/53.**C/L.**
After collision.

BOILERS:
280 14/3/02.
1199 *(new)* 19/6/15.
44 *(exD7 5565)* 30/8/24.
1571 *(exJ10 5117)* 17/9/32.
960 *(ex 5904)* 4/1/36.
4203 *(exJ10 5832)* 6/8/38.
4200 *(ex 5924)* 10/7/43.
315 *(ex 5532)* 25/5/46.
4212 *(ex 9268)* 31/7/48.
4212 reno.22666 11/11/50.
22819 *(exJ10 65141)* 23/5/53.

SHEDS:
Gorton.
Trafford Park 7/12/36.
Northwich 9/4/55.
Trafford Park 25/6/55.

RENUMBERED:
5520 30/8/24.
9255 8/12/46.
69255 31/7/48.

CONDEMNED: 4/6/56.
Cut up at Gorton 30/6/56.

5521

Beyer, Peacock 3555.

To traffic 9/1893.

REPAIRS:
Gor. ?/?—31/1/03.**G.**
Gor. 27/11/15—19/2/16.**G.**
Gor. 9/12/22—3/2/23.**G.**
Gor. 28/3—23/5/25.**G.**
Gor. 11/2—17/3/28.**G.**
Gor. 28/3—18/4/31.**G.**
Gor. 20/1—3/2/34.**G.**
Altered to LNE gauge.

BOILERS:
605 *(new)* 31/1/03.
1601 *(new)* 19/2/16 *(sup.).*
1092 *(ex 5539 & spare)* 17/3/28.
441 *(ex 5021)* 3/2/34 *(sat,).*

SHEDS:
Barnsley.
New England 21/11/34.

RENUMBERED:
5521 23/5/25.

CONDEMNED: 9/11/36.
Cut up at Doncaster 16/1/37.

5522

Beyer, Peacock 3556.

To traffic 9/1893.

REPAIRS:
Gor. 8/7—10/9/08.**G.**
Gor. 31/3—5/8/11.**G.**
Gor. 27/1—28/7/17.**G.**
Gor. 30/10/20—29/1/21.**G.**
Gor. 16/6—4/8/23.**G.**
Gor. 20/3—22/5/26.**G.**
Gor. 4/10—1/11/30.**G.**
Gor. 28/10—25/11/33.**G.**
Altered to LNE gauge.
New cylinders fitted.
Gor. 10—24/4/37.**G.**
Gor. 26/8—2/9/39.**G.**
Gor. 23/12/42—16/1/43.**G.**
Gor. 2—23/3/46.**G.**
Gor. 5—19/6/48.**L.**
Loose eccentric.
Gor. 6—20/11/48.**G.**
Gor. 26/2/49.**L.**
Burst ejector pipe.
Gor. 20/10—17/11/51.**G.**

BOILERS:
944 10/9/08.
1127 *(ex 518)* 5/8/11.
578 *(ex 545)* 28/7/17.
1820 *(new)* 25/11/33.
4215 *(new)* 24/4/37.
4202 *(ex 5935)* 2/9/39.
4185 *(exN4 5628)* 16/1/43.
310 *(ex 5751)* 23/3/46.
315 *(ex 9255)* 20/11/48.
22718 *(new, reno from 4337)* 17/11/51.

SHEDS:
Gorton.
Heaton Mersey 18/1/34.
Gorton 30/1/37.
Trafford Park 31/10/37.
Gorton 1/7/39.
Wrexham 31/7/41.
Gorton 8/3/42.
Colwick 16/2/47.
Bradford 21/2/47.
Boston 14/5/50.

RENUMBERED:
5522 22/5/26.
9256 13/7/46.
69256 19/6/48.

CONDEMNED: 18/11/55.
Condemned & cut up at Darlington.

5523

Beyer, Peacock 3557.

To traffic 10/1893.

REPAIRS:
Gor. 7/12/08—13/2/09.**G.**
New cylinders.
Gor. 23/4—20/8/21.**G.**
Wrx. 8/7—9/12/24.**G.**
Gor. 31/8—5/10/29.**G.**
Gor. 18/3/30. **L.**
Heating app. both ends.
Gor. 27/8—24/9/32.**G.**
Altered to LNE gauge.
New cylinders.
Gor. 7—21/12/35.**G.**
Gor. 31/12/38—14/1/39.**G.**
Gor. 3—20/12/41.**G.**
Gor. 9—18/4/42.**G.**
Vac control p&p gear.
Gor. 5—26/8/44.**G.**
Gor. 2—30/8/47.**G.**
Gor. 23/9—14/10/50.**G.**
Gor. 28/7—11/8/51.**G.**
Gor. 10/1—7/2/53.**G.**
New cylinders.
Gor. 25/8—22/9/56.**G.**

BOILERS:
613 *(ex 925)* 13/2/09.
467 *(exN4 613)* 20/8/21.
469 *(ex 5908)* 21/12/35.
376 *(exJ10 5842)* 14/1/39.
4259 *(new)* 20/12/41.
4262 *(ex 5752)* 26/8/44.
4278 *(exJ10 5174)* 30/8/47.
22660 *(ex 69272)* 14/10/50.
22806 *(new, reno from 4344)* 7/2/53.
22798 *(exJ10 65169)* 22/9/56.

From March 1899 to December 1900, Gorton built thirty-one more, Nos.894 to 924. Beginning with No.895, this batch had the more modern design of brake block with a lug cast on the back for attaching to the hanger. No.894 had the older type of two long plates with block pinned between them. By August 1920 it had been changed to the later design, but none of the earlier engines were altered – *see* page 65, 2nd from top.

Beyer, Peacock continued to supply the GCR and from April to July 1900 they turned out sixteen numbered 925 to 940. Like all the previous engines their tanks and bunker had snap-head rivets.

The last additions to the class, six numbered 941 to 946, were again built by Beyer, Peacock & Co., during February and March 1901. They had tanks and bunker fastened by rivets with countersunk head.

In the 1940s when a tank needed new plates, they were fixed by welding instead of riveting.

(below) **Between May 1915 and April 1916 eight were fitted with superheaters, which needed a longer smokebox and a frame extension: 1915 - 539 (8th May), 544 (10th July), 771 (6th November); 1916 – 200 (5th February), 530 (12th February), 521 (19th February), 127 (4th March), 410 (1st April). Two more, Nos.518 and 763, were superheated in 1923 by the LNER –** ***see*** **page 36, bottom.**

The LNER changed all these engines, except No.5410, back to non-superheated when they went in for repairs at: 5127 (8th November 1924), 5544 (10th March 1928), 5200 (14th April 1928), 5771 (20th September 1930), 5521 (20th January 1934), 5539 (25th August 1934), 5530 (9th March 1940), No.5410 being still superheated when withdrawn on 6th February 1936. Nos.5127 and 5771 kept their 3ft 8in. long smokebox but the others reverted to normal 2ft 9˘in. pattern making the frame extension quite prominent. No.5539 also kept its longer smokebox – ***see*** **page 36, middle.**

5523 cont./
SHEDS:
Gorton.
Walton-on-the-Hill 6/6/39.
Gorton 8/3/40.
Neasden 19/4/42.
King's Cross 18/3/51.
Neasden 9/9/51.
Annesley 9/8/53.
Neasden 30/8/53.
Stratford 3/10/54.
Neasden 31/10/54.

RENUMBERED:
5523 9/12/24.
9257 25/5/46.
69257 14/10/50.

CONDEMNED: 7/12/59.
Cut up at Gorton 30/4/60.

5524

Beyer, Peacock 3558.

To traffic 10/1893.

REPAIRS:
Gor. 2/8—10/9/08.**G**.
Gor. 19/4—23/8/13.**G**.
New cylinders.
Gor. 19/7—6/12/19.**G**.
Gor. 2/12/22—13/1/23.**G**.
Gor. 12/12/25—30/1/26.**G**.
Gor. 8—29/6/29.**G**.
Gor. 16—30/4/32.**G**.
Altered to LNE gauge.
Gor. 26/10—9/11/35.**G**.
Gor. 19/11—3/12/38.**G**.
Gor. 2—16/8/41.**G**.
New cylinders.
Gor. 10—24/6/44.**G**.
Gor. 12/10—2/11/46.**G**.
Gor. 19/3—2/4/49.**G**.
Gor. 15/3—5/4/52.**H/I**.
Gor. 25/12/54—29/1/55.**G**.
New cylinders.
Gor. 24/12/55.**C/L**.

BOILERS:
406 10/9/08.
612 *(ex 189)* 23/8/13.
1823 *(new)* 6/12/19.
1751 *(exN4 5633)* 30/4/32.
1588 *(exJ9 5741)* 9/11/35.
183 *(ex 5899)* 3/12/38.
4244 *(ex 5899)* 24/6/44.
4229 *(exN4 9242)* 2/4/49.
4229 reno.22750 5/4/52.
22842 *(ex69262 & sp.)* 29/1/55.

SHEDS:
Gorton 6/2/20.
Wrexham 31/7/29.
Chester 1/9/30.
Wrexham 2/10/30
Northwich 11/1/37.
Gorton 28/3/41.
Brunswick 9/11/41.
New England 27/4/58.
Sheffield 7/12/58.

RENUMBERED:
5524 30/1/26.
9258 28/9/46.
69258 5/3/49.

CONDEMNED: 10/9/60.
Into Don. for cut up 14/9/60.

5525

Beyer, Peacock 3559.

To traffic 10/1893.

REPAIRS:
Gor. 20/3—25/4/03.**G**.
Gor. 9/11/18—28/6/19.**G**.
Gor. 30/7—1/10/21.**G**.
New cylinders.
Gor. 8/11—20/12/24.**G**.
Gor. 6/10—17/11/28.**G**.
Gor. 1—22/2/30.**L**.
After collision.
Gor. 8/11—6/12/30.**G**.
Altered to LNE gauge.
Gor. 23/6—14/7/34.**G**.
Gor. 8—22/5/37.**G**.
Gor. 2—23/3/40.**G**.
Gor. 6—22/8/42.**G**.
Gor. 30/9—9/10/43.**G**.
Gor. 15/12/45—12/1/46.**G**.
Gor. 21/8—11/9/48.**G**.
Gor. 5/1—2/2/52.**G**.
Gor. 12/3—16/4/55.**G**.

BOILERS:
618 *(new)* 25/4/03.
1349 *(ex935)* 28/6/19.
644 *(ex5752)* 17/11/28.
243 *(ex5922)* 6/12/30.
471 *(ex5540)* 14/7/34.
1820 *(ex5522)* 22/5/37.
106 *(ex5931)* 23/3/40.
53 *(exJ10 5818)* 22/8/42.
401 *(ex5921)* 9/10/43.
4248 *(ex5772)* 12/1/46.
4287 *(ex9315)* 11/9/48.
22734 *(ex69252)* 2/2/52.
22785 *(ex69275 & sp.)* 16/4/55.

SHEDS:
Gorton.
Ardsley 17/8/34.
Bradford 18/8/34.
Ardsley 11/5/36.
Barnsley 21/12/37.
Sheffield 3/2/38.
Annesley 6/3/38.
Neasden 13/10/46.
Sheffield 12/12/54.

RENUMBERED:
5525 20/12/24.
9259 11/8/46.
69259 11/9/48.

CONDEMNED: 14/11/58.
Cut up at Gorton 27/12/58.

5526

Beyer, Peacock 3560.

To traffic 10/1893.

REPAIRS:
Gor. 2/10—18/12/15.**G**.
New cylinders.
Gor. 1/4—19/8/22.**G**.
Gor. 8/11—6/12/24.**G**.
Gor. 6/10—3/11/28.**G**.
Gor. 12—31/12/31.**G**.
Altered to LNE gauge.
Gor. 23—30/3/35.**G**.
Gor. 15/8—5/9/36.**G**.
Gor. 21/5—11/6/38.**G**.
Gor. 1—15/6/40.**G**.
Gor. 5—16/8/41.**H**.
Gor. 3—15/1/44.**G**.
Gor. 26/1—16/2/46.**G**.
Gor. 10—17/8/46.**L**.
Gor. 27/8—17/9/49.**G**.
New cylinders.
Gor. 18/10—1/11/52.**G**.

BOILERS:
573.
1590 *(new)* 18/12/15.
326 *(new)* 19/8/22.
1105 *(exJ10 5079)* 31/12/31.
1654 *(ex 5516)* 30/3/35.
538 *(ex 5757)* 5/9/36.
4231 *(new)* 11/6/38.
4256 *(new)* 16/8/41.
4221 *(exF1 5589)* 15/1/44.
4256 *(ex 5051)* 16/2/46.
4189 *(exJ10 5167)* 17/9/49.
22793 *(ex 69293)* 1/11/52.

SHEDS:
Gorton.
Langwith Jct. 29/6/35.
Neasden 1/1/42.
Derby 3/5/42.
Annesley 26/7/42.
Gorton 18/8/46.
Retford 14/8/55.

RENUMBERED:
5526 6/12/24.
9260 27/10/46.
69260 17/9/49.

CONDEMNED: 23/7/56.
Cut up at Gorton 29/9/56.

5527

Beyer, Peacock 3561.

To traffic 10/1893.

REPAIRS:
Gor. 3/9—27/12/01.**G**.
Gor. 25/3—20/5/16.**G**.
Gor. 11/2—8/4/22.**G**.
Gor. 7/3—25/4/25.**G**.
Gor. 8/12/28—2/2/29.**G**.
Altered to LNE gauge.
Gor. 2—23/5/31.**G**.
Gor. 22/12/34—19/1/35.**G**.
Gor. 3/4/37—1/5/37.**G**.
Gor. 20/1—10/2/40.**G**.
Gor. 10/6—4/7/42.**G**.
New cylinders.
Gor. 11—18/12/43.**L**.
New R.H. piston fitted.
Gor. 24/2—24/3/45.**G**.
Gor. 29/11—20/12/47.**G**.
Gor. 15—22/1/49.**L**.
Gor. 22/7—12/8/50.**G**.
New cylinders.
Gor. 7—21/11/53.**G**.
Gor. 9/12/57. *Not repaired.*

BOILERS:
231 27/12/01.
1618 *(new)* 20/5/16.
1345 *(exJ12 5495)* 2/2/29.
535 *(exJ10 5118)* 19/1/35.
36 *(exJ10 5851)* 1/5/37.
505 *(ex 5924)* 10/2/40.
563 *(ex 5935)* 4/7/42.
4243 *(ex 5929)* 24/3/45.
435 *(ex 9320)* 20/12/47.
4265 *(exN4 9247)* 12/8/50.
22829 *(exJ10 65209)* 21/11/53.

SHEDS:
Gorton.
Trafford Park 29/6/31.
Wigan 25/1/32.
Gorton 15/5/33.
Bradford 19/4/41.
Boston 14/5/50.
Immingham 30/10/55.
Langwith Jct. 17/2/57.

RENUMBERED:
5527 25/4/25.
9261 20/10/46.
69261 22/1/49.

5527 cont./
CONDEMNED: 23/12/57.
Cut up at Gorton 18/10/58.

5528

Beyer, Peacock 3562.

To traffic 10/1893.

REPAIRS:
Gor. ?/?—2/3/07.**G.**
Gor. 25/2—15/7/22.**G.**
New cylinders.
Gor. 7/11—26/12/25.**G.**
Gor. 19/1—23/2/29.**G.**
Gor. ?—?/1/30. **L.**
Heating app. both ends.
Gor. 13—27/2/32.**G.**
Altered to LNE gauge.
Gor. 17—24/3/34.**G.**
Gor. 28/11—12/12/36.**G.**
Gor. 18/2—4/3/39.**G.**
Gor. 2—13/6/42.**G.**
Gor. 20/11—12/12/42.**L.**
After collision.
Gor. 17—28/4/45.**G.**
Gor. 17/1—14/2/48.**G.**
Gor. 19/11—3/12/49.**G.**
Gor. 18/10—1/11/52.**G.**
Gor. 26/11—24/12/55.**G.**
Gor. 12/12/59. *Not repaired.*

BOILERS:
404 *(new)* 2/3/07.
207 *(exD7 686)* 15/7/22.
378 *(ex 5529)* 27/2/32.
401 *(new)* 24/3/34.
97 *(ex 5529)* 12/12/36.
142 *(ex 5901)* 4/3/39.
193 *(ex 5548)* 13/6/42.
4277 *(new)* 28/4/45.
490 *(ex 9272)* 14/2/48.
4211 *(ex 9308)* 3/12/49.
22749 *(ex 69343)* 1/11/52.
22801 *(ex 69276)* 24/12/55.

SHEDS:
Gorton.
Wrexham 12/5/39.
Gorton 21/9/39.
Northwich 7/4/40.
Heaton Mersey 6/12/52.
New England 27/4/58.

RENUMBERED:
5528 26/12/25.
9262 5/5/46.
E9262 14/2/48.
69262 5/3/49.

CONDEMNED: 22/12/59.
Cut up at Gorton 20/2/60.

5529

Beyer, Peacock 3563.

To traffic 11/1893.

REPAIRS:
Gor. 10/8—9/11/07.**G.**
Gor. 5/8—28/10/22.**G.**
Gor. 7/8—16/10/26.**G.**
Gor. 23/2—23/3/29.**G.**
Gor. 19/12/31—9/1/32.**G.**
Altered to LNE gauge.
Gor. 12—26/1/35.**G.**
Gor. 7—21/11/36.**G.**
Gor. 17/6—8/7/39.**G.**
Gor. 28/11—19/12/42.**G.**
Gor. 19/5—9/6/45.**G.**
Gor. 22/11—20/12/47.**G.**
Gor. 21/10—4/11/50.**G.**
Gor. 8/8—5/9/53.**G.**
Gor. 30/6—11/8/56.**G.**

BOILERS:
1343 *(new)* 9/11/07.
378 *(new)* 28/10/22.
1594 *(exJ10 5813)* 9/1/32.
97 *(exJ10 5810)* 26/1/35.
425 *(exN4 5617)* 21/11/36.
4199 *(ex 5774)* 8/7/39.
4239 *(exJ10 5839)* 19/12/42.
193 *(ex 5528)* 9/6/45.
716 *(ex 9334)* 20/12/47.
22665 *(exN4 9237)* 4/11/50.
22667 *(ex spare)* 5/9/53.
22728 *(exJ10 65175)* 11/8/56.

SHEDS:
Gorton 17/3/17.
Ardsley 11/5/27.
Gorton 16/627.
Chester 1/2/32.
Gorton 21/9/34.
Trafford Park 22/2/37.
Gorton 21/9/39.
Colwick 19/4/43.
Woodford 19/6/49.
Colwick 29/11/53
Staveley 31/10/54.
Langwith Jct. 25/10/59.

RENUMBERED:
5529 16/10/26.
9263 17/11/46.
69263 4/11/50.

CONDEMNED: 17/11/60.
Into Don. for cut up 17/11/60.

5530

Beyer, Peacock 3564.

To traffic 11/1893.

REPAIRS:
Gor. ?/?—22/2/08.**G.**
Gor. 13/11/15—12/2/16.**G.**
Gor. 19/3—14/5/21.**G.**
Gor. 18/8—3/11/23.**G.**
Gor. 13/3—12/6/26.**G.**
Gor. 27/12/30—31/1/31.**G.**
Gor. 28/4—5/5/34.**G.**
Altered to LNE gauge.
Gor. 23/1—13/2/37.**G.**
New cylinders.
Gor. 9/3—6/4/40.**G.**
Gor. 30/1—13/2/43.**G.**
Gor. 21/9—19/10/46.**G.**
Gor. 23—30/4/49.**G.**
Gor. 24/2—17/3/51.**G.**

BOILERS:
1360 *(new)* 22/2/08.
1598 *(new)* 12/2/16 (sup.).
1092 *(ex 5521)* 5/5/34.
144 *(ex 5926)* 6/4/40 (sat.).
357 *(ex 5946)* 13/2/43.
1230 *(ex 9341)* 19/10/46.
443 *(ex 69329)* 30/4/49.
22684 *(ex 9300)* 17/3/51.

SHEDS:
Wrexham 14/5/20.
Bidston ?/?/?.
Wrexham 24/7/28.
Bidston 11/10/28.
Wrexham 18/2/29.
Gorton 9/12/30.
Ardsley 6/2/36.
Mexborough 10/12/44.

RENUMBERED:
530c 10/11/23.
5530 12/6/26.
9264 2/6/46.
69264 30/4/49.

CONDEMNED: 14/2/55.
Cut up at Gorton 2/4/55.

5531

Beyer, Peacock 3565.

To traffic 11/1893.

REPAIRS:
Gor. 11/4—16/5/08.**G.**
Gor. 23/9/10—14/1/11.**G.**
Gor. 1/10—5/11/21.**G.**
Gor. 30/8—25/10/24.**G.**
Gor. 9/2—9/3/29.**G.**
Gor. 20/6—11/7/31.**G.**
Gor. 19/5—2/6/34.**G.**
Altered to LNE gauge.
Gor. 16—23/11/35.**G.**

BOILERS:
501 16/5/08.
194 *(new)* 14/1/11.
214 *(new)* 5/11/21.
137 *(ex 5546)* 11/7/31.
541 *(exJ10 5674)* 2/6/34.
1656 *(ex 5772)* 23/11/35.

SHEDS:
Wrexham.
Bidston 21/10/28.
Wrexham 4/1/29.
Gorton 4/2/29.
Brunswick 31/8/34.
Walton-on-the-Hill 30/11/36.

RENUMBERED:
5531 25/10/24.

CONDEMNED: 29/12/38.
Cut up at Doncaster 11/2/39.

5532

Beyer, Peacock 3566.

To traffic 11/1893.

REPAIRS:
Gor. 2/3—18/6/10.**G.**
YECo. 5/3—26/7/21.**G.**
Gor. 17/7—9/10/26.**G.**
Gor. 28/9—26/10/29.**G.**
Gor. 27/8—17/9/32.**G.**
Altered to LNE gauge.
Gor. 8—29/2/36.**G.**
Gor. 15—29/4/39.**G.**
Gor. 4—19/12/42.**G.**
Gor. 6/4—4/5/46.**G.**
Gor. 12/2—5/3/49.**G.**
Gor. 1—15/12/51.**H/I.**
Gor. 15/1—12/2/55.**G.**

BOILERS:
989 *(new)* 18/6/10.
613 *(ex 523)* 26/7/21.
1099 *(ex 5931)* 17/9/32.
1642 *(ex 5911)* 29/2/36.
541 *(ex 5910)* 29/4/39.
315 *(exJ10 5809)* 19/12/42.
304 *(ex 5908)* 4/5/46.
4253 *(exJ10 5205)* 5/3/49.
4253 reno.22724 15/12/51.
22701 *(ex 69286)* 12/2/55.

SHEDS:
Gorton 16/6/22.
Heaton Mersey 30/1/37.
Gorton 20/9/39.
Walton-on-the-Hill 25/3/43.

RENUMBERED:
5532 9/10/26.
9265 27/10/46.

5532 cont./
69265 5/3/49.

CONDEMNED: 7/12/59.
Cut up at Gorton 7/5/60.

5533

Beyer, Peacock 3567.

To traffic 12/1893.

REPAIRS:
Gor. 5/8—17/12/10.**G**.
New cylinders.
Gor. 19/8—25/11/22.**G**.
New cylinders.
Gor. 18/7—19/9/25.**G**.
Gor. 15/9—3/11/28.**G**.
Gor. 15—29/8/31.**G**.
Gor. 24/2—10/3/34.**G**.
Altered to LNE gauge.
Gor. 1—15/2/36.**G**.
Gor. 27/11—11/12/37.**G**.
Gor. 28/10—4/11/39.**G**.
Gor. 4—19/9/42.**G**.
Gor. 9—30/3/46.**G**.
New cylinders.
Gor. 20/8—10/9/49.**G**.
Gor. 28/11—12/12/53.**G**.
Gor. 8/6—6/7/57.**G**.

BOILERS:
1074 17/12/10.
380 *(new)* 25/11/22.
101 *(exN4 5725)* 3/11/28.
302 *(exJ10 5822)* 29/8/31.
294 *(ex 5773)* 10/3/34.
1748 *(exJ10 5644)* 15/2/36.
4229 *(new)* 11/12/37.
313 *(exN4 5725)* 4/11/39.
4215 *(exN4 5635)* 19/9/42.
4237 *(exJ10 5141)* 30/3/46.
4190 *(ex 9277)* 10/9/49.
22831 *(ex 69294)* 12/12/53.
22810 *(ex 69356)* 6/7/57.

SHEDS:
Barnsley.
Lincoln 29/9/25.
Staveley 6/10/25.
King's Cross 16/3/34.
Hatfield 26/3/34.
Ardsley 29/3/41.
Copley Hill 4/4/41.
Ardsley 10/8/52
Sheffield 25/1/53.
New England 7/12/58.
Hatfield 26/7/59.
New England 27/9/59.

RENUMBERED:
5533 19/9/25.
9266 18/11/46.
69266 10/9/49.

CONDEMNED: 25/11/60.
Into Don. for cut up 25/11/60.

5534

Beyer, Peacock 3568.

To traffic 12/1893.

REPAIRS:
Gor. ?/?—13/2/03.**G**.
Gor. 10/6—19/8/16.**G**.
Gor. 12/8—14/10/22.**G**.
New cylinders.
Gor. 27/12/24—7/2/25.**G**.
Gor. 17/8—14/9/29.**G**.
Gor. 12—26/11/32.**G**.
Altered to LNE gauge.
Gor. 24/8—21/9/35.**G**.
Gor. 7—21/1/39.**G**.
Gor. 17/2—16/3/40.**L**.
After collision.
Gor. 21/6—5/7/41.**G**.
Gor. 28/9—9/10/43.**G**.
Second-hand cyls. ex 5251.
Gor. 13/4—4/5/46.**G**.
Gor. 19/6—24/7/48.**G**.
Gor. 24/6—22/7/50.**G**.
Gor. 13/9—4/10/52.**G**.
Gor. 29/1—26/2/55.**G**.
Gor. 25/1/60. *Not repaired.*

BOILERS:
640 13/2/03.
619 *(ex 127)* 19/8/16.
29 *(ex 5930)* 14/9/29.
193 *(new)* 26/11/32.
4192 *(new)* 21/9/35.
82 *(exN4 5720)* 21/1/39.
4207 *(ex 5762)* 5/7/41.
4221 *(ex 5526)* 4/5/46.
4257 *(exN4 9245)* 24/7/48.
4249 *(ex 69281)* 22/7/50.
22785 *(ex 69275)* 4/10/52.
22784 *(ex 69366)* 26/2/55.

SHEDS:
Gorton.
Walton-on-the-Hill 24/4/39.
Wrexham 28/12/41
Tyne Dock 26/8/57.
New England 13/7/58.

RENUMBERED:
5534 7/2/25.
9267 11/8/46.
69267 24/7/48.

CONDEMNED: 26/1/60.
Cut up at Gorton 5/3/60.

5535

Beyer, Peacock 3569.

To traffic 1/1894.

REPAIRS:
Gor. 12/8—17/9/10.**G**.
YECo. 29/1—29/4/21.**G**.
New cylinders.
Gor. 2/8—4/10/24.**G**.
Gor. 13/8—1/10/27.**G**.
Gor. 5—26/7/30.**G**.
Altered to LNE gauge.
Gor. 28/10—4/11/33.**G**.
Gor. 26/12/36—9/1/37.**G**.
Gor. 22/4—6/5/39.**G**.
Gor. 11—20/6/42.**G**.
Gor. 23—28/8/43.**L**.
Backplate fractured.
Gor. 22/9—13/10/45.**G**.
New cylinders.
Gor. 15/5—5/6/48.**G**.
Gor. 2—23/6/51.**H/I**.
Gor. 13—27/6/53.**G**.
Gor. 20/4—11/5/57.**G**.
Gor. 25/1/60. *Not repaired.*

BOILERS:
616 17/9/10.
793 *(ex 764)* 29/4/21.
377 *(ex??)* 26/7/30.
221 *(ex 5941)* 4/11/33.
511 *(ex 5545)* 9/1/37.
1763 *(ex 5541)* 6/5/39.
1750 *(exJ10 5851)* 20/6/42.
4212 *(ex 5937)* 13/10/45.
4216 *(ex 9281)* 5/6/48.
4216 reno.22698 23/6/51.
22822 *(ex 69267)* 27/6/53.
22788 *(exJ10 65132)* 11/5/57.

SHEDS:
Gorton.
Stratford 22/1/37.
Hatfield 12/4/37.
Ardsley 13/2/41.
Copley Hill 2/3/41.
Barnsley 25/6/44.
Langwith Jct. 11/10/59.

RENUMBERED:
5535 4/10/24.
9268 18/8/46.
69268 5/6/48.

CONDEMNED: 26/1/60.
Cut up at Gorton 5/3/60.

5127

Beyer, Peacock 3571.

To traffic 1/1894.

REPAIRS:
Gor. 17/3—9/7/10.**G**.
New cylinders.
Gor. 18/12/15—4/3/16.**G**.
Gor. 20/5—4/11/22.**G**.
New cylinders.
Gor. 8/11/24—14/2/25.**G**.
Superheater taken out.
Gor. 30/6—4/8/28.**G**.
Gor. 4/4—2/5/31.**G**.
Altered to LNE gauge.
Gor. 22/9—6/10/34.**G**.
Gor. 19/2—5/3/38.**G**.
Gor. 21/12/40—11/1/41.**G**.
Gor. 7—22/1/44.**G**.
Gor. 13/9—11/10/47.**G**.
Gor. 8—15/1/49.**L**.
Bunker plates.
Gor. 21/4—5/5/51.**G**.
Gor. 24/4—15/5/54.**G**.
Gor. 22/12/56—19/1/57.**C/H**.

BOILERS:
619 *(new)* 9/7/10.
1603 *(new)* 4/3/16 (sup.).
483 *(new)* 2/5/31.
479 *(ex 5932)* 5/3/38.
747 *(ex 5936)* 22/1/44.
758 *(exJ10 5176)* 11/10/47.
22692 *(ex??)* 5/5/51.
22699 *(ex 69370)* 15/5/54.
22793 *(ex 69260)* 19/1/57.

SHEDS:
Barnsley.
Staveley 2/3/25.
Sheffield 7/6/43.
Staveley 8/10/43.
Woodford 21/11/44.
Staveley 22/3/53.
Immingham 13/11/55.
Boston 11/3/56.
Staveley 22/7/56.

RENUMBERED:
538 *to* 1903.
5127 14/2/25.
9269 15/9/46.
69269 15/1/49.

CONDEMNED: 17/10/58.
Cut up at Gorton 15/11/58.

(above) **From 6th February 1926 to 25th August 1934 No.5539 carried the similar 1915 built boiler used to superheat the single J10 and which had a tall dome and cover. When taken from 5539, this boiler was scrapped.**

Ex works 22nd September 1934, No.5539 was non-superheated with a new boiler built in February 1933 which had the shorter dome. Note that it kept the long smokebox.

In March 1923 new boilers, each with a superheater, were put on Nos.518 (10th) and 763 (24th), their frames and smokeboxes being made longer accordingly. Ex works 20th December 1930 No.5763 had reverted to a saturated boiler but No.5518 still had a superheater until it went to works 20th May 1943, after which no N5 was superheated.

(above) **When a superheater was put in, all ten had the header discharge valve on the left hand side of the smokebox. These were removed by the LNER but – strangely – were not replaced by a Gresley anti-vacuum valve, even though No.5530 still had a superheater until it went to works 9th March 1940.**

At Grouping, all were fitted with Robinson type chimney – of two varieties – but both were 13ft 3in. high from rail.

Beginning with No.5536, ex works 14th March 1925, a 6¾in. shorter chimney of opposite taper was fitted to bring the height within the 13ft 0in. composite load gauge. All duly had the chimney height cut to 12ft 8½in., but this was only completed on 1st October 1938 when No.5770 was ex works.

5409

Beyer, Peacock 3866.

To traffic 10/1896.

REPAIRS:
Wrx. 24/11/08—23/4/09.**G**.
Wrx. 3/6/19—2/3/20.**G**.
Wrx. 3/6—25/1/22.**G**.
New cylinders.
Gor. 25/10—20/12/24.**G**.
Wrx. 12/1—3/5/27.**H**.
Gor. 3—31/8/29.**G**.
Gor. 13—27/5/33.**G**.
Altered to LNE gauge.
Gor. 28/11—5/12/36.**G**.
Gor. 20/4—11/5/40.**G**.
Gor. 4—16/10/43.**G**.
Gor. 15/2—15/3/47.**G**.
Gor. 11—25/3/50.**G**.
Gor. 11—25/10/52.**G**.
New cylinders.

BOILERS:
433 23/4/09.
1345 *(ex 929)* 2/3/20.
568 *(new)* 20/12/24.
28 *(ex 5775)* 27/5/33.
249 *(ex 5936)* 5/12/36.
496 *(exD7 5704)* 11/5/40.
573 *(exJ10 5132)* 16/10/43.
4304 *(new)* 15/3/47.
4223 *(ex 9351)* 25/3/50.
22790 *(ex 69328)* 25/10/52.

SHEDS:
Wrexham.
Northwich 26/10/34.
Gorton 27/12/36.
Northwich 4/10/40.
Chester 29/11/42.
Wrexham 13/12/42.
Gorton 14/8/43.
Wrexham 9/9/45.
Trafford Park 28/10/45.
Northwich 18/11/45.
Gorton 25/11/45.
Brunswick 9/12/45.
Gorton 20/1/46.

RENUMBERED:
409 1905 (exWMCQ 17).
5409 20/12/24.
9270 21/7/46.
69270 5/3/49.

CONDEMNED: 29/10/56.
Cut up at Gorton 23/11/57.

5410

Beyer, Peacock 3867.

To traffic 10/1896.

REPAIRS:
Gor. ?/?—18/2/05.**G**.
Gor. 5/2/15—1/4/16.**G**.
Gor. 25/2—22/4/22.**G**.
Wrx. 30/5—16/9/24.**H**.
Wrx. 20/4—25/8/26.**H**.
Gor. 1/12/28—19/1/29.**G**.
Gor. 12/3—2/4/32.**G**.
Altered to LNE gauge.

BOILERS:
447 18/2/05.
1609 *(new)* 1/4/16 (sup).
1060 *(ex 5771)* 19/1/29.

SHEDS:
Wrexham.
Ardsley ?/?.
Gorton 20/7/27.
Bidston ?/?.
Wrexham 4/4/28.
Bidston 24/7/28.
Wrexham 11/10/28.
Gorton 29/11/28.
Wrexham 8/2/29.
Bidston ?/?.
Wrexham 24/7/31.
Gorton 10/1/36.

RENUMBERED:
410 1905 (exWMCQ 18).
5410 16/9/24.

CONDEMNED: 6/2/36.
Cut up at Gorton 22/2/36.

5537

Beyer, Peacock 3570.

To traffic 11/1894.

REPAIRS:
Gor. 3/12/01—15/2/02.**G**.
Gor. 11/10—22/1/13.**G**.
Gor. 8/10—26/11/21.**G**.
Gor. 2/8—27/9/24.**G**.
Gor. 18/6—23/7/27.**G**.
Gor. 1/2—1/3/30.**G**.
Gor. 8—29/4/33.**G**.
Altered to LNE gauge.
Gor. 26/9—10/10/36.**G**.
Gor. 9/3—6/4/40.**G**.
Gor. 6—24/7/43.**G**.
Gor. 13/9—11/10/47.**G**.
Gor. 28/2—21/3/53.**G**.
New cylinders.
Gor. 11/2—10/3/56.**C/H**.

BOILERS:
292 15/2/02.
504 *(new)* 22/11/13.
197 *(new)* 26/11/21.
192 *(exJ9 5647)* 29/4/33.
1799 *(exN4 5723)* 10/10/36.
1820 *(ex5525)* 6/4/40.
1710 *(exN4 5620)* 24/7/43.
4309 *(new)* 11/10/47.
22811 *(ex??)* 21/3/53.
22702 *(69278)* 10/3/56.

SHEDS:
Gorton.
Wigan 15/5/33.
Gorton 7/7/33.
Trafford Park 11/9/33.
Ardsley 26/10/33.
Copley Hill 26/9/34.
Ardsley 21/12/34.
Copley Hill 2/2/35.
Ardsley 18/2/51.
Colwick 3/5/53.
Staveley 31/5/53.
Colwick 14/6/53.
Sheffield 11/12/55.

RENUMBERED:
5537 27/9/24.
9271 17/8/46.
69271 21/3/53.

CONDEMNED: 10/3/58.
Cut up at Gorton 21/6/58.

5539

Beyer, Peacock 3572.

To traffic 2/1894.

REPAIRS:
Gor. 21/12/09—26/3/10.**G**.
Gor. 13/2—8/5/15.**G**.
Gor. 27/11/20—15/1/21.**G**.
Gor. 20/1—10/3/23.**G**.
Gor. 19/12/25—6/2/26.**G**.
Altered to LNE gauge.
Gor. 1/9—20/10/28.**G**.
Gor. 11/7—8/8/31.**G**.
Gor. 25/8—22/9/34.**G**.
Gor. 16—30/10/37.**G**.
Gor. 13—27/4/40.**G**.
New cylinders.
Gor. 5—23/1/43.**G**.
Gor. 29/9—20/10/45.**G**.
Gor. 31/12/47—31/1/48.**G**.
Gor. 2—23/9/50.**G**.
Gor. 29/11—27/12/52.**G**.
Gor. 21/2/53.**C/L**.
Bunker patched.

BOILERS:
792 26/3/10.
1092 *(new)* 8/5/15 (sup.).
1573 *(exJ10 5810)* 6/2/26.
440 *(new)* 22/9/34 (sat.).
4225 *(new)* 30/10/37.
4202 *(ex 5522)* 23/1/43.
490 *(exJ10 5123)* 20/10/45.
4291 *(ex 9322)* 31/1/48.
22655 *(exN4 9240)* 23/9/50.
22798 *(ex??)* 27/12/52.

SHEDS:
Wrexham 14/5/20.
Gorton 15/8/28.
Wrexham 28/11/28.
Gorton 2/11/47.
Brunswick 6/2/49.

RENUMBERED:
5539 6/2/26.
9272 2/6/46.
E9272 31/1/48.
69272 5/3/49.

CONDEMNED: 16/4/56.
Cut up at Gorton 19/5/56.

5540

Beyer, Peacock 3573.

To traffic 2/1894.

REPAIRS:
Gor. 3/2—12/3/10.**G**.
Gor. 25/4—4/7/14.**G**.
New cylinders.
Gor. 2/10—13/11/20.**G**.
Gor. 10/5—5/7/24.**G**.
Gor. 23/4—16/7/27.**G**.
New cylinders.
Gor. 27/9—25/10/30.**G**.
Altered to LNE gauge.
Gor. 2—23/6/34.**G**.
Gor. 4—25/9/37.**G**.
Gor. 30/10/37.**L**.
Trip cock gear fitted.
Gor. 28/10—14/11/42.**G**.
Gor. 30/8—27/9/47.**G**.
Gor. 10—31/5/52.**G**.

BOILERS:
541 12/3/10.
716 *(exJ10 84)* 4/7/14.
1640 *(ex 5769)* 16/7/27.
471 *(ex 5939)* 25/10/30.
314 *(ex 5756)* 23/6/34.
1898 *(exN4 5622)* 25/9/37.
1785 *(ex5747)* 14/11/42.
4308 *(new)* 27/9/47.
22761 *(ex??)* 31/5/52.

SHEDS:
Gorton 18/11/08.
Brunswick 20/10/34.

5540 cont./
Gorton 24/3/37.
Neasden 30/10/37.
LPTB 1/11/37.
Neasden 17/4/38.
Mexborough 11/4/48.
Retford 25/4/48.
Neasden 21/12/52.

RENUMBERED:
5540 5/7/24.
9273 11/8/46.
69273 31/5/52.

CONDEMNED: 27/6/55.
Cut up at Gorton 5/11/55.

5541

Beyer, Peacock 3574.

To traffic 2/1894.

REPAIRS:
Gor. ?/?—14/2/03.**G**.
Gor. 3/4—24/7/15.**G**.
Gor. 24/9—3/12/21.**G**.
Gor. 4/10—15/11/24.**G**.
Gor. 8/6—13/7/29.**G**.
Gor. 27/8—17/9/32.**G**.
Altered to LNE gauge.
Gor. 15—29/2/36.**G**.
Gor. 11—18/2/39.**G**.
Gor. 18/5—13/6/42.**G**.
Gor. 18/11—9/12/44.**G**.
Gor. 22/11—12/12/47.**G**.
Gor. 14/1—4/2/50.**G**.
New cylinders.
Gor. 10—17/11/51.**C/L**.
Gor. 31/5—21/6/52.**G**.
Gor. 20/8—24/9/55.**G**.

BOILERS:
608 *(new)* 14/2/03.
1569 *(new)* 24/7/15.
1897 *(new)* 17/9/32.
1763 *(exJ10 5834)* 29/2/36.
4218 *(ex 5895)* 18/2/39.
4214 *(ex 5925)* 9/12/44.
4311 *(new)* 12/12/47.
4203 *(exJ10 5126)* 4/2/50.
4203 reno.22720 17/11/51.
22763 *(new reno. from 4341)* 21/6/52.
22685 *(ex 69338)* 24/9/55.

SHEDS:
Gorton 30/6/22.
Brunswick 6/3/37.
Gorton 21/9/39.
Northwich 7/4/40.
Chester 27/9/40.
New England 27/4/58.

RENUMBERED:
5541 15/11/24.
9274 29/9/46.
69274 26/3/49.

CONDEMNED: 26/11/60.
Into Don. for cut up 26/11/60.

5542

Beyer, Peacock 3575.

To traffic 2/1894.

REPAIRS:
Gor. 4/1—29/2/08.**G**.
Gor. 15/7—24/12/10.**G**.
YECo. 29/1—22/3/21.**G**.
Gor. 12/4—7/6/24.**G**.
Gor. 19/2—2/4/27.**G**.
Gor. 28/9—26/10/29.**G**.
Gor. 24/9—8/10/32.**G**.
Gor. 18/5—1/6/35.**G**.
Altered to LNE gauge.
Gor. 31/10—14/11/36.**G**.
Gor. 8—22/10/38.**G**.
Gor. 14/9—5/10/40.**G**.
Gor. 9—27/3/43.**G**.
Gor. 23/3—13/4/46.**G**.
Gor. 26/2—19/3/49.**G**.
Gor. 7—28/6/52.**G**.
New cylinders.

BOILERS:
456 29/2/08.
789 *(new)* 24/12/10.
1656 *(exN4 615)* 22/3/21.
1226 *(exN4 5632)* 8/10/32.
155 *(exJ9 5741)* 1/6/35.
1769 *(ex 5899)* 14/11/36.
4233 *(new)* 22/10/38.
208 *(exJ10 5819)* 5/10/40.
4264 *(new)* 27/3/43.
726 *(ex 5744)* 13/4/46.
4322 *(new)* 19/3/49.
22766 *(ex 9273)* 28/6/52.

SHEDS:
Gorton 16/1/15.
Wrexham 9/1/30.
Gorton 6/6/35.
Langwith Jct. 28/6/35.
Tuxford 30/1/42.
Lincoln 11/1/48.

RENUMBERED:
5542 7/6/24.
9275 13/4/46.
69275 19/3/49.

CONDEMNED: 19/11/55.
Cond. & cut up at Darlington.

5543

Beyer, Peacock 3576.

To traffic 3/1894.

REPAIRS:
Gor. ?/?—3/1/03.**G**.
Gor. 26/6—11/12/15.**G**.
Gor. 9/8/19—10/7/20.**G**.
Gor. 30/12/22—10/2/23.**G**.
Gor. 12/6—28/8/26.**G**.
Gor. 6/10—17/11/28.**G**.
Gor. 13—27/2/32.**G**.
Altered to LNE gauge.
Gor. 3—24/8/35.**G**.
Gor. 9—30/4/38.**G**.
Gor. 22/3—19/4/41.**G**.
Gor. 30/12/43—15/1/44.**G**.
Gor. 13/9—11/10/47.**G**.
Gor. 1—22/4/50.**G**.
Gor. 22/12/52—10/1/53.**H/I**.
Gor. 1—29/10/55.**G**.

BOILERS:
601 *(new)* 3/1/03.
521 *(ex 544)* 11/12/15.
1705 *(ex 748)* 10/7/20.
1793 *(ex 5915)* 27/2/32.
1710 *(ex 5754)* 24/8/35.
482 *(ex 5896)* 30/4/38.
316 *(exJ10 5132)* 19/4/41.
4184 *(ex 5545)* 15/1/44.
4310 *(new)* 11/10/47.
4192 *(ex 9299)* 22/4/50.
4192 reno.22801 10/1/53.
22776 *(ex spare)* 29/10/55.

SHEDS:
Gorton 20/8/20.
Heaton Mersey 21/9/39.
New England 27/4/58.

RENUMBERED:
5543 28/8/26.??
9276 14/7/46.
69276 19/2/49.

CONDEMNED: 22/12/59.
Cut up at Gorton 27/2/60.

5544

Beyer, Peacock 3577.

To traffic 3/1894.

REPAIRS:
Gor. 17/3—23/7/10.**G**.
Gor. 29/5—10/7/15.**G**.
Gor. 28/10—18/11/22.**G**.
Gor. 17/10—26/12/25.**G**.
Gor. 10/3—21/4/28.**G**.
Altered to LNE gauge.
New cylinders.
Gor. 2—30/8/30.**G**.
Gor. 5—12/8/33.**G**.
Gor. 21/11—5/12/36.**G**.
Gor. 2—16/12/39.**G**.
Gor. 12—21/8/43.**G**.
Gor. 18/5—8/6/46.**G**.
Gor. 14—28/5/49.**G**.
Gor. 22/12/51—12/1/52.**G**.
Gor. 20/2—13/3/54.**G**.

BOILERS:
521 23/7/10.
1570 *(new)* 10/7/15 (sup.).
654 *(ex 5941)* 21/4/28 (sat.).
425 *(new)* 30/8/30.
1768 *(exN4 5636)* 12/8/33.
520 *(exJ10 5822)* 5/12/36.
4241 *(new)* 16/12/39.
1783 *(ex 5934)* 21/8/43.
4190 *(exJ10 5799)* 8/6/46.
4295 *(exJ10 5193)* 28/5/49.
22730 *(ex??)* 12/1/52.
22835 *(ex 69266)* 13/3/54.

SHEDS:
Gorton.
Barnsley *by* 1/23.
Retford 27/11/49.

RENUMBERED:
5544 26/12/25.
9277 19/6/46.
69277 28/5/49.

CONDEMNED: 20/11/56.
Cut up at Gorton 1/6/57.

5545

Beyer, Peacock 3578.

To traffic 3/1894.

REPAIRS:
Gor. 28/10/10—11/3/11.**G**.
New cylinders.
Gor. 25/11/16—7/4/17.**G**.
Gor. 3/6—30/9/22.**G**.
Gor. 8/11—20/12/24.**G**.
Gor. 3/9—15/10/27.**G**.
Gor. 22/2—8/3/30.**G**.
Gor. 13—27/8/32.**G**.
Altered to LNE gauge.
Gor. 12—19/12/36.**G**.
Gor. 25/5—8/6/40.**G**.
Gor. 18/11—18/12/43.**G**.
Gor. 26/7—16/8/47.**G**.
Gor. 25/3—8/4/50.**G**.
Gor. 25/10—8/11/52.**G**.

BOILERS:
578 *(new)* 11/3/11.
1681 *(new)* 7/4/17.

(above) **The Robinson chimney which tapered inward to the top proved prone to cracking and in 1922 one with an opposite taper but no liner was fitted to Nos.200 and 922 (3rd June), 528 (15th July), 526 and 920 (19th August), 929 (26th September), 908 (4th November), 533 (25th November). This single-piece chimney was to drawing No.13685 but still gave 13ft 3in. height from the rail.**

Whilst No.5922 lost its single piece chimney in January 1928, this type only disappeared from N5 class when No.5920 went into works on 18th August 1934. Their replacements were the plant pot type to bring them within the 13ft 0in. gauge.

Boilers fitted prior to 1910 did not have washout plugs on the shoulders of the firebox and the safety valves were the open Ramsbottom type on a raised mounting. This boiler was No.922's original of December 1900 which it kept until it went to works 24th December 1927, when the boiler was scrapped.

(above) **What was known as GCR No.1 boiler, and which became LNER Diagram 21, began to be fitted to N5 class in 1910 and all had it when No.5904 was ex works on 3rd December 1932. The firebox had two washout plugs with covers on each shoulder. Until May 1935 the normal safety valve type was Ramsbottom fitted directly on to the firebox and in a neat cast iron casing.**

By the 1930s it became usual to dispense with the safety valve casing but No.9314 (ex 5775) still carried one until 23rd February 1952 – ***see*** **page 73, top.**

This was No.945's original boiler which started work in March 1901, and which was ex works 17th January 1914 on No.904 which had it to 19th November 1932. Although retaining the raised seating, at some repair its Ramsbottom safety valves had been replaced by Ross 'pops'. This was the last boiler in service not of No.1 design.

5545 cont./
405 *(exJ10 834)* 30/9/22.
645 *(ex 5548)* 15/10/27.
286 *(exJ10 5827)* 8/3/30.
511 *(exN4 5635)* 27/8/32.
1768 *(ex 5544)* 19/12/36.
4184 *(ex 5925)* 8/6/40.
402 *(ex 5518)* 18/12/43.
4315 *(ex 69253)* 8/4/50.
22702 *(ex 69330)* 8/11/52.

SHEDS:
Mexborough 12/3/98.
Ardsley 5/5/33.
Copley Hill 6/4/35.
Gorton 11/2/36.
Sheffield 18/5/37.
Barnsley 20/7/37.
Doncaster 4/3/41.
Barnsley 2/3/43.

RENUMBERED:
5545 20/12/24.
9278 28/8/46.
69278 8/4/50.

CONDEMNED: 19/11/55.
Cond. & cut up at Darlington.

5546

Beyer, Peacock 3579.

To traffic 3/1894.

REPAIRS:
Gor. ?/?—5/10/07.**G**.
Gor. 14/11/14—6/2/15.**G**.
Gor. 9/10/20—15/1/21.**G**.
Gor. 12/5—16/6/23.**G**.
Gor. 27/2—1/5/26.**G**.
Gor. 9/6—7/7/28.**G**.
Gor. 23/5—20/6/31.**G**.
Altered to LNE gauge.
Gor. 14—21/10/33.**G**.
Gor. 18/4—2/5/36.**G**.
Gor. 22/4—6/5/39.**G**.
Gor. 11—21/3/42.**G**.
Gor. 12—26/8/44.**G**.
Gor. 26/10—16/11/46.**G**.
New cylinders.
Gor. 14—28/5/49.**G**.
Gor. 8/11—6/12/52.**G**.
Gor. 6/3—3/4/54.**C/L**.

BOILERS:
310 *(new)* 5/10/07.
695 6/2/15.
155 *(exJ9 741)* 15/1/21.
137 *(exN5 5767)* 7/7/28.
296 *(ex 5516)* 20/6/31.
1123 *(exN4 5720)* 21/10/33.
326 *(ex 5764)* 2/5/36.
197 *(ex 5768)* 6/5/39.
4240 *(ex 5748)* 21/3/42.
4192 *(exJ10 5074)* 26/8/44.
4273 *(exJ10 5101)* 16/11/46.
4325 *(new)* 28/5/49.
22797 *(ex 69270)* 6/12/52.

SHEDS:
Barnsley.
Langwith Jct. 16/5/29.
Colwick 12/2/36.
Leicester 4/6/37.
Colwick 10/11/37.
Staveley 23/2/42.

RENUMBERED:
5546 1/5/26.
9279 30/8/46.
69279 28/5/49.

CONDEMNED: 13/6/55.
Cut up at Gorton 30/7/55.

5547

Beyer, Peacock 3580.

To traffic 3/1894.

REPAIRS:
Gor. ?/?—10/1/03.**G**.
YECo. 29/1—26/4/21.**G**.
New cylinders.
Gor. 2/2—12/4/24.**G**.
Gor. 2/10—4/12/26.**G**.
Gor. 21/12/29—25/1/30.**G**.
Gor. 17—24/9/32.**G**.
Altered to LNE gauge.
Gor. 5—26/11/32.**L**.
Boiler work.
Gor. 31/8—21/9/35.**G**.
Gor. 30/4—14/5/38.**G**.
Gor. 3—31/5/41.**G**.
Gor. 29/4—13/5/44.**G**.
Gor. 3/5—7/6/47.**G**.
Gor. 17/4/48.**L**. *Valve ports.*
Gor. 19/2/49.**L**.
Valve port faces worn.
Gor. 8—22/4/50.**G**.
New cylinders.
Gor. 23/8—6/9/52.**G**.
Gor. 10/12/55. *Not repaired.*

BOILERS:
602 *(new)* 10/1/03.
1653 *(exN4 621)* 26/4/21.
1660 *(exN4 5512)* 4/12/26.
756 *(ex 5766)* 25/1/30.
613 *(ex 5532)* 24/9/32.
4191 *(new)* 21/9/35.
449 *(exN4 5620)* 14/5/38.
1199 *(exJ10 5808)* 31/5/41.
405 *(ex 5517)* 13/5/44.
4304 *(ex 9270)* 22/4/50.
22777 *(ex??)* 6/9/52.

SHEDS:
Mexborough 18/11/21.
Boston 24/11/32.
Hitchin 7/4/34.
Ardsley 19/7/34.
Copley Hill 21/3/36.
Bradford 9/6/46.
Boston 14/5/50.
Louth 19/11/50.
Mexborough 21/6/53.

RENUMBERED:
5547 12/4/24.
9280 15/12/46.
69280 17/4/48.

CONDEMNED: 22/11/55.
Cond. & cut up at Darlington.

5548

Beyer, Peacock 3581.

To traffic 3/1894.

REPAIRS:
Gor. 11/4—6/6/08.**G**.
Gor. 2/3—2/7/10.**G**.
YECo. 29/1—25/3/21.**G**.
New cylinders.
Gor. 30/8—25/10/24.**G**.
Gor. 20/8—8/10/27.**G**.
Gor. 15/3—5/4/30.**G**.
Altered to LNE gauge.
Gor. 27/5—3/6/33.**G**.
Gor. 4—25/4/36.**G**.
Gor. 25/2—4/3/39.**G**.
Gor. 14/5—6/6/42.**G**.
Gor. 28/7—8/9/45.**G**.
New cylinders.
Gor. 20/3—17/4/48.**G**.
Gor. 20/5—3/6/50.**G**.
Gor. 6—29/12/52.**G**.
Gor. 31/12/55—4/2/56.**G**.

BOILERS:
968 6/6/08.
654 *(new)* 2/7/10.
645 *(exN4 636)* 25/3/21.
227 *(exD7 5562)* 8/10/27.
318 *(new)* 5/4/30.
1762 *(ex 5774)* 3/6/33.
770 *(ex 5054)* 25/4/36.
193 *(exN4 5628)* 4/3/39.
4227 *(exN4 5637)* 6/6/42.
4216 *(ex 5764)* 8/9/45.
4249 *(exN4 9236)* 17/4/48.
4307 *(ex 69298)* 3/6/50.
22799 *(ex 69309)* 29/12/52.
22749 *(ex spare)* 4/2/56.

SHEDS:
Gorton 19/8/10.
Wrexham 30/3/28.
Bidston 13/9/31.
Wrexham 10/10/31.
Chester 26/9/32.
Gorton 8/3/42.
Chester 8/9/46.
Wrexham 2/7/55.

RENUMBERED:
5548 25/10/24.
9281 21/7/46.
69281 17/4/48.

CONDEMNED: 15/8/58.
Cut up at Gorton 6/9/58.

5744

Beyer, Peacock 3615.

To traffic 8/1894.

REPAIRS:
Gor. 3/3—4/6/10.**G**.
New cylinders.
Gor. 13/8—22/10/21.**G**.
Gor. 1/12/23—9/2/24.**G**.
Gor. 11/12/26—29/1/27.**G**.
Gor. 12/10—23/11/29.**G**.
Altered to LNE gauge.
Gor. 12—26/3/32.**G**.
Gor. 11—25/5/35.**G**.
Gor. 24/6—8/7/39.**G**.
Gor. 30/7—14/8/43.**G**.
Gor. 9—30/3/46.**G**.
Gor. 5—19/6/48.**G**.
New cyls. & valves.
Gor. 26/4—17/5/52.**G**.

BOILERS:
790 4/6/10.
394 *(new)* 9/2/24.
695 *(ex 5761)* 29/1/27.
207 *(ex 5528)* 26/3/32.
4183 *(new)* 25/5/35.
425 *(ex 5529)* 8/7/39.
726 *(ex 5762)* 14/8/43.
4185 *(ex 5522)* 30/3/46.
316 *(ex 9366)* 19/6/48.
22758 *(ex 69352)* 17/5/52.

SHEDS:
Mexborough.
Retford 31/10/48.

RENUMBERED:
5744 9/2/24.
9282 13/10/46.
69282 19/6/48.

CONDEMNED: 25/7/55.
Into Dar. for cut up 29/2/56.

5745

Beyer, Peacock 3616.

To traffic 8/1894.

REPAIRS:
Gor. 3/9—8/10/10.**G**.
Gor. 3/5—26/7/13.**G**.
New cylinders.
Gor. 5/7—1/11/19.**G**.
Gor. 14/1—11/3/22.**G**.
Gor. 22/5—7/8/26.**G**.
Gor. 14/6—19/7/30.**G**.
Gor. 14—28/4/34.**G**.
Altered to LNE gauge.
Gor. 9/10—6/11/37.**G**.
New cylinders.
Gor. 3—17/8/40.**G**.
Gor. 24/11—4/12/43.**G**.
Gor. 27/9—1/11/47.**G**.
Gor. 14—21/2/48.**L**.
Boiler short of water.
Gor. 21/7—4/8/51.**G**.
Gor. 22/1—19/2/55.**G**.

BOILERS:
1356 *(new)* 8/10/10.
1342 *(ex 54)* 26/7/13.
1810 *(new)* 1/11/19.
504 *(ex 537)* 11/3/22.
1810 *(exN4 5637)* 19/7/30.
917 *(exN4 5602)* 28/4/34.
564 *(exJ10 5809)* 6/11/37.
4196 *(exJ10 5832)* 4/12/43.
29 *(ex 9325)* 1/11/47.
22703 *(ex 69316)* 4/8/51.
22729 *(exJ10 65159)* 19/2/55.

SHEDS:
Neasden 28/4/22.
Retford 21/12/52.

RENUMBERED:
5745 7/8/26.
9283 20/1/46.
E9283 21/2/48.
69283 4/8/51.

CONDEMNED: 12/6/58.
Cut up at Gorton 16/8/58.

5746

Beyer, Peacock 3617.

To traffic 8/1894.

REPAIRS:
Gor. 22/2—11/4/08.**G**.
Gor. 12/7—8/11/13.**G**.
Gor. 2/9—18/11/22.**G**.
Gor. 6/12/24—17/1/25.**G**.
Gor. 24/3—5/5/28.**G**.
Gor. 6—31/12/30.**G**.
Altered to LNE gauge.
Gor. 25/8—22/9/34.**G**.
New cylinders.
Gor. 14/5—4/6/38.**G**.
Gor. 15/3—5/4/41.**G**.
Gor. 31/7—8/8/42.**H**.
Gor. 21/2—4/3/44.**G**.
Gor. 21/9—26/10/46.**G**.
Gor. 9—30/10/48.**G**.
Gor. 30/9—14/10/50.**G**.
Gor. 29/5—3/7/54.**L/I**.
Boiler re-tubed.

BOILERS:
952 11/4/08.
1197 *(ex 757)* 8/11/13.
174 *(exJ10 814)* 18/11/22.
52 *(exN4 5616)* 5/5/28.
222 *(ex 5928)* 31/12/30.
52 *(exN4 5621)* 22/9/34.
167 *(ex 5905)* 4/6/38.
736 *(exJ10 5789)* 5/4/41.
435 *(ex 5911)* 8/8/42.
483 *(exJ10 5823)* 4/3/44.
951 *(ex 9368)* 30/10/48.
22661 *(ex 69304)* 14/10/50.

SHEDS:
Mexborough.
Staveley 22/7/38.
Langwith Junction 17/12/38.
Boston 22/7/56.
Langwith Junction 27/1/57.

RENUMBERED:
5746 17/1/25.
9284 30/8/46.
69284 30/10/48.

CONDEMNED: 17/2/58.
Cut up at Gorton 29/3/58.

5747

Beyer, Peacock 3618.

To traffic 9/1894.

REPAIRS:
Gor. 13/1—16/4/10.**G**.
Gor. 5/7—25/10/19.**G**.
Gor. 16/12/22—13/1/23.**L**.
Gor. 1/12/23—2/2/24.**G**.
New cylinders.
Gor. 14/5—25/6/27.**G**.
Gor. 14/9—12/10/29.**G**.
Gor. 26/11—10/12/32.**G**.
Altered to LNE gauge.
Gor. 15—29/2/36.**G**.
Gor. 18—25/3/39.**G**.
Gor. 23/9—3/10/42.**G**.
Gor. 14/9—5/10/46.**G**.
Gor. 13—27/8/49.**G**.
Gor. 15/8—12/9/53.**H/I**.
New cylinders.

BOILERS:
1336 16/4/10.
1809 *(new)* 25/10/19.
680 *(exJ9 5661)* 2/2/24.
1775 *(ex 5911)* 10/12/32.
294 *(ex 5533)* 29/2/36.
1785 *(exJ10 5678)* 25/3/39.
84 *(ex 5025)* 3/10/42.
4297 *(new)* 5/10/46.
479 *(ex 9251)* 27/8/49.
479 reno.22826 12/9/53.

SHEDS:
Barnsley.
Doncaster 2/9/51.
Retford 27/4/52.
Doncaster 1/6/52.
Sheffield 25/1/53.

RENUMBERED:
5747 2/2/24.
9285 26/8/46.
69285 27/8/49.

CONDEMNED: 5/11/55.
Cond. & cut up at Darlington.

5748

Beyer, Peacock 3619.

To traffic 9/1894.

REPAIRS:
Gor. 29/7—2/12/11.**G**.
Gor. 27/6—18/10/17.**G**.
Gor. 14/2/19—8/5/20.**G**.
Gor. 11/11—30/12/22.**G**.
New cylinders.
Gor. 26/9—28/11/25.**G**.
Gor. 10/3—21/4/28.**G**.
Altered to LNE gauge.
Gor. 15/3—19/4/30.**G**.
Gor. 29/7—12/8/33.**G**.
Gor. 12—26/10/35.**G**.
Reverted to GC gauge.
Gor. 10—31/7/37.**G**.
Altered back to LNE gauge.
Gor. 25/11—9/12/39.**G**.
Gor. 17/2—7/3/42.**G**.
Gor. 27/5—17/6/44.**G**.
Gor. 1—22/2/47.**G**.
Gor. 23—30/4/49.**C/H**.
Gor. 16/6—21/7/51.**G**.
Gor. 10—31/10/53.**G**.
Gor. 15/6—13/7/57.**G**.

BOILERS:
680 *(new)* 2/12/11.
1705 *(new)* 18/10/17.
1896 *(new)* 8/5/20.
243A *(exJ8 5551)* 21/4/28.
587 *(exN4 5719)* 12/8/33.
78 *(exJ10 5788)* 26/10/35.
4190 *(exJ10 5845)* 31/7/37.
4240 *(new)* 9/12/39.
1713 *(exJ10 5848)* 7/3/42.
551 *(ex 5918)* 17/6/44.
727 *(exN4 9242)* 22/2/47.
196 *(ex 9324)* 30/4/49.
22701 *(ex 69315)* 21/7/51.
22695 *(ex 69332)* 31/10/53.
22822 *(ex 69268)* 13/7/57.

SHEDS:
Barnsley.
Colwick 18/12/30.
Annesley 18/3/32.
Derby 24/7/42.
Annesley 13/6/48.
Woodford 4/12/49.
Colwick 15/11/53.
Sheffield 11/12/55.
Langwith Junction 12/4/59.

RENUMBERED:
5748 28/11/25.
9286 11/8/46.
69286 30/4/49.

CONDEMNED: 26/11/60.
Cut up at Doncaster.

5749

Beyer, Peacock 3620.

To traffic 9/1894.

REPAIRS:
Gor. 25/3—15.5.08.**G**.
Gor. 4/5—6/7/18.**G**.
Mex. 25/5—24/8/21.**H**.
Gor. 7/6—26/7/24.**G**.
Gor. 17/4—26/6/26.**G**.
Gor. 17/11—15/12/28.**G**.
Altered to LNE gauge.
Gor. 4—18/2/33.**G**.
Gor. 27/11—11/12/37.**G**.
Gor. 17—31/8/40.**G**.
Gor. 3—19/2/44.**G**.
Gor. 12/10—2/11/46.**G**.
Gor. 7/5—25/6/49.**G**.
Gor. 28/6—2/8/52.**G**.

BOILERS:
609 15/5/08.
1748 *(new)* 6/7/18.
272 *(ex 5515)* 26/6/26.
573 *(new)* 15/12/28.
85 *(exJ10 5643)* 18/2/33.
293 *(ex 5907)* 11/12/37.
4235 *(ex 5766)* 19/2/44.

Replacement boilers built from 1941 had safety valves of Ross 'pop' type.

Normal position for the whistle was above the cab roof.

(below) **As the cab roof height was only 11ft 5$^{9}/_{16}$in. it was never necessary to alter the whistle position.**

(above) **Engines built by Beyer, Peacock had that firm's works plates fitted on the cab sides. Over the years, most of these were removed, but at least two, Nos.69261 and 69289 still had them through to 1952. No.69255 had them in June 1953.**

The cab roof did not originally have any ventilator fitted.

During LNER days many had a sliding ventilator fitted at the front end of the cab roof.

5749 cont./
768 *(ex 9295)* 25/6/49.
22771 *(new reno. from 4342)* 2/8/52.

SHEDS:
Barnsley.
Lincoln 1/12/34.
Tuxford 25/2/35.
Lincoln 11/1/48.
Immingham 13/1/52.
Lincoln 15/6/52.
Sheffield 22/11/53.

RENUMBERED:
5749 26/7/24.
9287 9/8/46.
69287 25/6/49.

CONDEMNED: 11/7/55.
Cut up at Gorton 12/5/56.

5750

Beyer, Peacock 3621.

To traffic 10/1894.

REPAIRS:
Gor. 17/4—19/6/09.**G**.
Gor. 28/11/14—20/3/15.**G**.
Gor. 23/7—1/10/21.**G**.
Gor. 2/2—5/4/24.**G**.
Gor. 4/12/26—29/1/27.**G**.
Gor. 4/5—8/6/29.**G**.
Gor. 17/10—7/11/31.**G**.
Gor. 11—25/5/35.**G**.
Heating app. both ends.
Gor. 20/2—13/3/37.**G**.
Altered to LNE gauge.
Gor. 2—16/12/39.**G**.
Gor. 26/6—3/7/43.**G**.
Gor. 26/1—9/2/46.**G**.
Gor. 21/2—13/3/48.**G**.
Gor. 10—24/6/50.**G**.
Gor. 11—25/10/52.**G**.

BOILERS:
611 19/6/09.
1361 *(ex 25)* 20/3/15.
1703 *(exJ10 84)* 1/10/21.
1038 *(exN4 5719)* 29/1/27.
186 *(exJ10 5671)* 8/6/29.
155 *(ex 5905)* 7/11/31.
150 *(ex 5905)* 25/5/35.
105 *(exN4 5609)* 13/3/37.
4242 *(new)* 16/12/39.
4232 *(exJ10 5101)* 3/7/43.
313 *(exJ10 5828)* 9/2/46.
4280 *(exJ10 5134)* 13/3/48.
4246 *(ex 9325)* 24/6/50.
22789 *(ex 69327)* 25/10/52.

SHEDS:
Mexborough 16/9/07.
Darlington 23/7/24.
Mexborough 7/11/24.
Gorton 18/5/35.
Northwich 30/10/35.
Trafford Park 28/11/36.
Gorton 7/12/36.
Brunswick 24/3/37.
Wrexham 24/9/50.

RENUMBERED:
5750 5/4/24.
9288 11/8/46.
E9288 13/3/48.
69288 12/3/49.

CONDEMNED: 18/4/55.
Cut up at Gorton 29/10/55.

5751

Beyer, Peacock 3622.

To traffic 10/1894.

REPAIRS:
Gor. ?/?—30/3/07.**G**.
New cylinders.
Gor. 27/11/09—5/3/10.**G**.
Gor. 4/2—6/5/22.**G**.
Gor. 16/8—4/10/24.**G**.
Gor. 7/1—4/2/28.**G**.
Gor. 22/8—19/9/31.**G**.
Altered to LNE gauge.
Gor. 4—25/8/34.**G**.
Gor. 5—19/2/38.**G**.
Gor. 4—18/1/41.**G**.
Gor. 17/12/43—8/1/44.**G**.
Gor. 9/2—2/3/46.**G**.
Gor. 25/1/47.**L**.
R.H. valve port.
Gor. 27/12/47—31/1/48.**G**.
New cylinders.
Gor. 4—18/3/50.**G**.
Gor. 11—25/8/51.**C/H**.
Gor. 8—29/3/52.**H/I**.
Gor. 20—27/6/53.**C/L**.
Firehole patch fitted.

BOILERS:
990 *(new)* 30/3/07.
306 *(new)* 5/3/10.
56 *(exJ10 5835)* 4/2/28.
188 *(exJ10 5084)* 19/9/31.
764 *(exJ9 5743)* 25/8/34.
443 *(exN4 5637)* 19/2/38.
310 *(exF1 5586)* 8/1/44.
4209 *(ex 5898)* 2/3/46.
4284 *(exJ10 5159)* 31/1/48.
4247 *(ex 9293)* 18/3/50.
22705 *(exJ10 65205)* 25/8/51.

SHEDS:
Chester.
Trafford Park 7/2/34.
Gorton 7/11/34.
Northwich 21/9/39.
Bidston 13/11/42.
Wrexham 27/9/52.

RENUMBERED:
5751 4/10/24.
9289 27/1/46.
E9289 31/1/48.
69289 25/6/49.

CONDEMNED: 11/1/54.
Cut up at Gorton 27/2/54.

5752

Beyer, Peacock 3623.

To traffic 10/1894.

REPAIRS:
Gor. 4/2—27/3/09.**G**.
New cylinders.
Gor. 16/5—1/8/14.**G**.
Gor. 10/3—5/5/17.**G**.
Gor. 15/1—7/5/21.**G**.
Gor. 22/9—24/11/23.**G**.
New cylinders.
Gor. 25/4—20/6/25.**G**.
Gor. 31/3—28/4/28.**G**.
Gor. 21/2—14/3/31.**G**.
Gor. 2—16/2/35.**G**.
Altered to LNE gauge.
Gor. 5—19/11/38.**G**.
Gor. 21/10—8/11/41.**G**.
Gor. 16—21/2/42.**L**.
New crank pins in wheels.
Gor. 22/7—5/8/44.**G**.
Gor. 15—29/11/47.**G**.
Gor. 24/6—29/7/50.**G**.
Gor. 13—20/10/51.**C/L**.
Gor. 17—24/1/53.**C/L**.
Boiler work.
Gor. 23/5—27/6/53.**G**.
New cylinders.
Gor. 10/12/55—14/1/56.**L/I**.
Gor. 26/9/59. *Not repaired.*

BOILERS:
1382 *(new)* 27/3/09.
415 *(new)* 1/8/14.
644 *(exN4 609)* 7/5/21.
574 *(ex 5944)* 28/4/28.
4235 *(new)* 19/11/38.
4262 *(new)* 8/11/41.
4258 *(exJ10 5803)* 5/8/44.
4261 *(exJ10 5177)* 29/11/47.
4280 *(ex 69288)* 29/7/50.
4280 reno.22716 20/10/51.
22821 *(new reno. from 4346)* 27/6/53.

SHEDS:
Barnsley.
Gorton 19/3/36.
Northwich 22/9/39.
Chester 1/12/40.
Wrexham 14/12/47.
Tyne Dock 26/8/57.
New England 13/7/58.
Sheffield 7/12/58.

RENUMBERED:
752c 24/11/23.
5752 20/6/25.
9290 11/8/46.
69290 29/7/50.

CONDEMNED: 2/10/59.
Cut up at Gorton 31/10/59.

5753

Beyer, Peacock 3624.

To traffic 11/1894.

REPAIRS:
Gor. ?/?—2/12/05.**G**.
Gor. 9/5—15/8/08.**G**.
Gor. 5/7—20/12/19.**G**.
Gor. 4/2—18/3/22.**G**.
Gor. 26/7—1/11/24.**G**.
Gor. 5/11—3/12/27.**G**.
Gor. 26/4—31/5/30.**G**.
Gor. 5—19/8/33.**G**.
Altered to LNE gauge.
Gor. 10—24/10/36.**G**.
Gor. 14—28/9/40.**G**.
Gor. 31/3—9/5/42.**H**.
New cylinders.
Gor. 8/7—5/8/44.**G**.
Gor. 5/7—9/8/47.**G**.
Gor. 12—19/3/49.**C/H**.
New cylinders.
Gor. 17/6—1/7/50.**G**.
Gor. 3—17/1/53.**L/I**.

BOILERS:
1168 2/12/05.
610 15/8/08.
168 *(exJ10 827)* 20/12/19.
917 *(ex 5775)* 3/12/27.
227 *(ex 5548)* 31/5/30.
1767 *(exN4 5613)* 19/8/33.
192 *(ex 5537)* 24/10/36.
188 *(exJ10 5788)* 28/9/40.
183 *(ex 5524)* 5/8/44.
417 *(exJ10 5175)* 9/8/47.
4186 *(ex 69356)* 1/7/50.
4186 reno.22803 17/1/53.

5753 cont./
SHEDS:
Mexborough ?/1/97.
Barnsley 1/4/45.

RENUMBERED:
5753 1/11/24.
9291 18/8/46.
69291 19/3/49.

CONDEMNED: 4/11/55.
Cond. & cut up at Darlington.

5200

Gorton.

To traffic 9/1895.

REPAIRS:
Gor. 20/4—27/8/10.**G**.
New cylinders.
Gor. 9/10/15—5/2/16.**G**.
Gor. 12/7—20/9/19.**G**.
Gor. 21/1—3/6/22.**G**.
Gor. 6/6—8/8/25.**G**.
Gor. 14/4—19/5/28.**G**.
Gor. 29/11—20/12/30.**G**.
Altered to LNE gauge.
Gor. 30/6—14/7/34.**G**.
Gor. 23/10—13/11/37.**G**.
Gor. 12/10—2/11/40.**G**.
Gor. 9—25/3/44.**G**.
Gor. 11/11/44.**L**.
Steam chest fractured.
Gor. 24/3—14/4/45.**G**.
New cylinders.
Gor. 7—21/12/46.**G**.
Gor. 5—19/2/49.**C/H**.
Gor. 13—27/1/51.**G**.
Gor. 28/11—12/12/53.**G**.
Gor. 29/9—27/10/56.**G**.
Gor. 25/1/60. *Not repaired.*

BOILERS:
1096 27/8/10.
1599 *(new)* 5/2/16 (sup.).
151 *(exN4 5607)* 19/5/28(sat).
437 *(new)* 20/12/30.
405 *(new)* 14/7/34.
440 *(ex 5539)* 13/11/37.
92 *(ex 5515)* 25/3/44.
4250 *(ex 9367)* 21/12/46.
4197 *(ex 9360)* 19/2/49.
22680 *(ex 9257)* 27/1/51.
22675 *(ex spare)* 12/12/53.
22806 *(ex 69257)* 27/10/56.

SHEDS:
Barnsley.
Sheffield 12/4/43.
Staveley 31/8/43.
Sheffield 8/3/53.
New England 7/12/58.

RENUMBERED:
200 6/1/96 *(ex200A)*.
5200 8/8/25.
9292 2/11/46.
69292 19/2/49.

CONDEMNED: 29/1/60.
Cut up at Gorton 19/3/60.

5536

Gorton.

To traffic 5/1895.

REPAIRS:
Gor. 28/5—24/7/09.**G**.
Gor. 25/5—29/6/12.**G**.
Gor. 14/10—11/11/22.**G**.
Gor. 27/12/24—14/3/25.**G**.
Altered to LNE gauge.
New cylinders.
Gor. 12/1—16/2/29.**G**.
Gor. 19/12/31—16/1/32.**G**.
Gor. 25/1—8/2/36.**G**.
Gor. 6—20/5/39.**G**.
Gor. 28/12/40—11/1/41.**G**.
New cylinders.
Gor. 19/11—11/12/43.**G**.
Gor. 3/5—7/6/47.**G**.
Gor. 28/1—11/2/50.**G**.
Gor. 13—27/9/52.**G**.
Gor. 7/1—4/2/56.**G**.

BOILERS:
172 24/7/09.
669 29/6/12.
1787 *(exJ10 5827)* 14/3/25.
190 *(ex 5946)* 16/1/32.
140 *(ex 5025)* 8/2/36.
1642 *(ex 5532)* 20/5/39.
4247 *(exJ10 5794)* 11/12/43.
4275 *(exN4 9243)* 11/2/50.
22783 *(ex 69342)* 27/9/52.
22770 *(ex 69367)* 4/2/56.

SHEDS:
Gorton.
Northwich 4/1/34.
Gorton 3/1/36.
Walton-on-the-Hill 23/5/36.
Gorton 24/4/39.
Northwich 30/6/39.
Gorton 22/9/39.
Northwich 23/3/40.
Chester 7/12/41.
Northwich 10/2/46.
Chester 27/8/50.
New England 27/4/58.

RENUMBERED:
5536 14/3/25.
9293 13/10/46.
69293 12/3/49.

CONDEMNED: 29/11/60.
Into Don. for cut up 29/11/60.

5756

Gorton.

To traffic 12/1895.

REPAIRS:
Gor. ?/?—21/2/03.**G**.
Gor. 25/12/09—19/3/10.**G**.
Gor. 6/11/15—18/3/16.**G**.
Gor. 13/8—19/11/21.**G**.
Wrx. 19/2—19/5/24.**H**.
Gor. 21/8—13/11/26.**G**.
Gor. 28/9—26/10/29.**G**.
Gor. 19/3—9/4/32.**G**.
Altered to LNE gauge.
Gor. 14—28/4/34.**G**.
Gor. 25/4—16/5/36.**G**.

BOILERS:
609 21/2/03.
990 *(ex 751)* 19/3/10.
1604 *(new)* 18/3/16.
202 *(new)* 19/11/21.
314 *(exN4 5615)* 9/4/32.
1640 *(ex 5928)* 28/4/34.
1762 *(ex 5548)* 16/5/36.

SHEDS:
Chester.
Immingham 13/12/29.
Lincoln 16/12/29.

RENUMBERED:
5756 19/5/24.

CONDEMNED: 1/10/38.
Cut up at Doncaster 3/12/38.

5021

Gorton.

To traffic 10/1896.

REPAIRS:
Gor. 24/3—2/5/03.**G**.
Gor. ?/?—?/12/09.**G**.
Gor. 16/1—27/3/15.**G**.
Gor. 26/2—30/7/21.**G**.
Gor. 19/7—30/8/24.**G**.
Gor. 30/7—24/9/27.**G**.
Gor. 18/1—15/2/30.**G**.
Gor. 25/11—25/12/33.**G**.
Altered to LNE gauge.
Gor. 15/5—5/6/37.**G**.
Gor. 29/6—20/7/40.**G**.
Gor. 26/4—17/5/41.**G**.
New cylinders.
Gor. 29/3—22/4/44.**G**.
Gor. 30/3—20/4/46.**G**.
Gor. 9/4—7/5/49.**G**.
Gor. 29/8—19/9/53.**G**.
Gor. 28/4—26/5/56.**G**.
Gor. 26/9/59. *Not repaired.*

BOILERS:
617 *(new)* 2/5/03.
607 ?/12/09.
1036 *(ex spare)* 27/3/15.
707 *(ex 25)* 30/7/21.
441 *(exJ12 5485)* 24/9/27.
1044 *(exD7 5701)* 25/12/33.
83 *(exN4 5634)* 5/6/37.
303 *(exN4 5633)* 22/4/44.
314 *(ex 5909)* 20/4/46.
4220 *(exF1 7099)* 7/5/49.
22716 *(ex 69290)* 19/9/53.
22771 *(ex 69287)* 26/5/56.

SHEDS:
Barnsley.
Retford 29/8/43.
Doncaster 4/6/52.
Sheffield 25/1/53.

RENUMBERED:
21 (ex202A) 27/10/00.
5021 30/8/24.
9294 18/4/46.
69294 7/5/49.

CONDEMNED: 2/10/59.
Cut up at Gorton 24/10/59.

5025

Gorton.

To traffic 12/1896.

REPAIRS:
Gor. 4/1—29/2/08.**G**.
Gor. 24/10—19/12/14.**G**.
Gor. 26/2—14/5/21.**G**.
Gor. 25/8—10/11/23.**G**.
Gor. 20/2—1/5/26.**G**.
Gor. 13/10—24/11/28.**G**.
Gor. 14/5—4/6/32.**G**.
Altered to LNE gauge.
Gor. 11—25/1/36.**G**.
Gor. 12/11—3/12/38.**G**.
Gor. 14/9—3/10/42.**G**.
Gor. 25/11—16/12/44.**G**.
New cylinders.
Gor. 3/5—7/6/47.**G**.
Gor. 19/2—5/3/49.**C/H**.
Gor. 1/7—5/8/50.**G**.
Gor. 5/7—9/8/52.**G**.
Gor. 19/2—19/3/55.**G**.

BOILERS:
1361 *(new)* 29/2/08.
707 *(exJ10 835)* 19/12/14.

(above) **Some cab roof ventilators differed and were probably not adjustable.**

Long before Grouping all had three open coal rails fitted on the top of the bunker.

Although the bunker rails began to be plated from 1930, this process was not completed until after Nationalisation, No.69299 still having open rails to July 1952, when it duly had them plated.

From about 1930 the open rails were replaced by sheet steel plating to help stop spillage of small coal.

There was no consistency about style of plating. Some which had the flared bunker top got vertical plating across the back.

(below) **Although the later built engines had a straight back to the bunker, the rails were stepped-in, flared style.**

5025 cont./
415 *(ex 752)* 14/5/21.
380 *(ex 5533)* 24/11/28.
140 *(exJ9 5646)* 4/6/32.
265 *(exN4 5718)* 25/1/36.
84 *(ex 5904)* 3/12/38.
249 *(exJ10 5080)* 3/10/42.
721 *(ex 5935)* 16/12/44.
768 *(exJ10 5209)* 7/6/47.
4215 *(ex 9333)* 5/3/49.
4182 *(ex F2 7113)* 5/8/50.
22720 *(ex 69274)* 9/8/52.
22724 *(ex 69265)* 19/3/55.

SHEDS:
Barnsley.
Sheffield 31/5/43.
Staveley 20/9/43.
Sheffield 23/11/43.
Staveley 16/2/44.
Sheffield 8/3/53.

RENUMBERED:
25 4/8/00 *(ex203A).*
25c 10/11/23.
5025 1/5/26.
9295 3/11/46.
69295 5/3/49.

CONDEMNED: 18/3/58.
Cut up at Gorton. 30/8/58

5054

Gorton.

To traffic 9/1896.

REPAIRS:
Gor. 23/4—4/7/03.**G**.
Gor. 10/8—30/11/07.**G**.
Gor. 8/3—24/5/13.**G**.
Gor. 4/2—18/3/22.**G**.
Gor. 16/2—5/4/24.**G**.
Gor. 8/1—26/2/27.**G**.
Gor. 9/3—18/5/29.**G**.
Altered to LNE gauge.
Gor. 17/9—1/10/32.**G**.
Gor. 21/3—4/4/36.**G**.
Gor. 19/8—16/9/39.**G**.
Gor. 25/11—26/12/42.**G**.
Gor. 1/6—6/7/46.**G**.
Gor. 21/12/46—11/1/47.**H**.
Gor. 1—22/10/49.**G**.
Gor. 28/2—14/3/53.**G**.
Gor. 16/11—14/12/57.**G**.

BOILERS:
718 *(new)* 4/7/03.
1342 *(new)* 30/11/07.
166 *(new)* 24/5/13.
127 *(exJ12 6439)* 26/2/27.
213 *(exD7 5701)* 18/5/29.
770 *(new)* 1/10/32.
1667 *(exJ10 5790)* 4/4/36.
318 *(ex 5766)* 16/9/39.
4272 *(exN4 5632)* 6/7/46.
1897 *(exN4 9225)* 22/10/49.
22812 *(ex??)* 14/3/53.
22824 *(ex spare)* 14/12/57.

SHEDS:
Barnsley.
Gorton 12/2/45.
Sheffield 19/12/54.

RENUMBERED:
54 4/8/00 *(ex201A).*
5054 5/4/24.
9296 16/12/46.
69296 12/3/49.

CONDEMNED: 6/12/60.
Into Don. for cut up 6/12/60.

5757

Gorton.

To traffic 2/1896.

REPAIRS:
Gor. 29/7—2/10/09.**G**.
New cylinders.
Gor. 7/6—27/9/13.**G**.
Gor. 4/2—6/5/22.**G**.
Gor. 12/7—20/9/24.**G**.
Gor. 9/6—4/8/28.**G**.
New cylinders.
Gor. 10—31/1/31.**G**.
Altered to LNE gauge.
Gor. 27/5—10/6/33.**G**.
Gor. 1—15/8/36.**G**.
Heating app. both ends.
Gor. 13/7—3/8/40.**G**.
Gor. 15—26/2/44.**G**.
Gor. 4/10—8/11/47.**G**.
Gor. 6—20/1/51.**G**.
Gor. 21/8—18/9/54.**G**.
Gor. 5—26/3/55.**C/L**.
After collision.

BOILERS:
1197 *(exJ10 819)* 2/10/09.
248 *(new)* 27/9/13.
1590 *(ex 526)* 6/5/22.
200 *(exJ10 5643)* 20/9/24.
1697 *(exJ10 5122)* 4/8/28.
460 *(exN4 5717)* 31/1/31.
538 *(exJ13 5571)* 10/6/33.
409 *(ex 5931)* 15/8/36.
4246 *(new)* 3/8/40.
4254 *(exJ10 5831)* 26/2/44.
4184 *(ex9276)* 8/11/47.
22679 *(ex??)* 20/1/51.
22680 *(ex 69280)* 18/9/54.

SHEDS:
Mexborough.
Immingham 13/11/55.
Barnsley 22/7/56.

RENUMBERED:
5757 20/9/24.
9297 10/11/46.
69297 20/1/51.

CONDEMNED: 8/8/58.
Cut up at Gorton 13/9/58.

5758

Gorton.

To traffic 3/1896.

REPAIRS:
Gor. 4/8—13/11/09.**G**.
Gor. 28/4—3/11/17.**G**.
Gor. 14/2—1/5/20.**G**.
Gor. 5/8—16/9/22.**G**.
Gor. 29/11/24—10/1/25.**G**.
Gor. 31/12/27—4/2/28.**G**.
Gor. 22/3—26/4/30.**G**.
Gor. 23/9—7/10/33.**G**.
Altered to LNE gauge.
Gor. 30/11—14/12/35.**G**.

BOILERS:
33 *(new)* 13/11/09.
1346 *(ex??)* 3/11/17.
87 *(ex 769)* 1/5/20.
1619 *(ex??)* 4/2/28.
493 *(ex 5929)* 7/10/33.
1618 *(ex 5895)* 14/12/35.

SHEDS:
Barnsley.
Colwick 18/12/30.
Annesley 7/3/32.

RENUMBERED:
5758 10/1/25.

CONDEMNED: 27/11/37.
Cut up at Doncaster 8/1/38.

5759

Gorton.

To traffic 4/1896.

REPAIRS:
Gor. 7/7—26/8/09.**G**.
New cylinders.
Gor. 25/5—27/7/12.**G**.
Gor. 24/11/17—13/4/18.**G**.
Gor. 25/9/20—5/2/21.**G**.
Gor. 17/3—5/5/23.**G**.
Gor. 28/3—16/5/25.**G**.
Gor. 18/2—7/4/28.**G**.
Altered to LNE gauge.
New cylinders.
Gor. 16/8—20/9/30.**G**.
Gor. 11—25/3/33.**G**.
Don. 20—22/4/33.**N/C**.
Gor. 10—24/11/34.**G**.
Gor. 7—28/5/38.**G**.
Gor. 22/2—8/3/41.**G**.
Gor. 24/3—15/4/44.**G**.
Gor. 23/8—20/9/47.**G**.
Gor. 22/4—13/5/50.**G**.
Gor. 20/9—11/10/52.**G**.
New cylinders.
Gor. 26/11—31/12/55.**H/I**.

BOILERS:
145 26/8/09.
714 27/7/12.
33 *(ex 758)* 13/4/18.
142 *(exN4 5712)* 7/4/28.
654 *(ex 5544)* 20/9/30.
573 *(ex 5749)* 25/3/33.
4191 *(ex 5547)* 28/5/38.
29 *(exJ10 5831)* 8/3/41.
4246 *(ex 5757)* 15/4/44.
4307 *(new)* 20/9/47.
4310 *(ex 9276)* 13/5/50.
22786 *(ex??)* 11/10/52.

SHEDS:
Mexborough.
Ardsley 24/11/34.
Wrexham 19/2/35.
Gorton 1/7/35.
Heaton Mersey 24/12/35.
Gorton 2/12/36.
Walton-on-the-Hill 29/12/38.

RENUMBERED:
5759 16/5/25.
9298 31/3/46.
69298 19/3/49.

CONDEMNED: 7/12/59.
Cut up at Gorton 23/4/60.

5760

Gorton.

To traffic 5/1896.

REPAIRS:
Gor. 21/7—16/10/09.**G**.
New cylinders.
Gor. 15/3—14/6/13.**G**.
Gor. 31/5—1/11/19.**G**.
New cylinders.
Gor. 21/1—8/4/22.**G**.
Gor. 2/5—27/6/25.**G**.
Gor. 12/5—16/6/28.**G**.
Gor. 9—23/5/31.**G**.

5760 cont./
Altered to LNE gauge.
Gor. 6—20/7/35.**G.**
Gor. 24/12/38—14/1/39.**G.**
Gor. 6—18/10/41.**G.**
Gor. 24/6—8/7/44.**G.**
Gor. 4/1—1/2/47.**G.**
Gor. 25/2—18/3/50.**G.**
Gor. 14/6—5/7/52.**G.**
Gor. 15/10—19/11/55.**G.**
Gor. 25/1/60. *Not repaired.*

BOILERS:
682 16/10/09.
126 *(exD7 700)* 14/6/13.
521 *(ex 543)* 1/11/19.
989 *(ex 532)* 8/4/22.
78 *(ex 5764)* 16/6/28.
22 *(exN4 5604)* 23/5/31.
4185 *(new)* 20/7/35.
1609 *(exJ10 5827)* 14/1/39.
4193 *(exN4 5605)* 18/10/41.
4194 *(exN4 5718)* 8/7/44.
4192 *(ex 9279)* 1/2/47.
293 *(ex 69317)* 18/3/50.
22768 *(exN4 69244)* 5/7/52.
22735 *(ex 69313)* 19/11/55.

SHEDS:
Barnsley.
Wrexham 10/1/36.
Gorton 3/11/46.
Northwich 18/9/49.
Gorton 25/9/49.
Heaton Mersey 5/10/52.
Sheffield 27/4/58.
Langwith Jct. 22/6/58.

RENUMBERED:
5760 27/6/25.
9299 13/10/46.
69299 18/3/50.

CONDEMNED: 29/1/60.
Cut up at Gorton 12/3/60.

5761

Gorton.

To traffic 5/1896.

REPAIRS:
Gor. 15/3—12/6/09.**G.**
Gor. 28/10/11—13/1/12.**G.**
Gor. 9/10/20—8/1/21.**G.**
Gor. 12/5—7/7/23.**G.**
Gor. 14/11—31/12/25.**G.**
Altered to LNE gauge.
Gor. 18/8—22/9/28.**G.**
Gor. 2—16/4/32.**G.**
Gor. 5—26/11/32.**L.***Boiler work.*
Gor. 17/8—14/9/35.**G.**
New cylinders.
Gor. 1—22/6/40.**G.**
Gor. 18/11—4/12/43.**G.**
Gor. 31/12/47—24/1/48.**G.**
Gor. 27/1—17/2/51.**G.**
Gor. 10/4—8/5/54.**G.**
Gor. 16/12/57. *Not repaired.*

BOILERS:
1036 12/6/09.
114 13/1/12.
695 *(ex 546)* 8/1/21.
457 *(exJ9 5656)* 31/12/25.
695 *(ex 5744)* 16/4/32.
169 *(exJ10 5172)* 14/9/35.
241 *(ex 5755)* 22/6/40.
1765 *(ex??)* 4/12/43.
4314 *(new)* 24/1/48.
22681 *(ex 9369)* 17/2/51.
22730 *(ex 69277)* 8/5/54.

SHEDS:
Barnsley.
Sheffield ?/?.
Grantham 5/5/32.
Boston 14/12/32.
Lincoln 28/12/35.
Neasden 29/1/36.
Retford 21/12/52.
Barnsley 11/12/55.

RENUMBERED:
5761 31/12/25.
9300 9/11/46.
E9300 24/1/48.
69300 17/2/51.

CONDEMNED: 10/2/58.
Cut up at Gorton 6/12/58.

5762

Gorton.

To traffic 6/1896.

REPAIRS:
Gor. 30/7—10/10/08.**G.**
New cylinders.
Gor. 7/10—9/12/11.**G.**
Gor. 12/2—14/5/21.**G.**
Gor. 3/11/23—2/2/24.**G.**
Gor. 11/12/26—12/2/27.**G.**
Gor. 3—24/8/29.**G.**
Gor. 24/10—14/11/31.**G.**
Altered to LNE gauge.
Gor. 18/5—1/6/35.**G.**
New cylinders.
Gor. 6—20/8/38.**G.**
Gor. 3—17/5/41.**G.**
Gor. 12—26/6/43.**G.**
Gor. 11/8—1/9/45.**G.**
Gor. 28/2—20/3/48.**G.**
Gor. 13—18/3/50.**C/H.**
Gor. 19/1—9/2/52.**G.**
Gor. 16/12/55. *Not repaired.*

BOILERS:
781 10/10/08.
1065 *(new)* 9/12/11.
170 *(ex 907)* 14/5/21.
1771 *(exJ12 7B)* 2/2/24.
576 *(exJ12 6458)* 12/2/27.
394 *(ex 5767)* 24/8/29.
765 *(exJ8 5555)* 14/11/31.
4207 *(ex 5894)* 20/8/38.
726 *(exJ10 5823)* 17/5/41.
437 *(ex 5940)* 26/6/43.
502 *(ex 5926)* 1/9/45.
4188 *(exJ10 5206)* 20/3/48.
4271 *(ex 69366)* 18/3/50.
22736 *(ex 69346)* 9/2/52.

SHEDS:
Mexborough.
Langwith Junction 23/3/39.
Staveley 23/12/41.

RENUMBERED:
5762 2/2/24.
9301 10/3/46.
69301 20/3/48.

CONDEMNED: 16/12/55.
Cond. & cut up at Darlington.

5754

Beyer, Peacock 3813.

To traffic 1/1896.

REPAIRS:
Gor. 7/1—6/3/09.**G.**
Gor. 3/6—28/10/11.**G.**
Gor. 7/3—25/4/14.**G.**
Gor. 13/3—17/4/20.**G.**
Gor. 16/9—11/11/22.**G.**
Gor. 14/2—16/5/25.**G.**
Gor. 2/6—7/7/28.**G.**
Altered to LNE gauge.
Gor. 2—23/5/31.**G.**
Gor. 29/6—13/7/35.**G.**

BOILERS:
285 6/3/09.
590 28/10/11.
450 *(new)* 25/4/14.
449 *(new)* 17/4/20.
1710 *(new)* 7/7/28.
207 *(ex 5744)* 13/7/35.

SHED:
Barnsley.

RENUMBERED:
5754 16/5/25.

CONDEMNED: 19/12/38.
Cut up at Doncaster 4/3/39.

5755

Beyer, Peacock 3814.

To traffic 1/1896.*(Record card gives 'built' date as Dec.1894.)*

REPAIRS:
Gor. 18/6—18/9/08.**G.**
Gor. 14/9—26/10/12.**G.**
Gor. 9/11/18—5/7/19.**G.**
Gor. 24/9—26/11/21.**G.**
Gor. 8/12/23—16/2/24.**G.**
Gor. 26/3—14/5/27.**G.**
New cylinders.
Gor. 22/6—27/7/29.**G.**
Gor. 31/10—28/11/31.**G.**
Gor. 23/3—6/4/35.**G.**
Gor. 5—26/6/37.**G.**
Altered to LNE gauge.
Gor. 8/6—6/7/40.**G.**
Gor. 14—22/5/43.**G.**
Gor. 6—27/12/47.**G.**
Gor. 14/10—4/11/50.**G.**
Gor. 11/4—2/5/53.**G.**
Gor. 19/11/57. *Not repaired.*

BOILERS:
460 18/9/08.
1055 *(new)* 26/10/12.
1785 *(new)* 5/7/19.
1895 *(exE2 509B)* 16/2/24.
212 *(ex 5774)* 14/5/27.
1618 *(ex 5527)* 27/7/29.
186 *(ex 5750)* 28/11/31.
144 *(exN4 5715)* 6/4/35.
241 *(ex 5895)* 26/6/37.
314 *(exJ10 5799)* 6/7/40.
4265 *(new)* 22/5/43.
4214 *(ex 9274)* 27/12/47.
22663 *(ex 9334)* 4/11/50.
22815 *(exJ10 65193)* 2/5/53.

SHEDS:
On loan to WM&CQ from 16th March 1896 to 31st January 1901.
Mexborough 29/11/08.
York 23/7/24.
Mexborough 7/11/24.
Doncaster 18/6/44.
Mexborough 17/9/44.
Immingham 25/10/45.
Neasden 14/7/46.
Sheffield 12/12/54.

RENUMBERED:
5755 16/2/24.
9302 10/2/46.
69302 4/11/50.

5755 cont./
CONDEMNED: 23/12/57.
Cut up at Gorton 25/10/58.

5763

Beyer, Peacock 3967.

To traffic 3/1898.

REPAIRS:
Gor. 10/3—24/4/09.**G**.
New cylinders.
Gor. 17/6—4/11/11.**G**.
Gor. 25/11/22—24/3/23.**G**.
Gor. 11/4—30/5/25.**G**.
Gor. 26/5—7/7/28.**G**.
Gor. 6—20/12/30.**G**.
Gor. 17/11—1/12/34.**G**.
Altered to LNE gauge.
New cylinders.
Gor. 6/8—3/9/38.**G**.
Gor. 15—30/8/41.**G**.
Gor. 27/5—10/6/44.**G**.
Gor. 28/6—9/8/47.**G**.
Gor. 1—22/4/50.**G**.
Gor. 18/10—1/11/52.**G**.

BOILERS:
645 *(new)* 24/4/09.
587 *(new)* 4/11/11.
400 *(new)* 24/3/23 (sup.).
644 *(ex 5525)* 20/12/30 (sat.).
202 *(exJ10 5802)* 1/12/34.
4194 *(exJ10 5644)* 3/9/38.
4230 *(exJ10 5847)* 30/8/41.
1199 *(ex 5547)* 10/6/44.
711 *(exJ10 5136)* 9/8/47.
4284 *(ex 69289)* 22/4/50.
22791 *(ex 69280)* 1/11/52.

SHEDS:
Barnsley.
Ardsley 1/12/34.
Copley Hill 21/12/34.
Ardsley 2/2/35.
Copley Hill 1/2/36.
Lincoln 20/3/36.
Sheffield 10/2/37.
Barnsley 23/7/37.

RENUMBERED:
5763 30/5/25.
9303 20/10/46.
69303 22/4/50.

CONDEMNED: 19/11/55.
Cond. & cut up at Darlington.

5764

Beyer, Peacock 3968.

To traffic 3/1898.

REPAIRS:
Gor. ?/?—21/11/03.**G**.
Gor. 14/11/14—30/1/15.**G**.
Yec. 5/3—28/5/21.**G**.
New cylinders.
Gor. 14/6—9/8/24.**G**.
Gor. 29/1—26/3/27.**G**.
Gor. 9/2—6/4/29.**G**.
Altered to LNE gauge.
Gor. 23/1—6/2/32.**G**.
Gor. 29/2—14/3/36.**G**.
Gor. 15—22/7/39.**G**.
Gor. 27/1/40. **L**.
Heating app. both ends.
Gor. 12/3—3/4/43.**G**.
Gor. 7/7—18/8/45.**G**.
New cylinders.
Gor. 20/3—17/4/48.**G**.
Gor. 8—22/4/50.**G**.
Gor. 9/2—1/3/52.**H/I**.

BOILERS:
920 21/11/03.
793 *(new)* 30/1/15.
78 *(exJ10 845)* 28/5/21.
1771 *(ex 5762)* 26/3/27.
1715 *(exD7 5685)* 6/4/29.
326 *(ex 5526)* 6/2/32.
1897 *(ex 5541)* 14/3/36.
4183 *(ex 5744)* 22/7/39.
4216 *(exJ10 5098)* 3/4/43.
428 *(exN4 5622)* 18/8/45.
4199 *(ex 9338)* 17/4/48.
4240 *(ex 69349)* 22/4/50.
4240 reno.22742 1/3/52.

SHEDS:
Annesley ?/12/17.
Ardsley 4/5/33.
Copley Hill 6/7/34.
Ardsley 26/9/34.
Gorton 11/3/36.
Walton-on-the-Hill 23/5/36.
Gorton 6/6/39.
Bidston 9/5/43.
Wrexham 18/6/44.
Gorton 18/7/44.
Trafford Park 30/9/45.

RENUMBERED:
5764 9/8/24.
9304 12/5/46.
69304 17/4/48.

CONDEMNED: 7/3/55.
Cut up at Gorton 8/10/55.

5765

Beyer, Peacock 3969.

To traffic 5/1898.

REPAIRS:
Gor. 18/1—12/4/13.**G**.
Tux. 14/4—17/6/21.**G**.
Gor. 23/2—17/5/24.**G**.
New cylinders.
Gor. 1/10—12/11/27.**G**.
Gor. 5/4—3/5/30.**G**.
Altered to LNE gauge.
Gor. 1—8/7/33.**G**.
Gor. 19/10—2/11/35.**G**.
Gor. 13—27/11/37.**G**.
Gor. 11—18/5/40.**G**.
Heating app. both ends.
Gor. 5/12/42—2/1/43.**G**.
Gor. 12—30/9/44.**G**.
Gor. 26/7—23/8/47.**G**.
Gor. 19/8—9/9/50.**G**.
Gor. 7—28/11/53.**G**.
Gor. 19/1/58. *Not repaired.*

BOILERS:
96 12/4/13.
1768 *(exJ8 5556)* 17/5/24.
405 *(ex 5545)* 12/11/27.
1689 *(ex 5944)* 3/5/30.
730 *(ex 5906)* 8/7/33.
272 *(ex??)* 2/11/35.
4228 *(new)* 27/11/37.
428 *(exN4 5637)* 18/5/40.
959 *(exJ10 5828)* 2/1/43.
142 *(exN4 5606)* 30/9/44.
1199 *(ex 9303)* 23/8/47.
22651 *(ex 9290)* 9/9/50.
22673 *(ex 69350)* 28/11/53.

SHEDS:
Annesley 8/3/10.
Colwick 8/5/38.
Langwith Jct. 9/6/40
Lincoln 25/1/45.
Immingham 15/7/45.
Mexborough 13/11/55.

RENUMBERED:
5765 17/5/24.
9305 14/4/46.
69305 9/9/50.

CONDEMNED: 10/2/58.
Cut up at Gorton 30/8/58.

5766

Beyer, Peacock 3970.

To traffic 5/1898.

REPAIRS:
Gor. ?/?—2/12/11.**G**.
New cylinders.
YECo. 5/3—28/5/21.**G**.
Gor. 13/10—15/12/23.**G**.
Gor. 11/6—23/7/27.**G**.
Gor. 7—28/12/29.**G**.
Altered to LNE gauge.
Gor. 24/6—15/7/33.**G**.
Gor. 8—22/8/36.**G**.
New cylinders.
Heating app. both ends.
Gor. 8—15/7/39.**G**.
Gor. 1—22/11/41.**G**.
Gor. 3—15/1/44.**G**.
Gor. 29/6—10/8/46.**G**.
Gor. 28/5—18/6/49.**G**.
Gor. 22/3—12/4/52.**G**.
New cylinders.

BOILERS:
620 *(ex 516)* 2/12/11.
756 *(exE2 507B)* 28/5/21.
921 *(exJ10 5679)* 28/12/29.
318 *(ex 5548)* 15/7/33.
219 *(ex 5906)* 15/7/39.
4235 *(ex 5752)* 22/11/41.
175 *(exF1 5729)* 15/1/44.
4252 *(ex 9340)* 18/6/49.
22751 *(ex 69225)* 12/4/52.

SHEDS:
Barnsley.
New England 21/11/34.
Immingham 15/9/37.
Louth 20/4/38.
Mexborough 21/6/53.

RENUMBERED:
766c 15/12/23.
5766 23/7/27 ??
9306 5/5/46.
69306 18/6/49.

CONDEMNED: 8/11/55.
Cond. & cut up at Darlington.

5767

Beyer, Peacock 3971.

To traffic 5/1898.

REPAIRS:
Gor. 21/4—1/10/10.**G**.
Wrx. 2/5—23/6/21.**G**.
Gor. 16/2—19/4/24.**G**.
Gor. 29/1—12/3/27.**G**.
Gor. 18/5—15/6/29.**G**.
New cylinders.
Gor. 19/11—10/12/32.**G**.
Altered to LNE gauge.
Gor. 22/2—7/3/36.**G**.
Gor. 22/10—12/11/38.**G**.

Some which had a straight back to the bunker were fitted with flared plating.

During the 1939-45 war, No.5898 acquired an upward extension to increase its bunker coal capacity. This was between the cab rear windows and was a local fitting by Immingham shed.

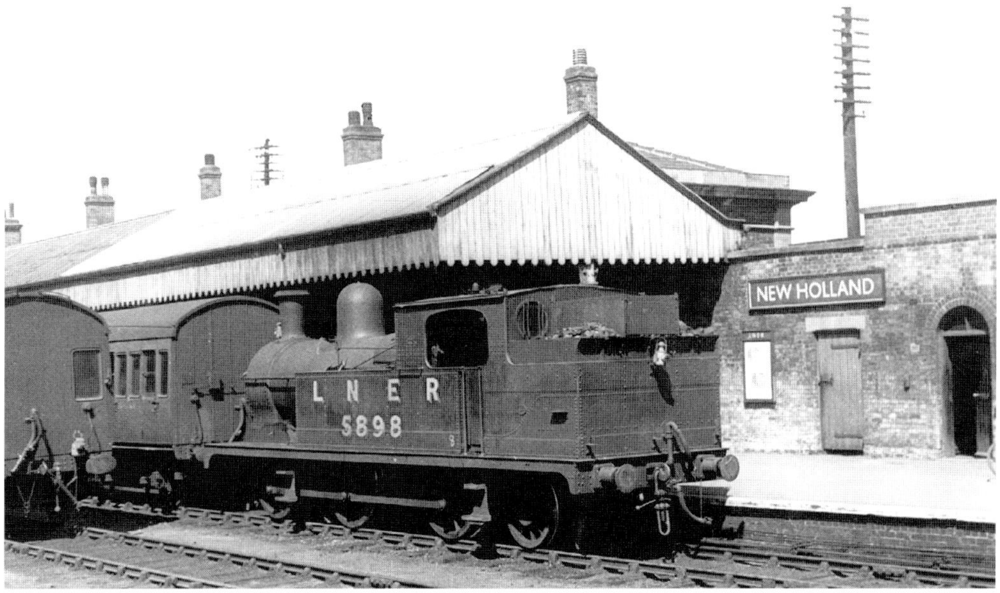

This shows the open topped well in the right hand side tank between the filler and cab front. This accommodated the reach rod from the screw reverse gear mounted on top of the lowered portion of the tank, evidenced by the line of rivet heads. Classes F1, F2 and N4 had a similar arrangement.

Fastening of the smokebox door was by two handles and this style was still in use when the LNER took over – *see* page 68, top and below.

Robinson preferred a wheel and handle and as early as 1902 change to that method had begun.

By the 1930s most, and probably all, were fitted with wheel and handle on the smokebox door.

5767 cont./
Gor. 22/4—3/6/39.**L.**
Gor. 1—6/6/42.**G.**
Gor. 17/11—15/12/45.**G.**
Gor. 8—29/1/49.**G.**
Gor. 18/2/50.**C/L.**
Washout hole welded.
Gor. 26/4—10/5/52.**G.**
Gor. 11/2—10/3/56.**G.**
Gor. 8/12/60. *Not repaired.*

BOILERS:
137 *(new)* 1/10/10.
394 *(ex 5744)* 12/3/27.
265 *(exJ10 5175)* 15/6/29.
196 *(new)* 10/12/32.
1099 *(ex 5532)* 7/3/36.
1594 *(ex 5770)* 12/11/38.
4211 *(exJ10 5820)* 6/6/42.
4289 *(new)* 15/12/45.
1917 *(ex 9341)* 29/1/49.
22755 *(ex 9313)* 10/5/52.
22718 *(ex 69256)* 10/3/56.

SHEDS:
Annesley 2/11/18.
Woodford 20/9/33.
Ardsley 13/12/40.
Bradford 31/12/40.
Ardsley 10/2/41.
Colwick 12/4/42.
Woodford 13/12/42.
Gorton 23/8/43.
LMR 23/5/49.
Gorton 26/6/49.

RENUMBERED:
5767 19/4/24.
9307 14/4/46.
69307 29/1/49.

CONDEMNED: 9/12/60.
Cut up at Gorton 11/2/61.

5768

Beyer, Peacock 3972.

To traffic 5/1898.

REPAIRS:
Gor. 23/1—24/2/06.**G.**
Gor. 13/12/13—7/2/14.**G.**
Gor. 9/12/22—10/2/23.**G.**
Gor. 19/3—4/6/27.**G.**
New cylinders.
Gor. 31/5—28/6/30.**G.**
Gor. 25/3—15/4/33.**G.**
Altered to LNE gauge.
Gor. 25/7—15/8/36.**G.**
Gor. 15—29/4/39.**G.**
Gor. 25/8—12/9/42.**G.**
Gor. 1/12/45—19/1/46.**G.**
New cylinders.
Gor. 13/8—3/9/49.**G.**
Gor. 27/9—11/10/52.**G.**
Gor. 22/12/56—19/1/57.**G.**
Gor. 15/2/60. *Not repaired.*

BOILERS:
911 *(ex 937)* 24/2/06.
4 *(new)* 7/2/14.
1722 *(exJ10 5822)* 4/6/27.
219 *(exJ9 5664)* 15/4/33.
197 *(ex 5929)* 15/8/36.
4201 *(ex 5942)* 29/4/39.
736 *(ex 5746)* 12/9/42.
4211 *(ex 5767)* 19/1/46.
537 *(exF1 7101)* 3/9/49.
22788 *(exN4 69229)* 11/10/52.
22686 *(exJ10 65205)* 19/1/57.

SHEDS:
Trafford Park 28/7/16.
Neasden 18/3/26.
Trafford Park 9/11/26.
Northwich 12/7/37.
Gorton 21/9/39.
Northwich 4/12/49.
Gorton 4/1/50.
Retford 10/4/55.
Mexborough 11/12/55.

RENUMBERED:
5768 4/6/27.
9308 11/8/46.
69308 12/3/49.

CONDEMNED: 17/2/60.
Cut up at Gorton 2/4/60.

5769

Beyer, Peacock 3973.

To traffic 7/1898.

REPAIRS:
Gor. 3/3—14/5/10.**G.**
Gor. 15/2—24/5/13.**G.**
New cylinders.
Gor. 20/9/19—7/2/20.**G.**
Gor. 22/4—3/6/22.**G.**
Gor. 12/7—4/10/24.**G.**
Gor. 23/4—11/6/27.**G.**
Gor. 4—25/1/30.**G.**
Gor. 9—23/7/32.**G.**
Altered to LNE gauge.
Gor. 22/12/34—12/1/35.**G.**
Gor. 1—15/1/38.**G.**
Gor. 12—26/7/41.**G.**
New cylinders.
Gor. 17/6—1/7/44.**G.**
Gor. 4/10—1/11/47.**G.**
Gor. 22/4—6/5/50.**G.**
Gor. 8—29/11/52.**G.**
Gor. 16/3—6/4/57.**G.**

BOILERS:
475 14/5/10.
87 *(new)* 24/5/13.
712 *(exJ8 552)* 7/2/20.
1640 *(ex 5939)* 4/10/24.
166 *(ex 5054)* 11/6/27.
469 *(exN4 5624)* 25/1/30.
1629 *(exN4 5606)* 23/7/32.
282 *(exJ13 5570)* 12/1/35.
408 *(exN4 5716)* 15/1/38.
954 *(exJ10 5849)* 26/7/41.
609 *(exJ10 5121)* 1/7/44.
4193 *(ex 69370)* 6/5/50.
22795 *(ex 69298)* 29/11/52.
22820 *(ex spare)* 6/4/57.

SHEDS:
Mexborough 12/8/07.
Ardsley 27/7/32.
Mexborough 27/2/35.
Immingham 22/12/46.
Louth 21/6/53.
Staveley 13/11/55.

RENUMBERED:
5769 4/10/24.
9309 7/4/46.
69309 6/5/50.

CONDEMNED: 23/11/60.
Into Doncaster for c/u 23/11/60.

5770

Beyer, Peacock 3974.

To traffic 7/1898.

REPAIRS:
Gor. 31/3—13/5/11.**G.**
New cylinders.
Gor. 17/6—7/10/16.**G.**
Gor. 23/10—27/11/20.**G.**
Gor. 1/12/23—9/2/24.**G.**
Gor. 14/1—25/2/28.**G.**
New cylinders.
Gor. 17/1—7/2/31.**G.**
Gor. 2—9/2/35.**G.**
Gor. 3/9—1/10/38.**G.**
Altered to LNE gauge.
Gor. 10/12/41—3/1/42.**G.**
Gor. 22/7—5/8/44.**G.**
Gor. 31/12/47—24/1/48.**G.**
Gor. 17/12/49—28/1/50.**G.**
Gor. 23/12/52—3/1/53.**G.**
New cylinders.

BOILERS:
300 13/5/11.
1641 *(new)* 7/10/16.
177 *(exD8 511B)* 9/2/24.
1761 *(exJ10 5080)* 25/2/28.
795 *(exN4 5610)* 7/2/31.
1594 *(ex 5529)* 9/2/35.
765 *(ex 5762)* 1/10/38.
376 *(ex 5523)* 3/1/42.
4193 *(ex 5760)* 5/8/44.
4243 *(ex 9261)* 24/1/48.
347 *(ex 69342)* 28/1/50.
22800 *(new reno. From 4343)* 3/1/53.

SHEDS:
Annesley 19/2/01.
York 8/8/24.
Annesley 7/11/24.
Colwick 21/2/34.
Annesley 26/6/35.
Langwith Jct. 14/8/35.
Barnsley 1/10/35.
Sheffield 12/4/43.
Staveley 30/9/43.
Woodford 21/11/44.
Colwick 29/11/53.

RENUMBERED:
5770 9/2/24.
9310 10/11/46.
E9310 24/1/48.
69310 14/1/50.

CONDEMNED: 18/11/55.
Cut up at Darlington.

5771

Beyer, Peacock 3975.

To traffic 7/1898.

REPAIRS:
Shf. 27/12/07—25/3/08.**H.**
Gor. 21/10/10—21/1/11.**G.**
New cylinders.
Gor. 15/5—6/11/15.**G.**
Rebuilt from 9F to 9O.
Gor. 27/3/16. **L.**
Intensifore lubrication fitted.
Gor. 20/8—12/11/21.**G.**
Gor. 20/9/24—3/1/25.**G.**
Gor. 21/4—9/6/28.**G.**
Altered to LNE gauge.
Gor. 20/9—25/10/30.**G.**
Gor. 27/1—17/2/34.**G.**
Wakefield lubricator fitted.
Gor. 16—30/10/37.**G.**
Gor. 26/2—19/3/38.**L.**
New cylinders.
Gor. 26/10—9/11/40.**G.**
Gor. 18/2—11/3/44.**G.**
Gor. 13—27/4/46.**G.**
Gor. 14—28/8/48.**G.**
Gor. 12/1/52. *Not repaired.*

BOILERS:
745 *(new)* 25/3/08.
957 21/1/11.
1060 *(new)* 6/11/15 (sup.).

5771 cont./
1599 *(ex 5200)* 9/6/28.
1586 *(ex 5933)* 25/10/30 (sat.).
98 *(exN4 5723)* 17/2/34.
1637 *(exJ10 5825)* 30/10/37.
4251 *(new)* 9/11/40.
316 *(ex 5543)* 11/3/44.
4264 *(ex 5542)* 27/4/46.
4239 *(exN4 9239)* 28/8/48.

SHEDS:
Woodford 28/4/19.
Neasden 1/5/35.
Tuxford 7/2/36.
Walton-on-the-Hill 2/1/41.
Gorton 31/7/43.
Mexborough 3/12/44.
Lincoln 20/5/45.

RENUMBERED:
5771 3/1/25.
9311 27/4/46.
69311 28/8/48.

CONDEMNED: 4/2/52.
Cut up at Gorton 15/3/52.

5772

Beyer, Peacock 3976.

To traffic 7/1898.

REPAIRS:
Gor. ?/?—24/5/05.**G**.
Gor. 20/10/17—23/3/18.**G**.
Gor. 16—23/7/21.**G**.
Gor. 21/11—31/12/25.**G**.
Gor. 27/4—1/6/29.**G**.
Gor. 22/10—5/11/32.**G**.
Altered to LNE gauge.
Gor. 26/10—9/11/35.**G**.
Gor. 1—15/1/38.**G**.
Gor. 6/4—4/5/40.**G**.
Gor. 9—27/3/43.**G**.
Gor. 24/11—15/12/45.**G**.
Gor. 31/12/48—22/1/49.**G**.
Gor. 31/5—21/6/52.**G**.
Gor. 4/9—2/10/54.**H/I**.
Gor. 9/9/57. *Not repaired.*

BOILERS:
1126 *(new)* 24/5/05.
10 *(exJ10 116)* 23/3/18.
1656 *(ex 5542)* 5/11/32.
1625 *(ex 5907)* 9/11/35.
275 *(exJ10 5846)* 15/1/38.
4248 *(exJ10 5122)* 27/3/43.
463 *(exJ10 5680)* 15/12/45.
523 *(ex 9332)* 22/1/49.
22764 *(ex??)* 21/6/52.

SHEDS:
Neasden 10/6/18.
Ardsley 16/1/26.
Gorton 22/2/26.
Neasden 18/3/26.
Gorton 9/11/26.
Walton-on-the-Hill 18/12/40.
Gorton 5/2/43.
Colwick 19/4/43.
Woodford 2/5/48.
Colwick 9/4/50.
Sheffield 10/6/51.

RENUMBERED:
5772 31/12/25.
9312 29/9/46.
69312 22/1/49.

CONDEMNED: 7/10/57.
Cut up at Gorton 11/1/58.

5773

Beyer, Peacock 3977.

To traffic 8/1898.

REPAIRS:
Gor. ?/?—10/10/03.**G**.
Gor. 13/6—22/8/14.**G**.
New cylinders.
Gor. 18/3—13/5/22.**G**.
Gor. 16/1—13/3/26.**G**.
Gor. 22/2—29/3/30.**G**.
Gor. 10—242/34.**G**.
Altered to LNE gauge.
Gor. 28/8—18/9/37.**G**.
New cylinders.
Gor. 28/6—5/7/41.**G**.
Gor. 17/6—1/7/44.**G**.
Gor. 29/3—3/5/47.**G**.
Gor. 19/1—9/2/52.**G**.

BOILERS:
901 10/10/03.
440 *(new)* 22/8/14.
294 *(exJ10 5833)* 29/3/30.
136 *(exJ10 5842)* 24/2/34.
4224 *(new)* 18/9/37.
167 *(ex 5746)* 5/7/41.
4230 *(ex 5763)* 1/7/44.
22735 *(ex 69368)* 9/2/52.

SHEDS:
Neasden 16/1/15.
Mexborough 11/4/48.
Retford 25/4/48.

RENUMBERED:
5773 13/3/26.
9313 7/4/46.
69313 9/2/52.

CONDEMNED: 21/3/55.
Cut up at Gorton 1/10/55.

5774

Beyer, Peacock 3978.

To traffic 8/1898.

REPAIRS:
Gor. ?/?—17/11/06.**G**.
Gor. 25/4—4/7/08.**G**.
Gor. 21/5—27/8/21.**G**.
Gor. 2/2—12/4/24.**G**.
Gor. 19/3—7/5/27.**G**.
Gor. 10—31/8/29.**G**.
Gor. 1—15/4/33.**G**.
Altered to LNE gauge.
Gor. 7—21/3/36.**G**.

BOILERS:
512 *(exJ10 831)* 17/11/06.
691 4/7/08.
212 *(exD7 689)* 27/8/21.
4 *(ex 5768)* 7/5/27.
1762 *(exJ10 5824)* 31/8/29.
324 *(exN4 5637)* 15/4/33.
4199 *(new)* 21/3/36.

SHEDS:
Annesley.
York 8/8/24.
Annesley 7/11/24.
Colwick 21/2/34.
Leicester 7/3/34.
Langwith Jct. 8/11/34.
Leicester 26/11/35.
Colwick 15/4/36.

RENUMBERED:
5774 12/4/24.

CONDEMNED: 26/1/39.
Cut up at Doncaster 18/3/39.

5775

Beyer, Peacock 3979.

To traffic 8/1898.

REPAIRS:
Gor. 20/1—2/3/06.**G**.
Gor. 6/2—15/5/15.**G**.
New cylinders.
Gor. 6/3—17/4/20.**G**.
Ann. 2/5—4/7/23.**H**.
Gor. 14/6—2/8/24.**G**.
Gor. 26/3—21/5/27.**G**.
New cylinders.
Gor. 17/8—28/9/29.**G**.
Altered to LNE gauge.
Gor. 25/2—4/3/33.**G**.
Gor. 24/8—14/9/35.**G**.
Gor. 14—28/8/37.**G**.
Gor. 22/6—20/7/40.**G**.
New cylinders.
Gor. 12—27/11/43.**G**.
Gor. 23/8—20/9/47.**G**.
Gor. 23/2—15/3/52.**G**.
Gor. 12/3—2/4/55.**G**.
Gor. 16/1/60. *Not repaired.*

BOILERS:
731 2/3/06.
917 *(new)* 15/5/15.
1688 *(exJ8 5559)* 21/5/27.
28 *(exJ8 5557)* 28/9/29.
608 *(ex 5913)* 4/3/33.
1793 *(ex 5543)* 14/9/35.
306 *(exD7 5708)* 28/8/37.
1647 *(ex 5941)* 27/11/43.
22745 *(ex 69259)* 15/3/52.
22846 *(exJ10 65146)* 2/4/55.

SHEDS:
Annesley.
Colwick 4/2/39.
Mexborough 21/3/40.
Retford 18/3/51.
New England 2/11/58.
Sheffield 7/12/58.

RENUMBERED:
5775 2/8/24.
9314 10/11/46.
69314 15/3/52.

CONDEMNED: 20/1/60.
Cut up at Gorton 5/3/60.

5051

Gorton.

To traffic 4/1898.

REPAIRS:
Gor. 28/3—16/5/08.**G**.
Gor. 6/5—10/6/16.**G**.
Gor. 18/11/22—28/4/23.**G**.
Gor. 14/11/25—9/1/26.**G**.
Altered to LNE gauge.
Gor. 25/8—6/10/28.**G**.
Gor. 15—29/11/30.**G**.
Reverted to GC gauge.
Gor. 11—25/3/33.**G**.
Altered back to LNE gauge.
New cylinders.
Gor. 24/8—21/9/35.**G**.
Gor. 26/6—10/7/37.**G**.
Gor. 21—28/10/39.**G**.
Gor. 2—20/12/41.**G**.
Gor. 4—26/2/44.**G**.
New cylinders.
Gor. 17/11—1/12/45.**G**.
Gor. 3/7—14/8/48.**G**.
Gor. 3—17/3/51.**G**.
Gor. 9/10—13/11/54.**H/I**.

5051 cont./
BOILERS:
495 *(ex 918)* 16/5/08.
990 *(ex 756)* 10/6/16.
82 *(exD7 5711)* 9/1/26.
1917 *(exJ12 6450)* 6/10/28.
1197 *(ex 5943)* 29/11/30.
293 *(new)* 25/3/33.
1643 *(exN4 5618)* 21/9/35.
56 *(exN4 5607)* 10/7/37.
727 *(exN4 5635)* 28/10/39.
219 *(ex 5766)* 20/12/41.
4256 *(ex 5526)* 26/2/44.
4287 *(new)* 1/12/45.
4318 *(new)* 14/8/48.
22687 *(exN4 69245)* 17/3/51.

SHEDS:
Mexborough.
Doncaster 21/7/24.
Colwick 9/12/30.
Leicester 5/8/32.
Annesley 3/12/32.
Neasden 13/10/46.
Barnsley 11/11/56.

RENUMBERED:
51 31/8/00 *(ex204A)*.
5051 9/1/26.
9315 26/10/46.
69315 14/8/48.

CONDEMNED: 3/6/58.
Cut up at Gorton 23/8/58.

5173

Gorton.

To traffic 5/1898.

REPAIRS:
Gor. 24/6—7/10/11.**G**.
New cylinders.
Gor. 12/1—23/3/18.**G**.
Gor. 2/4—28/5/21.**G**.
Gor. 23/6—25/8/23.**G**.
Gor. 30/1—20/3/26.**G**.
Gor. 2/3—27/4/29.**G**.
Gor. 3—31/10/31.**G**.
Gor. 12—26/5/34.**G**.
Altered to LNE gauge.
Gor. 13/2—6/3/37.**G**.
Gor. 2—30/12/39.**G**.
Heating app. both ends.
Gor. 28/8—4/9/43.**G**.
Gor. 8/6—27/7/46.**G**.
Gor. 2—16/10/48.**G**.
Gor. 3—31/3/51.**G**.
Gor. 9—23/5/53.**G**.

BOILERS:
583 *(exJ10 809)* 7/10/11.
1727 *(new)* 23/3/18.
29 *(new)* 25/8/23.
990 *(ex 5051)* 20/3/26.
106 *(exN4 5618)* 27/4/29.
393 *(ex 5924)* 26/5/34.
357 *(ex 5927)* 6/3/37.
527 *(exJ10 5824)* 16/12/39.
1799 *(exJ10 5850)* 4/9/43.
367 *(ex 5903)* 27/7/46.
4248 *(ex 9259)* 16/10/48.
22688 *(ex 69292)* 31/3/51.
22818 *(ex??)* 23/5/53.

SHEDS:
Mexborough 30/8/98.
Doncaster 21/7/24.
Bradford 13/2/31.
Doncaster 4/3/31.
Mexborough 18/3/39.
Sheffield 28/11/54.

RENUMBERED:
173 5/8/00 *(ex205A)*.
173c 15/9/23.
5173 20/3/26.
9316 27/7/46.
69316 16/10/48.

CONDEMNED: 11/3/57.
Cut up at Gorton 6/4/57.

5189

Gorton.

To traffic 2/1898.

REPAIRS:
Gor. ?/?—4/1/08.**G**.
Gor. 25/1—15/3/13.**G**.
Gor. 7/12/18—3/5/19.**G**.
New cylinders.
Gor. 23/7—3/9/21.**G**.
Gor. 9/8—25/10/24.**G**.
Gor. 13/8—1/10/27.**G**.
Gor. 22/2—22/3/30.**G**.
Altered to LNE gauge.
Gor. 23/9—7/10/33.**G**.
Gor. 6—20/11/37.**G**.
Gor. 17/5—14/6/41.**G**.
Gor. 28/2—18/3/44.**G**.
Gor. 16/8—6/9/47.**G**.
Gor. 14/1—4/2/50.**G**.
Gor. 18/10—1/11/52.**G**.

BOILERS:
612 4/1/08.
211 *(new)* 15/3/13.
1230 *(exJ12 7B)* 3/5/19.
707 *(ex 5021)* 1/10/27.
1769 *(exD7 5711)* 22/3/30.
735 *(exN4 5617)* 7/10/33.
4186 *(exN4 5513)* 20/11/37.
293 *(ex 5749)* 18/3/44.
4303 *(ex 9323)* 4/2/50.
22792 *(ex 69362)* 1/11/52.

SHEDS:
Barnsley.
Sheffield 18/7/29.
Barnsley 4/11/29.
Lincoln 1/12/34.
Tuxford 17/12/34.
Louth 7/11/35.
Gorton 19/11/37.
Heaton Mersey 17/9/39.

RENUMBERED:
189 ?/8/00 *(ex206A)*.
5189 25/10/24.
9317 19/5/46.
69317 12/2/49.

CONDEMNED: 6/2/56.
Into Dar. for cut up 23/2/56.

5251

Gorton.

To traffic 2/1898.

REPAIRS:
Gor. ?/?—4/4/03.**G**.
Gor. 8/8—21/11/14.**G**.
Gor. 5/6—6/11/20.**G**.
Gor. 3/3—7/4/23.**G**.
Gor. 16/5—18/7/25.**G**.
Gor. 26/1—2/3/29.**G**.
Gor. 27/8—17/9/32.**G**.
Altered to LNE gauge.
New cylinders.
Gor. 4/4—2/5/36.**G**.
Gor. 26/8—16/9/39.**G**.

BOILERS:
614 *(new)* 4/4/03.
1382 *(ex 752)* 21/11/14.
648 *(exE2 509B)* 6/11/20.
606 *(ex 5908)* 17/9/32.
1641 *(ex 5912)* 2/5/36.
4222 *(exN4 5604)* 16/9/39.

SHED:
Barnsley.

RENUMBERED:
251 ?/8/00 *(ex207A)*.
5251 18/7/25.

CONDEMNED: 1/3/43.
Dismantled at Gorton and 'converted' to Boiler Truck 27/11/43.

5894

Gorton.

To traffic 3/1899.

REPAIRS:
Gor. 19/12/14—6/3/15.**G**.
Gor. 19/6—14/8/20.**G**.
Gor. 27/1—3/3/23.**G**.
Gor. 23/4—30/7/27.**G**.
New cylinders.
Gor. 1—22/8/31.**G**.
Altered to LNE gauge.
Gor. 14—28/7/34.**G**.
Gor. 8—22/8/36.**G**.
Gor. 16—30/7/38.**G**.
Gor. 17/8—14/9/40.**G**.
Gor. 2—18/4/42.**G**.
After collision.
Gor. 24—27/11/43.**L**.
Boiler work.
Gor. 10—24/2/45.**G**.
Gor. 31/1—21/2/48.**G**.
Gor. 28/10—18/11/50.**H/I**.
Gor. 4/7—1/8/53.**G**.

BOILERS:
761.
310 *(ex 546)* 6/3/15.
711 *(ex 5938)* 30/7/27.
727 *(new)* 22/8/31.
437 *(ex 5200)* 28/7/34.
4207 *(new)* 22/8/36.
959 *(exJ10 5787)* 30/7/38.
324 *(exJ10 5841)* 14/9/40.
197 *(ex 5546)* 18/4/42.
249 *(ex 5025)* 24/2/45.
4277 *(ex 9262)* 21/2/48.
4277 reno.22667 18/11/50.
22823 *(exJ10 65126)* 1/8/53.

SHEDS:
Neasden 17/9/20.
Sheffield 28/7/34.
Barnsley 20/11/34.
Langwith Jct. 4/10/35.
Immingham 11/11/45.
Neasden 14/7/46.

RENUMBERED:
5894 30/7/27.
9318 24/3/46.
E9318 21/2/48.
69318 18/11/50.

CONDEMNED: 5/11/56.
Cut up at Gorton 8/6/57.

Reversion to two handles had begun by 1946 and the wheel then gradually disappeared.

The whole class were at first fitted with taper shank buffers which had a solid spindle and No.5902 – *see* page 72, top – still had this type to October 1947.

By LNER days many had been changed to a later GCR design which had a parallel shank with end collar, and a hollow spindle.

The later type had a variant with longer shank and no end collar.

By 1946, as replacement buffers were required, Group Standard type with stepped shank were used. No.9327 had them by 12th October 1946 and 9257 by 30th August 1947.

Many spent all their life on goods shunting so had 3-link couplings and no carriage heating equipment.

(below) For passenger station pilot duties some were changed to screw coupling although No.5173 did not have carriage heating equipment fitted until ex works in December 1939.

5895

Gorton.

To traffic 3/1899.

REPAIRS:
Gor. 6/7—19/10/07.**G**.
Gor. 10/12/21—28/1/22.**G**.
Gor. 9/2—29/3/24.**G**.
Gor. 29/1—19/3/27.**G**.
Gor. 5—31/12/31.**G**.
Altered to LNE gauge.
New cylinders.
Gor. 19/10—2/11/35.**G**.
Gor. 15—29/5/37.**G**.
Gor. 28/1—11/2/39.**G**.
Gor. 10/2—9/3/40.**H**.
Re-tubed & re-stayed.
Gor. 12—27/6/42.**G**.
Gor. 28/2—18/3/44.**G**.
Gor. 31/8—21/9/46.**G**.
Gor. 10/2—13/3/48.**G**.
Gor. 10/9—15/10/49.**G**.
New cylinders.
Gor. 26/7—16/8/52.**G**.
Gor. 25/4—9/5/53.**C/H**.
Gor. 28/4—2/6/56.**G**.

BOILERS:
1337 *(new)* 19/10/07.
516 *(exJ10 5840)* 19/3/27.
1618 *(ex 5755)* 31/12/31.
241 *(exD7 5562)* 2/11/35.
4218 *(new)* 29/5/37.
469 *(ex 5523)* 11/2/39.
4206 *(ex 5906)* 27/6/42.
479 *(ex 5127)* 18/3/44.
425 *(ex 5913)* 21/9/46.
313 *(ex 9288)* 13/3/48.
4329 *(new)* 15/10/49.
22772 *(ex 69324)* 16/8/52.
22817 *(ex 69325)* 9/5/53.
22850 *(exJ10 65192)* 2/6/56.

SHEDS:
Brunswick 24/11/07.
Neasden 10/4/24.
Langwith Jct. 1/11/35.
Neasden 27/1/57.

RENUMBERED:
5895 29/3/24.
9319 17/9/46.
E9319 13/3/48.
69319 15/10/49.

CONDEMNED: 7/12/59.
Cut up at Gorton 14/5/60.

5896

Gorton.

To traffic 4/1899.

REPAIRS:
Gor. 11/11/11—20/1/12.**G**.
Gor. 1/1—19/2/21.**G**.
Gor. 25/8—17/11/23.**G**.
Gor. 25/9—4/12/26.**G**.
Gor. 27/8—3/9/27.**L**.
Boiler work.
Gor. 26/1—9/3/29.**G**.
New cylinders.
Gor. 25/7—22/8/31.**G**.
Gor. 4—18/5/35.**G**.
Altered to LNE gauge.
Gor. 19/3—2/4/38.**G**.
Gor. 1—15/3/41.**G**.
Gor. 27/3—8/4/44.**G**.
Gor. 27/9—18/10/47.**G**.
Gor. 28/10—11/11/50.**G**.
New cylinders.
Gor. 6—13/12/52.**C/L**.
Gor. 31/10—21/11/53.**G**.
Gor. 1—22/12/56.**G**.
Gor. 3/10/59. *Not repaired.*

BOILERS:
476.
1118 *(exJ10 797)* 20/1/12.
1046 *(ex 914)* 19/2/21.
214 *(ex 5531)* 22/8/31.
482 *(exN4 5604)* 18/5/35.
483 *(ex 5127)* 2/4/38.
4191 *(ex 5759)* 15/3/41.
435 *(ex 5746)* 8/4/44.
747 *(ex 9269)* 18/10/47.
22668 *(ex??)* 11/11/50.
22828 *(ex 69321)* 21/11/53.
22813 *(ex 69334)* 22/12/56.

SHEDS:
Gorton 20/2/12.
Walton-on-the-Hill 2/1/25.
Gorton 18/3/35.
Mexborough 18/5/35.
Barnsley 7/1/39.

RENUMBERED:
896c 17/11/23.
5896 4/12/26.
9320 18/8/46.
69320 11/11/50.

CONDEMNED: 6/10/59.
Cut up at Gorton 14/11/59.

5897

Gorton.

To traffic 5/1899.

REPAIRS:
Gor. 20/1—12/2/10.**G**.
New cylinders.
Gor. 27/7—26/10/12.**G**.
Gor. 27/11/20—8/1/21.**G**.
Gor. 1/3—26/4/24.**G**.
Gor. 30/7—3/9/27.**G**.
New cylinders.
Gor. 24/1—14/2/31.**G**.
Altered to LNE gauge.
Gor. 3—17/2/34.**G**.
Gor. 22/8—5/9/36.**G**.
Gor. 30/9—7/10/39.**G**.
Gor. 21/4—8/5/43.**G**.
Gor. 23/12/44—10/2/45.**G**.
Gor. 29/3—26/4/47.**G**.
Gor. 5—26/8/50.**G**.
Gor. 23/5—13/6/53.**G**.

BOILERS:
455 12/2/10.
945 *(exJ10 5829)* 26/10/12.
1643 *(exJ12 5493)* 26/4/24.
400 *(ex 5763)* 14/2/31.
1917 *(exN4 5610)* 17/2/34.
452 *(ex 5906)* 5/9/36.
950 *(ex 5909)* 7/10/39.
36 *(ex 5900)* 8/5/43.
4218 *(ex 5541)* 10/2/45.
393 *(exN4 5611)* 26/4/47.
4257 *(ex 9267)* 26/8/50.
22820 *(exJ10 65189)* 13/6/53.

SHEDS:
Neasden 20/9/18.
Woodford 7/2/28.
Ardsley 13/12/40.
Bradford 4/4/41.
Doncaster 20/4/42.
Sheffield 9/5/42.
Retford 29/8/43.

RENUMBERED:
5897 26/4/24.
9321 11/8/46.
69321 26/8/50.

CONDEMNED: 8/10/56.
Cut up at Gorton 27/4/57.

5898

Gorton.

To traffic 6/1899.

REPAIRS:
Wrx. 12/8—16/10/08.**G**.
Wrx. 20/4—9/8/14.**G**.
Gor. 28/8—6/11/20.**G**.
New cylinders.
Wrx. 12/1—4/4/23.**G**.
Gor. 7/11—31/12/25.**G**.
Gor. 9/6—7/7/28.**G**.
Gor. 16/5—13/6/31.**G**.
Gor. 17/11—8/12/34.**G**.
Altered to LNE gauge.
Heating app. both ends.
Gor. 8—29/10/38.**G**.
Gor. 28/9—12/10/40.**G**.
Gor. 4—12/6/43.**G**.
Gor. 5/1—2/2/46.**G**.
Gor. 20/12/47—24/1/48.**G**.
New cylinders.
Gor. 4—18/11/50.**G**.
Gor. 17/1—7/2/53.**G**.
Gor. 2—30/6/56.**G**.

BOILERS:
542 16/10/08.
672 *(ex 943)* 9/8/14.
937 7/7/28.
501 *(new)* 8/12/34.
4209 *(ex 5909)* 12/6/43.
4291 *(new)* 2/2/46.
448 *(exN4 5724)* 24/1/48.
22669 *(ex??)* 18/11/50.
22805 *(ex 69288)* 7/2/53.
22754 *(ex 69354)* 30/6/56.

SHEDS:
Wrexham 17/12/20.
Bidston 24/7/31.
Wrexham 21/9/31.
Ardsley 19/2/35.
Lincoln 13/2/36.
Immingham 29/3/37.
Lincoln 30/10/38.
Immingham 1/7/45.
Louth 21/6/53.
Langwith Jct. 23/9/56.
Retford 17/2/57.
New England 2/11/58.

RENUMBERED:
5898 31/12/25.
9322 18/8/46.
E9322 24/1/48.
69322 18/11/50.

CONDEMNED: 24/6/59.
Cut up at Gorton 29/8/59.

The Engine History Cards listed ninety-four of the class as being fitted at both ends for carriage heating, most of them so equipped from 1934 to 1940.

(above) **In 1937 the LNER took over the goods workings on the former Metropolitan Railway and on 30th October 1937 Nos.5540 and 5930 of Neasden shed were fitted with trip cock apparatus. The trigger was between the driving and trailing coupled wheels.**

By July 1946 No.9313 had trip cock fitted and in October 1946 Nos.9315 and 9350 were also equipped. Curiously the trigger position was the same on both sides of the engine.

5899

Gorton.

To traffic 6/1899.

REPAIRS:
Gor. 29/10/09—29/1/10.**G.**
Gor. 11/11/22—31/3/23.**G.**
New cylinders.
Wrx. 9/12/25—4/2/26.**H.**
Gor. 21/1—25/2/28.**G.**
Gor. 9/8—20/9/30.**G.**
Gor. 4—11/11/33.**G.**
Altered to LNE gauge.
Gor. 11—25/7/36.**G.**
Gor. 29/10—12/11/38.**G.**
Gor. 27/4—11/5/40.**G.**
Heating app. both ends.
Gor. 16/9—3/10/42.**G.**
Gor. 6—13/5/44.**G.**
Gor. 27/10—10/11/45.**L.**
Boiler tubes.
Gor. 21/12/46—18/1/47.**G.**
Gor. 24/12/49—21/1/50.**G.**
Gor. 18/4—9/5/53.**G.**
New cylinders.

BOILERS:
617 *(ex 21)* 29/1/10.
423 *(exJ10 825)* 31/3/23.
1769 *(ex 5189)* 11/11/33.
183 *(exJ10 5803)* 25/7/36.
382 *(exJ10 5841)* 12/11/38.
222 *(exJ10 5083)* 11/5/40.
4244 *(exJ10 5126)* 3/10/42.
4255 *(ex 5932)* 13/5/44.
4303 *(new)* 18/1/47.
4269 *(exN4 9226)* 21/1/50.
22816 *(exJ10 65130)* 9/5/53.

SHEDS:
Wrexham 1/1/05.
Gorton 13/10/30.
Colwick 18/12/30.
Leicester 11/12/31.
Colwick 7/3/34.
Langwith Jct. 16/10/36.
Sheffield 15/8/54.

RENUMBERED:
5899 4/2/26.
9323 11/8/46.
69323 21/1/50.

CONDEMNED: 26/11/56.
Cut up at Gorton 19/1/57.

5900

Gorton.

To traffic 7/1899.

REPAIRS:
Gor. ?/?—26/3/04.**G.**
Gor. 3/6—11/11/22.**G.**
Gor. 12/12/25—23/1/26.**G.**
Gor. 27/10—24/11/28.**G.**
Gor. 20/2—5/3/32.**G.**
Altered to LNE gauge.
Gor. 23/3—6/4/35.**G.**
Heating app. both ends.
Gor. 13—27/3/37.**G.**
Gor. 10—17/2/40.**G.**
Gor. 10—17/8/40.**L.**
After collision.
Gor. 3—17/4/43.**G.**
Gor. 27/7—10/8/46.**G.**
Gor. 19/3—7/5/49.**G.**
New cylinders.
Gor. 31/5—14/6/52.**G.**

BOILERS:
487 26/3/04.
373 *(new)* 11/11/22.
275 *(exJ10 5121)* 5/3/32.
373 *(exN4 5724)* 6/4/35.
747 *(ex 5943)* 27/3/37.
36 *(ex 5527)* 17/2/40.
4183 *(ex 5764)* 17/4/43.
196 *(exN4 5625)* 10/8/46.
4298 *(exJ10 5154)* 7/5/49.
22762 *(ex??)* 14/6/52.

SHEDS:
Gorton 3/11/20.
Brunswick *by* 18/9/26.
Gorton 31/8/34.
Woodford 6/4/35.
Colwick 25/3/42.
Woodford 2/5/48.
Colwick 2/4/50.
Sheffield 10/6/51.

RENUMBERED:
5900 23/1/26.
9324 10/8/46.
69324 7/5/49.

CONDEMNED: 8/11/54.
Cut up at Doncaster 9/12/54.

5901

Gorton.

To traffic 8/1899.

REPAIRS:
Gor. ?/?—8/10/04.**G.**
Gor. 10/6—26/8/16.**G.**
Gor. 2/9—16/12/22.**G.**
New cylinders.
Wrx. 14/8—26/11/25.**G.**
Gor. 5/5—16/6/28.**G.**
Gor. 19/12/31—9/1/32.**G.**
Altered to LNE gauge.
Gor. 4—18/6/32.**L.**
Boiler work.
Gor. 20/1—10/2/34.**G.**
Gor. 21/11—5/12/36.**G.**
Gor. 28/1—11/2/39.**G.**
Gor. 6/9—25/10/41.**G.**
Gor. 13/5—3/6/44.**G.**
New cylinders.
Gor. 16/8—13/9/47.**G.**
Gor. 13/5—10/6/50.**G.**
Gor. 8—29/11/52.**G.**

BOILERS:
173 8/10/04.
1639 *(new)* 26/8/16.
34 *(exJ10 5174)* 9/1/32.
94 *(exN4 5634)* 10/2/34.
142 *(exJ10 5090)* 5/12/36.
375 *(ex 5914)* 11/2/39.
1787 *(ex 5938)* 25/10/41.
29 *(ex 5759)* 3/6/44.
4246 *(ex 9298)* 13/9/47.
4312 *(ex 69359)* 10/6/50.
22796 *(ex 69278)* 29/11/52.

SHEDS:
Wrexham 30/11/09.
Gorton 30/3/28.
Chester 30/1/32.
Wrexham 20/2//33.
Mexborough 12/12/34.
Ardsley 26/2/35.
Bradford 4/4/35.
Barnsley 22/6/44.

RENUMBERED:
5901 26/11/25.
9325 16/8/46.
69325 10/6/50.

CONDEMNED: 24/9/56.
Cut up at Gorton 3/11/56.

5902

Gorton.

To traffic 9/1899.

REPAIRS:
Gor. 14/12/07—1/2/08.**G.**
Gor. 1/4—15/7/22.**G.**
Gor. 10/1—21/2/25.**G.**
Gor. 22/6—20/7/29.**G.**
New cylinders.
Gor. 18/2—4/3/33.**G.**
Altered to LNE gauge.
Gor. 20/1—3/2/34.**L.**
Boiler work.
Gor. 7—21/12/35.**G.**
Gor. 22/7—5/8/39.**G.**
Heating app. both ends.
Gor. 27/11—12/12/42.**G.**
Gor. 21/7—11/8/45.**G.**
Gor. 25/10—15/11/47.**G.**
Gor. 1—22/10/49.**G.**
Gor. 26/1—23/2/52.**H/I.**
Gor. 21/8—25/9/54.**G.**
New cylinders.

BOILERS:
444.
1357 *(new)* 1/2/08.
404 *(ex 528)* 15/7/22.
1776 *(exJ10 5821)* 4/3/33.
563 *(exJ10 5835)* 21/12/35.
1897 *(ex 5764)* 5/8/39.
1898 *(ex 5540)* 12/12/42.
4223 *(ex 5946)* 11/8/45.
4254 *(ex 9297)* 15/11/47.
4237 *(ex 9266)* 22/10/49.
4237 reno.22741 23/2/52.
22732 *(exN4 69239)* 25/9/54.

SHEDS:
Wrexham 1/1/05.
Gorton 1/7/35.
Northwich 22/1/36.
Gorton 20/9/39.
Wrexham 3/11/46.
Trafford Park 17/10/48.

RENUMBERED:
5902 21/2/25.
9326 12/5/46.
69326 29/1/49.

CONDEMNED: 10/10/57.
Cut up at Gorton 23/11/57.

5903

Gorton.

To traffic 9/1899.

REPAIRS:
Gor. 14/12/01—28/2/02.**G.**
Gor. 27/2—8/4/05.**G.**
Gor. 19/7—22/11/19.**G.**
Gor. 4/3—8/4/22.**G.**
Wrx. 27/10/24—7/3/25.**G.**
Gor. 2/5—4/7/27.**G.**
Gor. 13/7—24/8/29.**G.**
Gor. 13—27/8/32.**G.**
Altered to LNE gauge.
Gor. 18/5—1/6/35.**G.**
Gor. 31/10—14/11/36.**G.**
Gor. 18/3—1/4/39.**G.**
New cylinders.
Gor. 10/1—7/2/42.**G.**
Gor. 1—18/3/44.**G.**

5903 cont./
Gor. 1—29/6/46.**G**.
Gor. 5—12/10/46.**L**.
After collision.
Gor. 5/2—12/3/49.**G**.
New cylinders.
Gor. 6—20/9/52.**G**.
Gor. 8/12/56—5/1/57.**G**.
Gor. 12/9/59. *Not repaired.*

BOILERS:
300 28/2/02.
1116 *(new)* 8/4/05.
1819 *(new)* 22/11/19.
1031 *(exJ10 5834)* 27/8/32.
44 *(ex spare)* 1/6/35.
1654 *(ex 5526)* 14/11/36.
97 *(ex 5528)* 1/4/39.
727 *(ex 5051)* 7/2/42.
367 *(ex 5905)* 18/3/44.
4225 *(ex 5942)* 29/6/46.
4330 *(new)* 12/3/49.
22781 *(ex 69357)* 20/9/52.
22802 *(ex 69344)* 5/1/57.

SHEDS:
Wrexham 6/2/20.
Gorton 6/7/29.
Langwith Jct. 29/6/35.
Lincoln 17/2/52.
Louth 19/7/53.
Sheffield 30/10/55.
New England 7/12/58.

RENUMBERED:
5903 7/3/25.
9327 22/6/46.
69327 12/3/49.

CONDEMNED: 17/9/59.
Cut up at Gorton 31/10/59.

5904

Gorton.

To traffic 10/1899.

REPAIRS:
Gor. 17/2—19/5/06.**G**.
Gor. 1/11/13—17/1/14.**G**.
Gor. 15/5—24/7/20.**G**.
New cylinders.
Gor. 4/8—3/11/23.**G**.
Gor. 29/1—19/3/27.**G**.
Gor. 4/1—1/2/30.**G**.
Gor. 19/11—3/12/32.**G**.
Altered to LNE gauge.
Gor. 16—30/11/35.**G**.
Gor. 29/10—12/11/38.**G**.
Gor. 29/1—21/2/42.**G**.
Gor. 31/3—15/4/44.**G**.
Gor. 20/12/47—17/1/48.**G**.
Gor. 5—26/11/49.**G**.
After collision.
Gor. 30/8—13/9/52.**G**.

BOILERS:
434.
650 19/5/06.
657 *(ex 906)* 17/1/14.
960 *(exJ10 5790)* 3/12/32.
84 *(exJ10 5787)* 30/11/35.
498 *(ex 5937)* 12/11/38.
4206 *(ex 5895)* 15/4/44.
193 *(ex 9263)* 17/1/48.
4254 *(ex 69326)* 26/11/49.
22780 *(exN5 9295)* 13/9/52.

SHEDS:
Brunswick 21/3/14.
Gorton 31/8/34.
Northwich 3/1/36.
Gorton 5/12/36.
Wrexham 21/9/39.
Gorton 28/12/41.
Heaton Mersey 30/4/42.
Gorton 5/10/52.

RENUMBERED:
904c 3/11/23.
5904 19/3/27.
9328 14/7/46.
E9328 17/1/48.
69328 12/2/49.

CONDEMNED: 9/1/57.
Cut up at Gorton 16/2/57.

5905

Gorton.

To traffic 11/1899.

REPAIRS:
Gor. ?/?—18/8/06.**G**.
Gor. 9/11/18—28/6/19.**G**.
Gor. 3/6—29/7/22.**G**.
Gor. 14/3—9/5/25.**G**.
Gor. 9/2—30/3/29.**G**.
Gor. 3—31/10/31.**G**.
Altered to LNE gauge.
Gor. 4—18/5/35.**G**.
Heating app. both ends.
Gor. 26/3—9/4/38.**G**.
Gor. 22/3—12/4/41.**G**.
Gor. 27/1—19/2/44.**G**.
Gor. 4/1—8/2/47.**G**.
Gor. 17/1/48.**L**.
Firehole ring fractured.
Gor. 17/4/48.**L**.
Firehole ring fractured.
Gor. 26/3—9/4/49.**G**.
Gor. 2—16/6/51.**G**.
Gor. 19/12/53—9/1/54.**G**.
Gor. 24/3—14/4/56.**C/L**.

BOILERS:
434 *(ex 904)* 18/8/06.
1782 *(new)* 28/6/19.
155 *(ex 5546)* 30/3/29.
150 *(exJ10 5641)* 31/10/31.
167 *(exJ10 5846)* 18/5/35.
367 *(exJ10 5096)* 9/4/38.
443 *(ex 5751)* 19/2/44.
726 *(ex 9275)* 9/4/49.
22696 *(ex 69297)* 16/6/51.
22651 *(ex 69305)* 9/1/54.

SHEDS:
Gorton.
Wrexham 26/6/29.

RENUMBERED:
5905 9/5/25.
9329 20/10/46.
69329 17/4/48.

CONDEMNED: 18/9/57.
Cut up at Gorton 26/10/57.

5906

Gorton.

To traffic 11/1899.

REPAIRS:
Gor. 3/6—5/8/11.**G**.
Gor. 21/6—27/9/13.**G**.
Gor. 15/7—26/8/22.**G**.
Gor. 27/6—29/8/25.**G**.
Altered to LNE gauge.
Gor. 7/12/29—11/1/30.**G**.
Gor. 6—20/5/33.**G**.
Gor. 8—22/8/36.**G**.
Gor. 16—23/10/37.**L**.
Gor. 17—24/6/39.**G**.
Gor. 2—20/6/42.**G**.
Gor. 2/11—23/12/44.**G**.
New cylinders.
Gor. 27/4/46.**L**.
Backplate fractured.
Gor. 22/3—19/4/47.**G**.
Gor. 3—24/9/49.**G**.
Gor. 30/6—21/7/51.**C/H**.
Gor. 26/7—16/8/52.**G**.

BOILERS:
442.
657 *(new)* 5/8/11.
287 *(new)* 27/9/13.
730 *(exJ12 36B)* 29/8/25.
452 *(ex 5912)* 20/5/33.
219 *(ex 5768)* 22/8/36.
4206 *(exN4 5623)* 24/6/39.
4269 *(new)* 20/6/42.
1897 *(exN4 5611)* 23/12/44.
162 *(ex 9342)* 19/4/47.
608 *(ex 69331)* 24/9/49.
22702 *(ex 69335)* 21/7/51.
22773 *(ex??)* 16/8/52.

SHEDS:
Wrexham 2/12/21.
Gorton 12/5/39.
Walton-on-the-Hill 8/3/40.
Gorton 27/12/41.
Wrexham 25/9/42.

RENUMBERED:
5906 29/8/25.
9330 13/10/46.
69330 25/6/49.

CONDEMNED: 7/2/55.
Cut up at Gorton 30/4/55.

5907

Gorton.

To traffic 11/1899.

REPAIRS:
Gor. 28/3—23/5/08.**G**.
Gor. 1/3—14/6/13.**G**.
Gor. 2/4—23/7/21.**G**.
New cylinders.
Gor. 13/10—15/12/23.**G**.
Gor. 12/6—7/8/26.**G**.
Gor. 4—25/5/29.**G**.
Gor. 25/6—9/7/32.**G**.
Altered to LNE gauge.
Gor. 5—19/10/35.**G**.
Gor. 20/11—4/12/37.**G**.
Gor. 1—15/2/41.**G**.
Gor. 6—15/5/43.**G**.
Gor. 3—10/3/45.**G**.
Gor. 14/6—5/7/47.**G**.
Gor. 20/8—10/9/49.**G**.
Gor. 14—28/6/52.**G**.
Gor. 15/10—19/11/55.**G**.

BOILERS:
477 23/5/08.
170 *(new)* 14/6/13.
771 *(exN4 717)* 23/7/21.
1625 *(exN4 5607)* 9/7/32.
293 *(ex 5051)* 19/10/35.
735 *(ex 5189)* 4/12/37.
4253 *(new)* 15/2/41.
950 *(ex 5897)* 15/5/43.
608 *(exF1 7095)* 5/7/47.
4191 *(ex 9363)* 10/9/49.
22767 *(exN4 69246)* 28/6/52.
22849 *(exJ10 65187)* 19/11/55.

SHED:
Heaton Mersey 15/5/15.

RENUMBERED:
907c 15/12/23.
5907 7/8/26.
9331 8/9/46.

Ex works 18th April 1942, No.5523 (9257 from 25th May 1946) was fitted with vacuum controlled push-and-pull gear in order to act as the reserve to the C13 class working the Chesham branch.

(above) **The vacuum controlled push and pull gear remained on No.69257 to its 7th December 1959 withdrawal, and was used in 1951 on the Alexandra Palace shuttle service, in October 1954 for trials on the Wickford-Southminster branch, and in 1955 to cover a temporary shortage of F5 class on the Epping-Ongar line.**

All had automatic vacuum brake, on engine, and for train working. The ejector exhaust pipe was inside the boiler even on those boilers built to 1950 – ***see*** **page 80, top. Note load class 2 collar fixed on the vacuum standpipe.**

This class was later than many others in retaining the upper lamp iron fixed at the top of the smokebox front plate, none being altered before BR took over.

By November 1948 – *see* page 75, 3rd from top – the upper lamp iron was being moved on to the smokebox door for easier access and less risk to the crew from overhead electric wiring.

Rated as goods engines by the GCR they were in unlined black and those numbered below 919 had transfer shaded numerals. Although No.894 was ex works 3rd March 1923 from General repair, the paint shop only touched it up and it remained in GC livery – as here in June 1925 – until it went to works on 23rd April 1927.

The last six, Nos.919 to 924, of the final batch built at Gorton, from September to December 1900, were the only ones to get the rectangular brass number plate which Robinson introduced.

5907 cont./
69331 2/4/49.

CONDEMNED: 21/1/57.
Cut up at Gorton 2/3/57.

5908

Gorton.

To traffic 12/1899.

REPAIRS:
Gor. 7/3—11/4/08.**G**.
Gor. 13/1—23/3/12.**G**.
Gor. 15/7—4/11/22.**G**.
Gor. 11/12/26—12/2/27.**G**.
Gor. 31/8—5/10/29.**G**.
Gor. 13—27/8/32.**G**.
Altered to LNE gauge.
New cylinders.
Gor. 16—30/11/35.**G**.
Gor. 5—19/11/38.**G**.
Gor. 16/3—3/4/43.**G**.
Gor. 30/3—13/4/46.**G**.
Gor. 30/10—13/11/48.**G**.
Gor. 19/5—9/6/51.**H/I**.
Gor. 6/6/53.**C/L**.
Gor. 15—29/8/53.**G**.
Gor. 9/2/59. *Not repaired.*

BOILERS:
941 11/4/08.
476 *(ex 896)* 23/3/12.
606 *(ex 917)* 4/11/22.
469 *(ex 5769)* 27/8/32.
1751 *(ex 5524)* 30/11/35.
1695 *(exN4 5724)* 19/11/38.
304 *(ex 5917)* 3/4/43.
523 *(exN4 5725)* 13/4/46.
4274 *(ex 9355)* 13/11/48.
4274 reno.22695 9/6/51.
22656 *(ex 69344)* 29/8/53.

SHEDS:
Walton-on-the-Hill.
Gorton 6/1/25.
Wrexham 23/1/28.
Gorton 28/8/29.
Northwich 4/1/34.
Gorton 30/10/35.
Barnsley 27/11/35.
Gorton 6/12/35.
Northwich 13/12/35.
Gorton 3/12/36.
Wrexham 21/9/39.
Gorton 8/3/42.
Heaton Mersey 23/5/43.
Chester 28/3/53.
Sheffield 27/4/58.
Barnsley 22/6/58.

RENUMBERED:
5908 12/2/27.
9332 29/9/46.
69332 13/11/48.

CONDEMNED: 11/2/59.
Cut up at Gorton 4/4/59.

5909

Gorton.

To traffic 12/1899.

REPAIRS:
Gor. 11/1—15/2/08.**G**.
YECo. 19/3—14/6/21.**G**.
Gor. 14/6—2/8/24.**G**.
Gor. 27/8—8/10/27.**G**.
Gor. 26/7—23/8/30.**G**.
Gor. 19—25/8/33.**G**.
Altered to LNE gauge.
Gor. 11—25/7/36.**G**.
Gor. 26/8—16/9/39.**G**.
Heating app. both ends.
Gor. 25/5—5/6/43.**G**.
Gor. 16/3—6/4/46.**G**.
Gor. 29/1—19/2/49.**G**.
Gor. 29/3—12/4/52.**G**.

BOILERS:
134 15/2/08.
789 *(ex 542)* 14/6/21.
1689 *(ex 5765)* 26/8/33.
950 *(exN4 5614)* 25/7/36.
4209 *(exN4 5721)* 16/9/39.
314 *(ex 5755)* 5/6/43.
4215 *(ex 5533)* 6/4/46.
4289 *(ex 9307)* 19/2/49.
22752 *(ex 69347)* 12/4/52.

SHEDS:
Heaton Mersey 17/3/17.
Gorton 17/9/39.
Wrexham 29/12/46.
Gorton 25/2/47.
Chester 4/1/50.
Gorton 4/6/50.

RENUMBERED:
5909 2/8/24.
9333 14/7/46.
69333 19/2/49.

CONDEMNED: 2/1/56.
Into Dar. for cut up 25/1/56.

5910

Gorton.

To traffic 1/1900.

REPAIRS:
Gor. 21/7—24/9/04.**G**.
YECo. 9/4—29/7/21.**G**.
Gor. 9/2—15/3/24.**G**.
Gor. 5—19/7/24.**L**.
Backplate fractured.
Gor. 9/10—18/12/26.**G**.
Gor. 8/6—6/7/29.**G**.
Gor. 19/3—9/4/32.**G**.
Altered to LNE gauge.
Gor. 27/1—17/2/34.**L**.
Crank pin.
Gor. 21/12/35—4/1/36.**G**.
Heating app. both ends.
Gor. 24/12/38—14/1/39.**G**.
Gor. 24/12/41—10/1/42.**G**.
New cylinders.
Gor. 26/8—2/9/44.**G**.
Gor. 8/11—6/12/47.**G**.
Gor. 23/9—7/10/50.**G**.
Gor. 14/3—4/4/53.**G**.

BOILERS:
542.
486 24/9/04.
1350 *(ex 941)* 29/7/21.
1652 *(exN4 5629)* 18/12/26.
1771 *(exN4 5638)* 9/4/32.
541 *(ex 5531)* 4/1/36.
265 *(ex 5025)* 14/1/39.
414 *(exJ10 5118)* 10/1/42.
716 *(exJ10 5675)* 2/9/44.
4258 *(ex 9290)* 6/12/47.
22659 *(ex 69301)* 7/10/50.
22813 *(new reno. from 4345)* 4/4/53.

SHEDS:
Heaton Mersey 30/6/22.
Barnsley 4/1/36.

RENUMBERED:
5910 15/3/24.
9334 25/8/46.
69334 7/10/50.

CONDEMNED: 9/7/56.
Cut up at Gorton 1/9/56.

5911

Gorton.

To traffic 2/1900.

REPAIRS:
Gor. 12/5—18/6/10.**G**.
Gor. 12/10/18—25/1/19.**G**.
New cylinders.
Gor. 11/3—15/4/22.**G**.
Gor. 17/11/23—12/1/24.**G**.
Gor. 29/5—7/8/26.**G**.
Gor. 17/8—5/10/29.**G**.
Gor. 5—12/11/32.**G**.
Altered to LNE gauge.
Gor. 8—22/2/36.**G**.
Gor. 19/11—10/12/38.**G**.
Gor. 3/7—1/8/42.**G**.
Gor. 21/10—4/11/44.**G**.
Gor. 31/7—28/8/48.**G**.
Gor. 30/9—14/10/50.**G**.
Gor. 4/11/50.**L**.
Fitting new vac. pan.
Gor. 13/9—4/10/52.**L/I**.
Gor. 2—16/5/53.**C/L**.
Collision damage.
Gor. 12/11—10/12/55.**C/L**.
Motion & brake work.

BOILERS:
1034 18/6/10.
1775 *(new)* 25/1/19.
1642 *(ex 5932)* 12/11/32.
736 *(exJ10 5677)* 22/2/36.
435 *(exJ10 5121)* 10/12/38.
4270 *(new)* 1/8/42.
959 *(ex 5765)* 4/11/44.
4228 *(exN4 9234)* 28/8/48.
22662 *(ex??)* 14/10/50.

SHEDS:
Brunswick.
Gorton 5/10/41.
Heaton Mersey 13/12/42.
Northwich 16/12/45.
Trafford Park 6/12/52.
Wrexham 18/6/55.

RENUMBERED:
911c 19/1/24.
5911 7/8/26.
9335 9/11/46.
69335 28/8/48.

CONDEMNED: 9/9/57.
Cut up at Gorton 5/10/57.

5912

Gorton.

To traffic 3/1900.

REPAIRS:
Gor. 12/6—20/11/20.**G**.
Gor. 21/7—22/9/23.**G**.
Gor. 31/1—14/3/25.**G**.
New cylinders.
Gor. 8/10—12/11/27.**G**.
Gor. 17/5—14/6/30.**G**.
Gor. 1—22/4/33.**G**.
Altered to LNE gauge.
Gor. 28/3—11/4/36.**G**.
Gor. 10/6—1/7/39.**G**.
Gor. 17—28/2/42.**G**.
Gor. 5—19/8/44.**G**.
Gor. 21/6—26/7/47.**G**.
New cylinders.
Gor. 4—11/9/48.**L**.
After collision.

5912 cont.
Gor. 29/10—12/11/49.**G**.
Gor. 18/2/50.**C/L**.
After collision.
Gor. 5—19/4/52.**G**.

BOILERS:
628.
450 *(ex 754)* 20/11/20.
452 *(exN4 5603)* 14/6/30.
1641 *(exD7 5687)* 22/4/33.
1797 *(ex 5945)* 11/4/36.
4229 *(exJ10 5103)* 28/2/42.
954 *(ex 5769)* 19/8/44.
4208 *(exJ10 5184)* 26/7/47.
455 *(exN4 9235)* 12/11/49.
22753 *(exN4 69235)* 19/4/52.

SHEDS:
Heaton Mersey 30/6/22.
Gorton 21/9/39.
Trafford Park 7/5/42.

RENUMBERED:
912c 29/9/23.
5912 14/3/25.
9336 11/8/46.
69336 11/9/48.

CONDEMNED: 7/12/54.
Cut up at Doncaster 28/12/54.

5913

Gorton.

To traffic 3/1900.

REPAIRS:
Gor. 14/11/08—9/1/09.**G**.
Gor. 10/7—10/12/10.**G**.
Gor. 8/10—24/12/21.**G**.
New cylinders.
Gor. 29/11/24—10/1/25.**G**.
Gor. 17/8—21/9/29.**G**.
Gor. 4—11/2/33.**G**.
Altered to LNE gauge.
Gor. 3—24/4/37.**G**.
Gor. 25/11—2/12/39.**G**.
Gor. 12—21/8/43.**G**.
New cylinders.
Gor. 24/8—14/9/46.**G**.
Gor. 25/1—1/2/47.**L**.
After collision.
Gor. 18/6—23/7/49.**G**.
Gor. 5—19/9/53.**G**.

BOILERS:
448 9/1/09.
465 10/12/10.
608 *(new)* 10/1/25.
1660 *(exJ10 5833)* 11/2/33.
1783 *(exJ10 5835)* 24/4/37.
4226 *(exN4 5513)* 2/12/39.
425 *(ex 5744)* 21/8/43.
4233 *(ex 5928)* 14/9/46.
4187 *(ex 9346)* 23/7/49.
22691 *(exJ10 65144)* 19/9/53.

SHEDS:
Neasden 18/4/11.
Ipswich 14/5/38.
Gorton 24/5/38.
Brunswick 19/1/40.
Spital Bridge 13/8/50.
New England 20/8/50.
Ardsley 17/9/50.
Bradford 19/4/53.
Mexborough 17/5/53.
Sheffield 28/11/54.

RENUMBERED:
5913 10/1/25.
9337 13/10/46.
69337 12/3/49.

CONDEMNED: 6/8/56.
Cut up at Gorton 22/9/56.

5914

Gorton.

To traffic 4/1900.

REPAIRS:
Wrx. 22/3—29/5/10.**G**.
Gor. 22/7—18/11/16.**G**.
Gor. 29/1—18/2/22.**G**.
Wrx. 25/2—20/7/25.**H**.
Gor. 25/2—31/3/28.**G**.
Gor. 27/9—25/10/30.**G**.
Gor. 5—19/8/33.**G**.
Altered to LNE gauge.
Gor. 23/5—13/6/36.**G**.
Gor. 21/1—4/2/39.**G**.
Gor. 26/6—11/7/42.**G**.
Gor. 22/9—6/10/45.**G**.
Gor. 20/3—10/4/48.**G**.
Gor. 24/2—17/3/51.**G**.

BOILERS:
685 29/5/10.
1046 *(ex 927)* 18/11/16.
1810 *(ex 745)* 18/2/22.
1384 *(exN4 5636)* 31/3/28.
304 *(exN4 5616)* 19/8/33.
375 *(exJ10 5832)* 13/6/36.
4236 *(new)* 4/2/39.
505 *(ex 5527)* 11/7/42.
4199 *(exJ10 5835)* 6/10/45.
502 *(ex 9301)* 10/4/48.
22685 *(ex 69295)* 17/3/51.

SHEDS:
Chester 16/8/07.
Wrexham ?/?.
Gorton 24/1/28.
Wrexham 15/8/28.
Gorton 12/9/30.
Wrexham 9/12/30.
Gorton 30/11/31.
Northwich 11/9/33.
Gorton 9/1/39.
Wrexham 26/6/39.
Gorton 21/9/39.
Walton-on-the-Hill 16/1/43.
Gorton 15/2/48.

RENUMBERED:
5914 20/7/25.
9338 21/7/46.
69338 10/4/48.

CONDEMNED: 14/3/55.
Cut up at Gorton 6/8/55.

5915

Gorton.

To traffic 5/1900.

REPAIRS:
Gor. 15/12/04—11/2/05.**G**.
Gor. 14/12/18—2/8/19.**G**.
Gor. 11/3—29/4/22.**G**.
Gor. 29/2—21/7/24.**G**.
Gor. 3/3—14/4/28.**G**.
Gor. 9—23/1/32.**G**.
Altered to LNE gauge.
Gor. 2—16/3/35.**G**.
Gor. 26/3—9/4/38.**G**.
Gor. 15/2—8/3/41.**G**.
Gor. 22/4—6/5/44.**G**.
Gor. 11/10—15/11/47.**G**.
New cylinders.
Gor. 22/4—6/5/50.**G**.
Gor. 7—21/2/53.**G**.

BOILERS:
446.
563 *(ex 932)* 11/2/05.
1793 *(new)* 2/8/19.
1787 *(ex 5536)* 23/1/32.
726 *(new)* 16/3/35.
958 *(exJ10 5176)* 9/4/38.
440 *(ex 5200)* 6/5/44.
402 *(ex 9278)* 6/5/50.
22808 *(ex??)* 21/2/53.

SHEDS:
Heaton Mersey 14/3/14.
Northwich *at* 4/30.
Gorton 5/12/36.
Brunswick 21/9/39.
Bidston 24/9/50.
Wrexham ?/8/52.

RENUMBERED:
5915 21/7/24.
9339 11/8/46.
69339 12/3/49.

CONDEMNED: 12/3/56.
Cut up at Gorton 28/4/56.

5916

Gorton.

To traffic 6/1900.

REPAIRS:
Gor. 13/5—24/7/09.**G**.
New cylinders.
Gor. 13/1—29/4/11.**G**.
Wrx. 17/5—22/8/21.**G**.
Gor. 7/7—6/10/23.**G**.
Wrx. 28/1—15/4/26.**G**.
Gor. 30/6—28/7/28.**G**.
Gor. 7—21/3/31.**G**.
Gor. 19/5—2/6/34.**G**.
Altered to LNE gauge.
Gor. 22/1—12/2/38.**G**.
Gor. 1—8/2/41.**G**.
Gor. 16/2—4/3/44.**G**.
Gor. 28/7/45.**L**.
Gor. 21/12/46—18/1/47.**G**.
Gor. 30/4—21/5/49.**G**.
Gor. 24/11—22/12/51.**G**.
Gor. 27/3—24/4/54.**G**.

BOILERS:
443 24/7/09.
783 *(new)* 29/4/11.
200 *(ex 5757)* 28/7/28.
448 *(exJ10 5122)* 2/6/34.
162 *(ex 5918)* 12/2/38.
4252 *(new)* 8/2/41.
1763 *(ex spare)* 4/3/44.
4252 *(ex 9363)* 18/1/47.
4250 *(ex 9292)* 21/5/49.
22725 *(ex 69370)* 22/12/51.
22837 *(ex 69261)* 24/4/54.

SHEDS:
Wrexham 16/6/11.
Bidston 4/1/29.
Gorton 19/1/31.
Wrexham 30/11/31.
Gorton 1/7/45.
Wrexham 12/8/45.

RENUMBERED:
916c 20/10/23.
5916 15/4/26.
9340 14/7/46.
69340 21/5/49.

CONDEMNED: 7/5/56.
Into Dar. for cut up 17/5/56.

(above) **Ex works 5th May 1923, No.919 was the only one to have a rectangular number plate in conjunction with L.&N.E.R. lettering.**

(left) **By the beginning of April 1923 those from a General repair got what Gorton paint shop listed as 'One coat black and varnished'. A standard LNER number plate was fitted on the bunker and small GCR numbers were then supplanted by 12 inch shaded transfers on the tank. Until June 1923 the ampersand and full points were included but were then discarded.**

(left) **From September 1923 (No.173 out on the 15th was probably the first) to the end of January 1924 the number had the area suffix C added. Fourteen are listed as getting it: 1923 – 173c (15th September), 912c (29th September), 938c (6th October), 916c (20th October), 904c (3rd November), 25c and 530c (10th November), 896c (17th November), 752c (24th November), 926c (1st December), 515c (8th December), 766c and 907c (15th December); 1924 – 911c (19th January). The dates are ex paint shop.**

Full LNER numbering began with No.5762 on 2nd February 1924 – ***see*** **page 28, middle – and this unlined style continued using 7½in. LNER letters until July 1942.**

5917

Gorton.

To traffic 6/1900.

REPAIRS:
Gor. 5/5—29/9/06.**G.**
Gor. 8/4—23/9/22.**G.**
Gor. 14/2—21/3/25.**G.**
Gor. 9/2—9/3/29.**G.**
Gor. 12—19/11/32.**G.**
Altered to LNE gauge.
Gor. 12—31/12/36.**G.**
Gor. 27/1—10/2/40.**G.**
Heating app. both ends.
Gor. 10—27/3/43.**G.**
Gor. 14/9—12/10/46.**G.**
Gor. 30/10—13/11/48.**G.**
Gor. 26/1—16/2/52.**G.**
Gor. 15/1—19/2/55.**G.**

BOILERS:
606 *(new)* 29/9/06.
248 *(ex 757)* 23/9/22.
415 *(ex 5927)* 19/11/32.
28 *(ex 5409)* 31/12/36.
304 *(ex 5944)* 10/2/40.
1230 *(exN4 5636)* 27/3/43.
1917 *(exJ10 5201)* 12/10/46.
4232 *(ex 9254)* 13/11/48.
22739 *(ex??)* 16/2/52.
22653 *(ex spare)* 19/2/55.

SHED:
Neasden 16/5/19.

RENUMBERED:
5917 21/3/25.
9341 11/8/46.
69341 13/11/48.

CONDEMNED: 7/12/59.
Cut up at Gorton 14/5/60.

5918

Gorton.

To traffic 6/1900.

REPAIRS:
Gor. 18/1—29/2/08.**G.**
Gor. 11/12/15—18/3/16.**G.**
Gor. 10/12/21—22/1/22.**G.**
Gor. 25/4—13/6/25.**G.**
New cylinders.
Gor. 12/5—23/6/28.**G.**
Altered to LNE gauge.
Gor. 3—31/10/31.**G.**
Gor. 6—20/10/34.**G.**
Gor. 26/12/37—8/1/38.**G.**
Gor. 8—22/3/41.**G.**
Gor. 29/4—13/5/44.**G.**
Gor. 1—29/3/47.**G.**
Gor. 10—31/12/49.**G.**
Gor. 24/5—7/6/52.**G.**
Gor. 1—29/10/55.**L/I.**
Motion and brakework.
Gor. 29/7/59. *Not repaired.*

BOILERS:
495.
444 *(ex 902)* 29/2/08.
1360 *(ex 530)* 18/3/16.
1893 *(exN4 5723)* 23/6/28.
162 *(exJ10 5807)* 20/10/34.
4187 *(exN4 5618)* 8/1/38.
551 *(exN4 5625)* 22/3/41.
162 *(ex 5939)* 13/5/44.
347 *(exJ10 5811)* 29/3/47.
4208 *(ex 69336)* 31/12/49.
22710 *(exN4 69231)* 7/6/52.

SHEDS:
Walton-on-the-Hill 6/9/01.
Gorton 22/12/28.
Brunswick 21/9/39.
Chester 24/9/50.
Sheffield 27/4/58.
Barnsley 22/6/58.

RENUMBERED:
5918 13/6/25.
9342 21/7/46.
69342 12/3/49.

CONDEMNED: 6/8/59.
Cut up at Gorton 29/9/59.

5919

Gorton.

To traffic 9/1900.

REPAIRS:
Gor. 5/8/16—20/1/17.**G.**
Gor. 8/11/19—10/1/20.**G.**
Gor. 31/3—5/5/23.**G.**
New cylinders.
Wrx. 6/7—7/10/27.**G.**
Gor. 19/1—9/3/29.**G.**
Gor. 27/2—12/3/32.**G.**
Altered to LNE gauge.
Gor. 16—23/3/35.**G.**
Gor. 1—22/10/38.**G.**
Gor. 30/11—21/12/40.**G.**
Gor. 8—18/12/43.**G.**
Gor. 17—26/3/45.**L.**
After collision.
Gor. 23/3—27/4/46.**G.**
New cylinders.
Gor. 14/2—6/3/48.**G.**
Gor. 6—20/5/50.**G.**
Gor. 22/3—12/4/52.**C/L.**
After collision.
Gor. 27/9—11/10/52.**G.**
Gor. 12/3—16/4/55.**G.**
Gor. 9/1/60. *Not repaired.*

BOILERS:
494.
1657 *(new)* 20/1/17.
1688 *(exN4 5715)* 12/3/32.
1787 *(ex 5915)* 23/3/35.
1778 *(ex 5920)* 22/10/38.
306 *(ex spare)* 27/4/46.
36 *(ex 9353)* 6/3/48.
4217 *(exF2 7109)* 20/5/50.
4217 reno.22749 12/4/52.
22787 *(ex 69349)* 11/10/52.
22779 *(ex 69362)* 16/4/55.

SHEDS:
Trafford Park 13/12/13.
Wrexham *by* 17/9/26.
Chester 2/10/30.
Gorton 6/2/32.
Wrexham 5/4/35.
Gorton 2/8/38.
Trafford Park 27/9/39.
Wrexham 22/10/55.
Trafford Park 24/11/56.
Sheffield 27/4/58.
Barnsley 22/6/58.
Mexborough 3/1/60.

RENUMBERED:
5919 7/10/27.
9343 20/7/46.
E9343 6/3/48.
69343 5/2/49.

CONDEMNED: 11/1/60.
Cut up at Gorton 6/2/60.

5920

Gorton.

To traffic 10/1900.

REPAIRS:
Gor. 3/2—19/3/10.**G.**
Gor. 8/11/13—14/2/14.**G.**
New cylinders.
Gor. 27/5—19/8/22.**G.**
Single piece chimney fitted.
Gor. 15/8—17/10/25.**G.**
Gor. 30/8—4/10/30.**G.**
Heating app. both ends.
Gor. 18/8—15/9/34.**G.**
Altered to LNE gauge.
Heating apparatus removed.
Gor. 3/9—8/10/38.**G.**
Gor. 22/11—13/12/41.**G.**
Gor. 5—23/9/44.**G.**
Gor. 5—19/5/45.**L.**
After collision.
Gor. 22/11—20/12/47.**G.**
Gor. 9—23/9/50.**G.**
Gor. 20/12/52—17/1/53.**G.**
Gor. 29/9—27/10/56.**G.**
Gor. 19/1/57.**C/L.**
Backplate welded.
Gor. 15/3/58.**C/L.**
Backplate welded.

BOILERS:
556 19/3/10.
1156 *(new)* 14/2/14.
1778 *(exD7 5684)* 15/9/34.
568 *(exJ10 5808)* 8/10/38.
4219 *(exJ10 5640)* 13/12/41.
414 *(ex 5910)* 23/9/44.
22656 *(ex 9348)* 23/9/50.
22802 *(ex 69279)* 17/1/53.
22650 *(exj10 65177)* 27/10/56.

SHEDS:
Wrexham 29/9/22.
Northwich 12/1/25.
Chester *by* 17/9/26.
Gorton 17/8/32.
Trafford Park 7/11/34.
Gorton 26/6/35.
Trafford Park 21/9/39.
Gorton 23/4/41.
Walton-on-the-Hill 28/12/41.

RENUMBERED:
5920 17/10/25.
9344 21/7/46.
69344 19/3/49.

CONDEMNED: 7/12/59.
Cut up at Gorton 23/4/60.

5921

Gorton.

To traffic 11/1900.

REPAIRS:
Gor. ?/?—18/4/03.**G.**
Gor. 12/2—3/6/16.**G.**
Gor. 22/7—23/9/22.**G.**
Gor. 17/10—26/12/25.**G.**
Gor. 15/9—13/10/28.**G.**
Altered to LNE gauge.
Gor. 14/2—7/3/31.**G.**
Gor. 16—30/12/33.**G.**
Gor. 1—29/9/34.**G.**
New cylinders.
Gor. 23/1—6/2/37.**G.**
Gor. 3—17/2/40.**G.**
Heating app. both ends.
Gor. 26/8—11/9/43.**G.**
Gor. 22/3—19/4/47.**G.**
Gor. 27/5—10/6/50.**G.**
Gor. 1—15/11/52.**G.**

BOILERS:
690 18/4/03.

5921 cont./
605 *(ex 521)* 3/6/16.
954 *(new)* 13/10/28.
1809 *(exJ10 5800)* 30/12/33.
221 *(ex 5535)* 6/2/37.
401 *(ex 5946)* 12/2/40.
472 *(ex??)* 11/9/43.
496 *(exJ10 5165)* 19/4/47.
408 *(exJ10 65192)* 10/6/50.
22794 *(ex 69260)* 15/11/52.

SHEDS:
Walton-on-the-Hill.
Gorton 3/12/36.
Sheffield 10/5/37.
Barnsley 17/5/37.

RENUMBERED:
5921 26/12/25.
9345 25/8/46.
69345 10/6/50.

CONDEMNED: 25/10/56.
Cut up at Gorton 24/8/57.

5922

Gorton.

To traffic 12/1900.

REPAIRS:
Gor. 22/4—3/6/22.**G**.
New cylinders.
Gor. 21/2—11/4/25.**G**.
Gor. 5—12/12/25.**L**.
Gor. 24/12/27—28/1/28.**G**.
Altered to LNE gauge.
Gor. 1—22/11/30.**G**.
Gor. 3—17/2/34.**G**.
Gor. 20/11—4/12/37.**G**.
Gor. 16/11—7/12/40.**G**.
Heating app. both ends.
Gor. 12—28/8/43.**G**.
Gor. 1—22/3/47.**G**.
Gor. 21/5—11/6/49.**G**.
Gor. 17/11—22/12/51.**G**.
New cylinders.
Gor. 24/4—15/5/54.**G**.
Gor. 5—26/11/55.**C/L**.
Motion and brakes.

BOILERS:
524.
243 *(exD7 5567)* 28/1/28.
1614 *(exN4 5714)* 22/11/30.
428 *(ex 5939)* 17/2/34.
1893 *(ex 5515)* 4/12/37.
567 *(exN4 5629)* 7/12/40.
735 *(exN4 5625)* 28/8/43.
4187 *(exJ10 5126)* 22/3/47.
4225 *(ex 9327)* 11/6/49.
22723 *(ex 69289)* 22/12/51.
22725 *(ex 69340)* 15/5/54.

SHEDS:
Brunswick 21/8/01.
Heaton Mersey 30/8/34.
Northwich 24/4/35.
Chester 30/3/38.
Wrexham 22/10/38.
Gorton 28/8/43.
Walton-on-the-Hill 23/9/43.
Gorton 11/8/46.
Wrexham 21/12/47.

RENUMBERED:
5922 11/4/25.
9346 21/7/46.
69346 11/6/49.

CONDEMNED: 30/9/57.
Cut up at Gorton 9/11/57.

5923

Gorton.

To traffic 12/1900.

REPAIRS:
Gor. 7/3—18/4/08.**G**.
YECo. 23/4—15/7/21.**G**.
Gor. 21/6—16/8/24.**G**.
New cylinders.
Gor. 18/2—24/3/28.**G**.
Altered to LNE gauge.
Gor. 2—30/8/30.**G**.
Gor. 6—20/10/34.**G**.
Gor. 6—20/2/37.**G**.
Gor. 30/12/39—13/1/40.**G**.
Heating app. both ends.
Gor. 16/9—3/10/42.**G**.
Gor. 14—28/10/44.**G**.
Gor. 16/11—14/12/46.**G**.
New cylinders.
Gor. 15—29/10/49.**G**.
Gor. 23/2—15/3/52.**G**.
Gor. 27/11/54—1/1/55.**H/I**.

BOILERS:
718 *(ex 54)* 18/4/08.
293 *(exJ10 675)* 15/7/21.
426 *(new)* 30/8/30.
1709 *(exJ10 5837)* 20/10/34.
1809 *(ex 5921)* 20/2/37.
4243 *(new)* 13/1/40.
4201 *(ex 5768)* 3/10/42.
4229 *(ex 5912)* 28/10/44.
4300 *(new)* 14/12/46.
4256 *(ex 9260)* 29/10/49.
22746 *(ex 69355)* 15/3/52.

SHEDS:
Leicester 20/10/22.
Langwith Jct. 2/6/28.
Colwick 9/11/33.
Annesley 8/5/38.
Gorton 18/8/46.
Trafford Park 27/8/50.

RENUMBERED:
5923 16/8/24.
9347 23/11/46.
69347 26/2/49.

CONDEMNED: 10/10/57.
Cut up at Gorton 1/2/58.

5924

Gorton.

To traffic 12/1900.

REPAIRS:
Gor. 23/5—18/7/08.**G**.
Gor. 20/3—12/6/15.**G**.
Gor. 22/7—25/11/22.**G**.
Gor. 13/6—15/8/25.**G**.
Gor. 17/3—12/5/28.**G**.
New cylinders.
Gor. 19/7—16/8/30.**G**.
Altered to LNE gauge.
Gor. 21/4—5/5/34.**G**.
Gor. 6—20/6/36.**G**.
Gor. 6—20/1/40.**G**.
Heating app. both ends.
Gor. 28/5—5/6/43.**G**.
Gor. 24/5—28/6/47.**G**.
Gor. 24/6—29/7/50.**G**.
New cylinders.
Gor. 3—24/1/53.**G**.

BOILERS:
568 18/7/08.
957 *(ex 771)* 12/6/15.
1655 *(exN4 5637)* 25/11/22.
393 *(new)* 16/8/30.
289 *(exJ9 5648)* 5/5/34.
505 *(exJ10 5789)* 20/6/36.
4200 *(exJ10 5643)* 20/1/40.
665 *(exJ10 5123)* 5/6/43.
4222 *(ex 9365)* 28/6/47.
496 *(ex 9345)* 29/7/50.
22804 *(ex??)* 24/1/53.

SHEDS:
Brunswick 21/8/01.
Gorton 24/5/33.
Walton-on-the-Hill 18/3/35.
Gorton 20/6/36.
Sheffield 12/2/37.
Barnsley 14/9/37.
Doncaster 4/7/54.
Sheffield 17/10/54.

RENUMBERED:
5924 15/8/25.
9348 20/10/46.
69348 29/7/50.

CONDEMNED: 25/1/57.
Cut up at Gorton 16/3/57.

5925

Beyer, Peacock 4185.

To traffic 4/1900.

REPAIRS:
Gor. ?/?—1/9/05.**G**.
Gor. 1/8—29/9/08.**G**.
Gor. 9/7—3/9/21.**G**.
Gor. 2/2—22/3/24.**G**.
Gor. 21/8—30/10/26.**G**.
Gor. 26/1—23/2/29.**G**.
Gor. 15/8—19/9/31.**G**.
Altered to LNE gauge.
Gor. 2—16/3/35.**G**.
Gor. 16—30/10/37.**G**.
Gor. 1—15/6/40.**G**.
Gor. 9—31/10/42.**G**.
Gor. 21—28/10/44.**G**.
Gor. 20/12/47—24/1/48.**G**.
Gor. 4—25/3/50.**G**.
Gor. 9—23/8/52.**G**.
Gor. 7/11—5/12/53.**C/L**.
After collision.
Gor. 27/8—8/10/55.**G**.

BOILERS:
613 *(new)* 1/9/05.
512 *(ex 774)* 29/9/08.
1361 *(ex 750)* 3/9/21.
1128 *(exN4 5617)* 19/9/31.
92 *(exJ10 5101)* 16/3/35.
4184 *(exJ10 5804)* 30/10/37.
1768 *(ex 5545)* 15/6/40.
4214 *(ex 5927)* 31/10/42.
4240 *(ex 5546)* 28/10/44.
4259 *(ex 69364)* 25/3/50.
22776 *(ex 69331)* 23/8/52.
22689 *(ex spare)* 8/10/55.

SHEDS:
Brunswick 8/2/13.
Gorton 15/1/29.
Wrexham 6/7/29.
Bidston 26/1/31.
Wrexham 8/8/31.
Bidston 10/10/31.
Wrexham 4/2/33.
Gorton 25/9/42.
Brunswick 1/4/45.
Gorton 20/5/45.
Heaton Mersey 24/6/45.
Northwich 16/12/45.
Wrexham 4/2/48.

RENUMBERED:
5925 22/3/24.
9349 14/7/46.
E9349 24/1/48.
69349 25/6/49.

5925 cont./
CONDEMNED: 21/8/58.
Cut up at Gorton 27/9/58.

5926

Beyer, Peacock 4186.

To traffic 4/1900.

REPAIRS:
Gor. 22/1—26/2/10.**G**.
Gor. 9/12/16—26/5/17.**G**.
New cylinders.
Gor. 5/6—31/7/20.**G**.
Gor. 18/8—1/12/23.**G**.
Gor. 17/12/27—21/1/28.**G**.
Gor. 28/6—26/7/30.**G**.
Gor. 10—17/11/34.**G**.
Altered to LNE gauge.
Gor. 26/6—10/7/37.**G**.
Gor. 2—23/3/40.**G**.
Gor. 21/10—21/11/42.**G**.
Gor. 5/5—2/6/45.**G**.
Gor. 16/8—6/9/47.**G**.
Gor. 25/11—16/12/50.**G**.
Gor. 10—24/10/53.**G**.

BOILERS:
1045 26/2/10.
745 *(ex 518)* 26/5/17.
504 *(ex 5745)* 26/7/30.
1668 *(ex??)* 17/11/34.
144 *(ex 5755)* 10/7/37.
1767 *(ex 5936)* 23/3/40.
502 *(ex 5929)* 21/11/42.
1823 *(ex??)* 2/6/45.
765 *(ex??)* 6/9/47.
22673 *(ex??)* 16/12/50.
22772 *(ex 69319)* 24/10/53.

SHEDS:
Leicester 20/10/22.
Langwith Jct. 17/3/28.
Colwick 9/11/33.
Leicester 3/2/36.
Colwick 10/11/37.
Annesley 27/3/38.
Neasden 13/10/46.

RENUMBERED:
926c 1/12/23.
5926 21/1/28 ??
9350 11/8/46.
69350 16/12/50.

CONDEMNED: 18/1/57.
Cut up at Gorton 23/2/57.

5927

Beyer, Peacock 4187.

To traffic 4/1900.

REPAIRS:
Gor. ?/?—23/7/04.**G**.
Gor. 1/4—22/7/16.**G**.
Gor. 28/1—18/3/22.**G**.
Gor. 28/3—23/5/25.**G**.
New cylinders.
Gor. 2/4—14/5/27.**G**.
Gor. 8/6—6/7/29.**G**.
Gor. 8—22/10/32.**G**.
Altered to LNE gauge.
Gor. 10—24/3/34.**G**.
Gor. 23/1—6/2/37.**G**.
Gor. 2—16/12/39.**G**.
Heating app. both ends.
Gor. 6—17/10/42.**G**.
New cylinders.
Gor. 3—24/3/45.**G**.
Gor. 8—29/11/47.**G**.
Gor. 10/12/49—7/1/50.**G**.
Gor. 21/3—11/4/53.**G**.
Gor. 9—23/1/54.**C/L**.
After collision.

BOILERS:
1046 *(new)* 23/7/04.
31 *(exJ10 125)* 22/7/16.
1356 *(ex 5519)* 14/5/27.
415 *(ex 5025)* 6/7/29.
756 *(ex 5547)* 22/10/32.
357 *(new)* 24/3/34.
4214 *(new)* 6/2/37.
451 *(exJ10 5141)* 17/10/42.
376 *(ex 5770)* 24/3/45.
4223 *(ex 9326)* 29/11/47.
4202 *(exN4 9246)* 7/1/50.
22719 *(ex 69366)* 11/4/53.

SHEDS:
Annesley 29/12/22.
Leicester 3/12/32.
Gorton 11/1/39.
Northwich 20/9/39.
Gorton 1/11/39.
Ardsley 14/4/41.
Doncaster 14/4/42.
Sheffield 9/5/42.
Staveley 26/8/43.
Gorton 11/12/55.

RENUMBERED:
5927 23/5/25.
9351 18/8/46.
69351 7/1/50.

CONDEMNED: 16/10/56.
Cut up at Gorton 12/1/57.

5928

Beyer, Peacock 4188.

To traffic 5/1900.

REPAIRS:
Gor. 7/4—24/9/10.**G**.
Gor. 23/4—11/6/21.**G**.
Wrx. 23/5—25/6/23.**H**.
Gor. 15/8—24/10/25.**G**.
Gor. 7/1—18/2/28.**G**.
Altered to LNE gauge.
Gor. 11/10—8/11/30.**G**.
Reverted to GC gauge.
Gor. 10—24/3/34.**G**.
Gor. 3—17/4/37.**G**.
Altered back to LNE gauge.
Gor. 30/3—20/4/40.**G**.
Gor. 12—19/6/43.**G**.
Gor. 3—25/8/46.**G**.
Gor. 13—20/12/47.**L**.
Gor. 10—24/4/48.**G**.
New cylinders.
Gor. 10/9—1/10/49.**G**.
Gor. 8—29/3/52.**G**.
Gor. 3—17/1/53.**C/L**.
After collision.

BOILERS:
796 24/9/10.
222 *(exJ12 6432)* 18/2/28.
1640 *(ex 5540)* 8/11/30.
387 *(new)* 24/3/34.
951 *(exJ10 5820)* 17/4/37.
4233 *(exN4 5632)* 19/6/43.
4242 *(exJ10 5099)* 25/8/46.
4273 *(ex 9279)* 1/10/49.
22748 *(new reno. from 4340)* 29/3/52.

SHEDS:
Wrexham 2/12/21.
Heaton Mersey *by* 1/32.
Brunswick 30/8/34.
Gorton 6/3/37.
Northwich 28/11/40.
Gorton 4/6/43.
Walton-on-the-Hill 8/10/43.
Wrexham 18/11/45.
Gorton 4/9/46.
Wrexham 6/10/46.

RENUMBERED:
5928 24/10/25.
9352 25/8/46.
69352 24/4/48.

CONDEMNED: 6/6/55.
Cut up at Gorton 27/8/55.

5929

Beyer, Peacock 4189.

To traffic 5/1900.

REPAIRS:
Gor. ?/?—30/7/04.**G**.
Wrx. 1/2—21/12/17.**G**.
Gor. 29/11/19—28/8/20.**G**.
New cylinders.
Wrx. 24/7—26/9/22.**G**.
Gor. 25/4—13/6/25.**G**.
Gor. 25/1—8/3/30.**G**.
Gor. 18/4—2/5/31.**L**.
Boiler work.
Gor. 12—26/8/33.**G**.
Altered to LNE gauge.
Gor. 18/7—1/8/36.**G**.
Gor. 14—21/10/39.**G**.
Gor. 2—24/10/42.**G**.
Gor. 3—24/2/45.**G**.
Gor. 24/1—28/2/48.**G**.
Gor. 16/12/50—6/1/51.**G**.
New cylinders.
Gor. 6—15/11/52.**C/L**.

BOILERS:
1047 *(new)* 30/7/04.
1345 *(exJ10 122)* 21/12/17.
493 *(exD7 5693)* 28/8/20.
197 *(ex 5537)* 26/8/33.
303 *(exJ10 5841)* 1/8/36.
502 *(exN4 5713)* 21/10/39.
4243 *(ex 5923)* 24/10/42.
36 *(ex 5897)* 24/2/45.
505 *(exN4 9240)* 28/2/48.
22677 *(ex??)* 6/1/51.

SHEDS:
Wrexham.
Gorton 10/3/30.
Northwich 11/9/33.
Chester 2/8/38
Gorton 21/10/39.
Northwich 28/10/39.
Gorton 3/3/46.
Trafford Park 18/12/49.
Gorton 8/5/50.
Walton-on-the-Hill 12/5/50.
Gorton 9/7/50.

RENUMBERED:
5929 13/6/25.
9353 6/4/46.
E9353 28/2/48.
69353 6/1/51.

CONDEMNED: 14/11/55.
To Darlington for c/u 18/2/56.

From July 1942 to January 1946 only the initials NE were applied, but for them, Gorton used 12 inch instead of the 7½in. shaded transfers.

Many still had only NE when re-numbered in 1946. When ex works on 1st December 1945 No.5051 got only NE and on 26th October 1946 Neasden shed changed it to 9315. It was one which did not have LNER restored as from its next works visit it was out 14th August 1948 carrying BRITISH RAILWAYS.

Unlike the other works, Gorton retained 12 inch transfers on tank engines when they restored LNER. No.5744 was so treated when ex works 30th March 1946.

No.5908 had 12 inch LNER put on ex works 13th April 1946 and when changed to 9332 on Sunday 29th September 1946, Stockport (Heaton Mersey) shed managed to get shaded transfers for it. Gorton was still using 12 inch LNER until at least December 1946.

By April 1947 reversion to 7½in. LNER had taken place but for No.9314, ex works 20th September 1947, Gorton was still able to use normal shaded transfers as they also did for No.9283, ex works 1st November 1947 – *see* bottom illustration.

No.9263 was ex works 20th December 1947, only eleven days before the LNER ceased to exist. Whilst it also got shaded transfers, the numerals were not the standard 12in. being only 10½in. tall, so no LNER N5 wore the yellow painted and unshaded Gill sans style.

(below) Because No.9283's boiler had been allowed to run short of water, it went to Gorton for light repair on 14th February 1948. When out on 21st February the regional prefix E had been added to its number.

5930

Beyer, Peacock 4190.

To traffic 5/1900.

REPAIRS:
Gor. ?/?—15/10/04.**G**.
Gor. 8/8—17/10/08.**G**.
Gor. 9/1—19/6/15.**G**.
Gor. 5/6—11/12/20.**G**.
New cylinders.
Gor. 10/11/23—26/1/24.**G**.
Gor. 1/5—24/7/26.**G**.
Gor. 9/3—4/5/29.**G**.
Gor. 28/1—11/2/33.**G**.
Altered to LNE gauge.
Gor. 30/3—13/4/35.**G**.
Gor. 20/3—3/4/37.**G**.
Gor. 21—30/10/37.**L**.
Trip cock gear fitted.
Gor. 9—25/4/42.**G**.
Gor. 16/12/44—17/3/45.**G**.
New cylinders.
Gor. 21/2—20/3/48.**G**.
Gor. 26/4—3/5/52.**G**.
Gor. 3—31/3/56.**G**.
Gor. 10/2/60. *Not repaired.*

BOILERS:
955 15/10/04.
1168 *(ex 753)* 17/10/08.
1564 *(new)* 19/6/15.
17 *(new)* 11/12/20.
29 *(ex 5173)* 24/7/26.
120 *(ex 5517)* 4/5/29.
1747 *(exJ9 5658)* 11/2/33.
426 *(exN4 5606)* 3/4/37.
322 *(exJ10 5095)* 25/4/42.
249 *(ex 9318)* 20/3/48.
22754 *(ex 69360)* 3/5/52.
22800 *(ex 69310)* 31/3/56.

SHEDS:
Annesley 2/10/15.
King's Cross 19/4/34.
Hatfield 4/5/34.
Hornsey 17/7/35.
Hatfield 5/10/35.
Gorton 4/4/37.
Neasden 1/11/37 (LPTB).
Neasden 17/4/38.
Retford 15/8/48.
Neasden 21/12/52.
Barnsley 30/9/56.
Mexborough 3/1/60.

RENUMBERED:
5930 26/1/24.
9354 11/8/46.
69354 20/3/48.

CONDEMNED: 12/2/60.
Cut up at Gorton 12/3/60.

5931

Beyer, Peacock 4191.

To traffic 5/1900.

REPAIRS:
Gor. 2/2—12/3/10.**G**.
Gor. 28/9—26/10/12.**G**.
Gor. 9/12/22—3/2/23.**G**.
Gor. 14/2—2/5/25.**G**.
Altered to LNE gauge.
Gor. 8/6—13/7/29.**G**.
Gor. 13—27/8/32.**G**.
New cylinders.
Gor. 25/7—8/8/36.**G**.
Gor. 10/2—2/3/40.**G**.
Heating app. both ends.
Gor. 17/10—7/11/42.**G**.
Gor. 26/1—16/2/46.**G**.
Gor. 2—23/10/48.**G**.
Gor. 1—29/12/51.**G**.
Gor. 27/11—18/12/54.**L/I**.

BOILERS:
773 12/3/10.
727 26/10/12.
1099 *(exJ10 5676)* 13/7/29.
409 *(ex 5938)* 27/8/32.
106 *(exN4 5611)* 8/8/36.
221 *(ex 5921)* 2/3/40.
222 *(ex 5899)* 7/11/42.
4274 *(exN4 5629)* 16/2/46.
4185 *(ex 9282)* 23/10/48.
22726 *(ex??)* 29/12/51.

SHEDS:
Heaton Mersey 18/1/13.
Neasden 10/3/23.
Gorton 6/8/36.
Barnsley 14/11/36.

RENUMBERED:
5931 2/5/25.
9355 25/8/46.
69355 23/10/48.

CONDEMNED: 21/4/58.
Cut up at Gorton 1/11/58.

5932

Beyer, Peacock 4192.

To traffic 5/1900.

REPAIRS:
Gor. 2/8—22/10/04.**G**.
Gor. 20/5—12/8/16.**G**.
New cylinders.
Gor. 12/8—21/10/22.**G**.
Gor. 20/2—24/4/26.**G**.
Gor. 21/9—19/10/29.**G**.
Gor. 27/8—3/9/32.**G**.
Altered to LNE gauge.
Gor. 1—22/9/34.**G**.
Gor. 5—19/2/38.**G**.
Gor. 24/7—9/8/41.**G**.
Gor. 15/4—6/5/44.**G**.
Gor. 4—25/10/47.**G**.
Gor. 27/5—10/6/50.**G**.
Gor. 28/2—14/3/53.**G**.

BOILERS:
563.
259 22/10/04.
1642 *(new)* 12/8/16.
1819 *(ex 5903)* 3/9/32.
479 *(new)* 22/9/34.
448 *(ex 5916)* 19/2/38.
4255 *(new)* 9/8/41.
498 *(ex 5904)* 6/5/44.
4186 *(exN4 9238)* 25/10/47.
405 *(ex 69280)* 10/6/50.
22810 *(ex 69281)* 14/3/53.

SHEDS:
Gorton 14/5/20.
Heaton Mersey 19/2/39.
Wrexham 15/4/45.
Walton-on-the-Hill 18/11/45.

RENUMBERED:
5932 24/4/26.
9356 17/3/46.
69356 19/3/49.

CONDEMNED: 18/2/57.
Cut up at Gorton 23/3/57.

5933

Beyer, Peacock 4193.

To traffic 5/1900.

REPAIRS:
Gor. 17/6—15/8/08.**G**.
Gor. 31/7—13/11/15.**G**.
Wrx. 15/9—21/12/22.**H**.
Gor. 4/7—26/9/25.**G**.
New cylinders.
Gor. 2—30/8/30.**G**.
Altered to LNE gauge.
Gor. 21—28/7/34.**G**.
Gor. 3—24/7/37.**G**.
Gor. 17/2—9/3/40.**G**.
Heating app. both ends.
Gor. 28/5—5/6/43.**G**.
Gor. 24/5—28/6/47.**G**.
Gor. 7—28/1/50.**G**.
Gor. 26/4—24/5/52.**G**.
Gor. 24—31/10/53.**C/L**.

BOILERS:
698 15/8/08.
1586 *(new)* 13/11/15.
1750 *(exD7 5565)* 30/8/30.
243 *(ex 5525)* 28/7/34.
459 *(exD7 5692)* 24/7/37.
4268 *(new)* 5/6/43.
4210 *(exN4 9230)* 28/1/50.
22759 *(ex??)* 24/5/52.

SHEDS:
Wrexham 8/1/16.
Chester *by* 1/1/23.
Wrexham 26/9/32.
Barnsley 31/3/38.
Mexborough 7/3/54.

RENUMBERED:
5933 26/9/25.
9357 31/3/46.
69357 28/1/50.

CONDEMNED: 11/11/55.
Cond. & cut up at Darlington.

5934

Beyer, Peacock 4194.

To traffic 5/1900.

REPAIRS:
Gor. 24/8—23/11/07.**G**.
Gor. 18/11/16—27/1/17.**G**.
Gor. 9/10—6/11/20.**G**.
Gor. 1/12/23—8/3/24.**G**.
Gor. 12/11—17/12/27.**G**.
Gor. 3—31/10/31.**G**.
Gor. 17—31/8/35.**G**.
Altered to LNE gauge.
Gor. 30/12/39—13/1/40.**G**.
Gor. 27/4—11/5/40.**L**.
Crank pin broken.
Gor. 28/6—24/7/43.**G**.
Gor. 29/3—3/5/47.**G**.
Gor. 14/10—4/11/50.**G**.
Gor. 14/3—4/4/53.**L/I**.

BOILERS:
446 23/11/07.
483 *(ex 517)* 27/1/17.
974 *(ex 5937)* 17/12/27.
1783 *(ex 5913)* 13/1/40.
501 *(ex 5898)* 24/7/43.
4204 *(exJ10 5181)* 3/5/47.
22664 *(ex??)* 4/11/50.

SHEDS:
Neasden 24/11/20.
Trafford Park 16/9/51.

RENUMBERED:
5934 8/3/24.
9358 7/4/46.
69358 4/11/50.

CONDEMNED: 5/11/56.
Cut up at Gorton 5/10/57.

In the two months when BRITISH RAILWAYS and the regional prefix E was in use during 1948, fourteen N5 acquired it: E9262 (5th March), E9272 (31st January), E9288 (13th March), E9289 (31st January), E9300 (24th January), E9310 (24th January), E9318 (21st February), E9319 (13th March), E9322 (24th January), E9328 (17th January), E9343 (6th March), E9349 (24th January), E9353 (28th February), E9370 (14th February). Note the change from transfers, but sizes and positions were unaltered.

With the change to figure 6 in place of E to the number, sizes remained at 7½in. and 12in. but positions were altered. All subsequent numbering was on the bunker, No.69361 being so treated ex works 24th April 1948. Note the modified LNER version of Gill sans 6 and 9.

No.69335 was ex works on 28th August 1948 and by then Gorton was using correct Gill sans 6 and 9 on the bunker with figures reduced in height to match letters on the tank. A smokebox number plate was fitted but had been cast with modified 6 and 9.

Further change had been made by 13th November 1948 when No.69341 was ex works. Letters and figures were both 10 inch, that height having become the BR standard. This style was then used until September 1949.

Under the LNER, this class was used frequently for local passenger work and so qualified for BR mixed traffic lined livery. On 19th June 1948 No.69366 was out with BR red, grey and cream lining, but was the only one done with BRITISH RAILWAYS on the tanks.

A further attempt to introduce lining was made in 1950. Ex works 4th February 1950, No.69317, and No.69325 on 10th June 1950, were lined out but no more were done, and by November 1952 all had reverted to unlined black.

From October 1949 the lettering was superseded by the BR emblem and all those then running except No.69252 (withdrawn 20th August 1951) and the single N5/3 No.69311 (*see* page 81, middle) were put into this style.

Although Gorton paint shop were using correct Gill sans 6 and 9 by August 1949 – *see* page 75, 3rd from top – many smokebox plates were cast with the LNER modified version, No.69275 being so fitted ex works on 19th March 1949, and No.69346 as late as 11th June 1949.

5935

Beyer, Peacock 4195.

To traffic 5/1900.

REPAIRS:
Gor. ?/?—14/12/07.**G.**
Gor. 26/10/18—26/4/19.**G.**
Wrx. 4/1—3/5/22.**H.**
Gor. 8/3—24/5/24.**G.**
New cylinders.
Gor. 7/7—4/8/28.**G.**
Gor. 26/3—9/4/32.**G.**
Altered to LNE gauge.
Gor. 28/3—11/4/36.**G.**
Gor. 12—26/8/39.**G.**
Gor. 3—20/6/42.**G.**
Gor. 3—14/10/44.**G.**
Gor. 29/11—20/12/47.**G.**
Gor. 22/4—6/5/50.**G.**
Gor. 7—21/2/53.**G.**

BOILERS:
1349 (*new*) 14/12/07.
921 *(exJ10 805)* 26/4/19.
1605 *(exJ10 5818)* 24/5/24.
1639 *(ex 5901)* 9/4/32.
4202 *(new)* 11/4/36.
563 *(ex 5902)* 26/8/39.
721 *(exJ10 5081)* 20/6/42.
4219 *(ex 5920)* 14/10/44.
4312 *(new)* 20/12/47.
4243 *(ex 9310)* 6/5/50.
22807 *(ex 69317)* 21/2/53.

SHEDS:
Wrexham ?/6/19.
Northwich *at* 4/30.
Gorton 27/6/35.
Heaton Mersey 20/9/39.

RENUMBERED:
5935 24/5/24.
9359 14/7/46.
69359 12/2/49.

CONDEMNED: 23/4/56.
Cut up at Gorton 26/5/56.

5936

Beyer, Peacock 4196.

To traffic 6/1900.

REPAIRS:
Gor. 8/12/06—1/6/07.**G.**
Gor. 21/2—4/4/14.**G.**
Gor. 29/1/21—11/2/22.**G.**
New cylinders.
Gor. 25/10—29/11/24.**G.**
Gor. 3/9—22/10/27.**G.**
Gor. 9/11—7/12/29.**G.**
Gor. 4—11/3/33.**G.**
Altered to LNE gauge.
Gor. 7—21/11/36.**G.**
Gor. 17/2—9/3/40.**G.**
Heating app. both ends.
Gor. 11—23/10/43.**G.**
Gor. 5—26/1/46.**G.**
Gor. 30/10—20/11/48.**G.**
Gor. 16/2—8/3/52.**G.**
Gor. 26/2—26/4/55.**G.**
Gor. 19/3/60. *Not repaired.*

BOILERS:
757 1/6/07.
603 *(ex 519)* 4/4/14.
194 *(ex 531)* 11/2/22.
249 *(new)* 11/3/33.
1767 *(ex 5753)* 21/11/36.
747 *(ex 5900)* 9/3/40.
1670 *(exJ10 5827)* 23/10/43.
4197 *(exJ10 5819)* 26/1/46.
4200 *(exN4 9237)* 20/11/48.
22743 *(ex 69277)* 8/3/52.
22703 *(ex 69283)* 26/4/55.

SHEDS:
Walton-on-the-Hill 30/6/22.
Gorton 22/12/28.
Trafford Park 11/9/33.
Gorton 24/1/34.
Sheffield 12/2/37.
Barnsley 27/7/37.
Sheffield 31/5/43.
Staveley 23/10/43.
Colwick 11/4/48.
Woodford 19/6/49.
Colwick 15/11/53.
Gorton 11/12/55.

RENUMBERED:
5936 29/11/24.
9360 18/8/46.
69360 20/11/48.

CONDEMNED: 17/3/60.
Cut up at Gorton 2/4/60.

5937

Beyer, Peacock 4197.

To traffic 6/1900.

REPAIRS:
Gor. 25/10—23/12/05.**G.**
Gor. 19/6—23/10/20.**G.**
Gor. 12/4—31/5/24.**G.**
Gor. 23/7—3/9/27.**G.**
Gor. 11/7—8/8/31.**G.**
Gor. 26/5—16/6/34.**G.**
Altered to LNE gauge.
New cylinders fitted.
Gor. 15/10—5/11/38.**G.**
Gor. 27/4—11/5/40.**L.**
After collision.
Gor. 10—27/2/43.**G.**
Gor. 22/9—13/10/45.**G.**
Gor. 3—24/4/48.**G.**
Gor. 11—25/3/50.**G.**
Gor. 23/8—6/9/52.**L/I.**
Gor. 20/8—17/9/55.**G.**

BOILERS:
911.
442 *(ex 906)* 23/12/05.
974 *(exN4 718)* 23/10/20.
632 *(exJ10 5809)* 3/9/27.
498 *(exJ10 5175)* 16/6/34.
289 *(exN4 5624)* 5/11/38.
4212 *(exN4 5611)* 27/2/43.
4283 *(new)* 13/10/45.
4206 *(ex 9328)* 24/4/48.
4334 *(new)* 25/3/50.
4334 reno.22778 6/9/52.
22753 *(ex 69336)* 17/9/55.

SHEDS:
Annesley 25/9/15.
Leicester 2/12/27.
Grantham 11/12/31.
Boston 4/8/32.
Lincoln 28/12/35.
Immingham 4/6/37.
Walton-on-the-Hill 19/12/39.
Gorton 26/7/41.
Trafford Park 31/5/43.
Sheffield 27/4/58.

RENUMBERED:
5937 31/5/24.
9361 20/7/46.
69361 24/4/48.

CONDEMNED: 8/6/59.
Cut up at Gorton 29/8/59.

5938

Beyer, Peacock 4198.

To traffic 6/1900.

REPAIRS:
Gor. 22/6—8/8/08.**G.**
Gor. 14/10—17/12/10.**G.**
Wrx. 8/5—10/8/22.**G.**
Gor. 7/7—29/9/23.**G.**
Wrx. 3/7—31/8/25.**G.**
Gor. 12/3—16/4/27.**G.**
Gor. 29/6—27/7/29.**G.**
Gor. 23—30/7/32.**G.**
Altered to LNE gauge.
Gor. 24—31/8/35.**G.**
Gor. 15—29/10/38.**G.**
Gor. 16—30/8/41.**G.**
Gor. 28/1—13/2/43.**G.**
New cylinders.
Gor. 1—22/9/45.**G.**
Gor. 8—29/11/47.**G.**
Gor. 6—20/5/50.**G.**
Gor. 30/8—20/9/52.**G.**
Gor. 12/2—12/3/55.**G.**

BOILERS:
998 8/8/08.
711 *(exF2 781)* 17/12/10.
409 *(exJ10 5817)* 16/4/27.
771 *(ex 5907)* 30/7/32.
173 *(exN4 5513)* 31/8/35.
1787 *(ex 5919)* 29/10/38.
448 *(ex 5932)* 30/8/41.
4282 *(new)* 22/9/45.
4194 *(exN4 9229)* 20/5/50.
22779 *(ex 69364)* 20/9/52.
22844 *(ex spare)* 12/3/55.

SHEDS:
Wrexham 2/12/21.
Gorton 26/6/29.
Wrexham 28/8/29.
Chester 20/12/29.
Wrexham 6/11/38.
Gorton 30/8/41.
Wrexham 2/12/41.

RENUMBERED:
938c 6/10/23.
5938 31/8/25.
9362 1/12/46.
69362 25/6/49.

CONDEMNED: 21/8/58.
Cut up at Gorton 13/9/58.

5939

Beyer, Peacock 4199.

To traffic 7/1900.

REPAIRS:
Gor. 9/6—9/7/10.**G.**
Gor. 10/6—9/9/16.**G.**
Gor. 30/10/20—8/1/21.**G.**
New cylinders.
Gor. 19/4—30/8/24.**G.**
Gor. 13/8—1/10/27.**G.**
Gor. 20/9—25/10/30.**G.**
Altered to LNE gauge.
Gor. 9—23/12/33.**G.**
Gor. 31/12/35—18/1/36.**G.**
Heating app. both ends.
Gor. 4—25/6/38.**G.**
Gor. 8—22/2/41.**G.**
Gor. 14/3—1/4/44.**G.**
Gor. 21/12/46—11/1/47.**G.**
Gor. 21/5—11/6/49.**G.**
Gor. 26/7—16/8/52.**G.**
New cylinders.
Gor. 19—26/8/52.**N/C.**

5939 cont./
BOILERS:
286 9/7/10.
1640 *(new)* 9/9/16.
1123 *(exD7 5563)* 30/8/24.
471 *(exJ9 5738)* 1/10/27.
428 *(new)* 25/10/30.
458 *(exJ9 5742)* 23/12/33.
1771 *(ex 5910)* 18/1/36.
573 *(ex 5759)* 25/6/38.
162 *(ex 5916)* 22/2/41.
4252 *(ex 5916)* 1/4/44.
4191 *(exN4 9233)* 11/1/47.
1230 *(ex 9264)* 11/6/49.
22774 *(ex 69306)* 16/8/52.

SHEDS:
Annesley 22/3/13.
Langwith Jct. 13/2/29.
Leicester 8/11/34.
Langwith Jct. 4/2/36.
Staveley 17/12/38.

RENUMBERED:
5939 30/8/24.
9363 22/9/46.
69363 11/6/49.

CONDEMNED: 9/7/56.
Cut up at Gorton 18/8/56.

5940

Beyer, Peacock 4200.

To traffic 7/1900.

REPAIRS:
Gor. ?/?—18/7/03.**G**.
Gor. 25/10/04—?/?.**G**.
Gor. ?/?—?/9/06.**L**.
Eyres patent buffers fitted.
Gor. ?/?—21/11/08.**G**.
Wrx. 27/12/17—2/8/18.**G**.
Gor. 15/5—9/10/20.**G**.
Gor. 17/5—5/7/24.**G**.
New cylinders.
Gor. 12/3—7/5/27.**G**.
Gor. 8—29/3/30.**G**.
Gor. 27/5—10/6/33.**G**.
Altered to LNE gauge.
Gor. ?—?/7/36.**L**.
Heating app. both ends.
Gor. 3—17/10/36.**G**.
Gor. 18—25/11/39.**G**.
Gor. 20—29/5/43.**G**.
Gor. 12—30/9/44.**G**.
Gor. 22/11—13/12/47.**G**.
Gor. 11/2—4/3/50.**G**.
Gor. 21/6—5/7/52.**G**.
Gor. 16—30/5/53.**C/L**.

BOILERS:
757 18/7/03.
1081 ?/?/04.
955 *(ex 930)* 21/11/08.
432 *(exJ13 570)* 9/10/20.
178 *(ex 5942)* 10/6/33.
1917 *(ex 5897)* 17/10/36.
437 *(exJ10 5103)* 25/11/39.
393 *(ex 5943)* 29/5/43.
4259 *(ex 5523)* 30/9/44.
4316 *(exN4 69236)* 4/3/50.
22769 *(exN4 69242)* 5/7/52.

SHEDS:
Gorton 3/11/20.
Heaton Mersey 7/1/28.
Gorton 23/10/39.
Trafford Park 18/12/40.

RENUMBERED:
5940 5/7/24.
9364 13/10/46.
69364 29/1/49.

CONDEMNED: 8/8/55.
Cut up at Gorton 24/9/55.

5941

Beyer, Peacock 4248.

To traffic 2/1901.

REPAIRS:
Gor. 27/4—4/6/10.**G**.
Gor. 9/5—20/6/14.**G**.
YECo. 19/3—30/6/21.**G**.
Gor. 19/8—7/10/22.**G**.
Gor. 22/11/24—3/1/25.**G**.
New cylinders.
Gor. 10/3—14/4/28.**G**.
Gor. 16/8—27/9/30.**G**.
Gor. 30/9—14/10/33.**G**.
Altered to LNE gauge.
Gor. 30/5—13/6/36.**G**.
Gor. 9—23/3/40.**G**.
Heating app. both ends.
Gor. 1—16/10/43.**G**.
New cylinders.
Gor. 26/4—24/5/47.**G**.
Gor. 2—30/4/49.**C/L**.
Gor. 2—16/9/50.**G**.
Gor. 14/2—7/3/53.**G**.
Gor. 9/2/57. *Not repaired.*

BOILERS:
1350 *(new)* 4/6/10.
654 *(ex 548)* 30/6/21.
221 *(exN4 5720)* 14/4/28.
1384 *(ex 5914)* 14/10/33.
1647 *(exJ10 5098)* 13/6/36.
4222 *(ex 5251)* 16/10/43.
501 *(ex 9358)* 24/5/47.
22654 *(ex??)* 16/9/50.
22809 *(ex??)* 7/3/53.

SHEDS:
Walton-on-the-Hill 29/6/10.
Gorton 13/6/36.
Sheffield 20/4/37.
Barnsley 30/7/37.

RENUMBERED:
5941 3/1/25.
9365 1/12/46.
69365 30/4/49.

CONDEMNED: 9/2/57.
Cut up at Darlington.

5942

Beyer, Peacock 4249.

To traffic 2/1901.

REPAIRS:
Gor. ?/?—16/5/03.**G**.
Gor. 28/3—9/5/14.**G**.
Gor. 15/11/19—3/1/20.**G**.
Gor. 31/3—12/5/23.**G**.
Gor. 9/10—18/12/26.**G**.
Gor. 18/1—15/2/30.**G**.
Gor. 29/4—13/5/33.**G**.
Altered to LNE gauge.
Gor. 21/3—11/4/36.**G**.
Gor. 1—15/4/39.**G**.
Gor. 20—30/1/43.**G**.
Gor. 11/5—1/6/46.**G**.
Gor. 22/5—19/6/48.**G**.
Gor. 18/2—4/3/50.**G**.
Gor. 3—24/11/51.**C/L**.
Gor. 13—27/9/52.**G**.
Gor. 25/12/54—22/1/55.**G**.

BOILERS:
715 16/5/03.
12 *(exJ10 788)* 9/5/14.
178 *(exJ9 5743)* 18/12/26.
194 *(ex 5936)* 13/5/33.
4201 *(new)* 11/4/36.
770 *(ex 5548)* 15/4/39.
4225 *(ex 5539)* 30/1/43.
316 *(ex 5771)* 1/6/46.
4271 *(exN4 9227)* 19/6/48.
4268 *(ex 9357)* 4/3/50.
4268 reno.22719 24/11/51.
22784 *(ex 69319)* 27/9/52.
22843 *(ex 69351)* 22/1/55.

SHEDS:
Neasden 5/12/14.
Gorton 20/12/26.
Trafford Park 7/1/28.
Gorton 1/1/29.
Brunswick 31/8/34.
Gorton 21/9/39.
Wrexham 14/8/43.
Gorton 17/1/45.
Wrexham 4/9/46.

RENUMBERED:
5942 18/12/26.
9366 1/12/46.
69366 19/6/48.

CONDEMNED: 6/8/56.
Cut up at Gorton 15/9/56.

5943

Beyer, Peacock 4250.

To traffic 2/1901.

REPAIRS:
Gor. 10/1—28/3/14.**G**.
Gor. 27/5—1/7/16.**G**.
Gor. 10/3—19/5/23.**G**.
Gor. 21/8—13/11/26.**G**.
New cylinders.
Gor. 25/10—15/11/30.**G**.
Gor. 24/2—10/3/34.**G**.
Altered to LNE gauge.
Gor. 6—20/3/37.**G**.
Gor. 2—16/3/40.**G**.
Heating app. both ends.
Gor. 10—24/4/43.**G**.
Gor. 9—30/11/46.**G**.
Gor. 21/8/48.**L**.
Gor. 5/2/49.**C/L**.
Gor. 15—29/10/49.**G**.
New cylinders.
Gor. 28/6—26/7/52.**G**.

BOILERS:
672.
556 *(ex 920)* 28/3/14.
1197 *(ex 746)* 19/5/23.
131 *(exJ10 5832)* 15/11/30.
747 *(exJ10 5828)* 10/3/34.
393 *(ex 5173)* 20/3/37.
4250 *(exJ10 5819)* 24/4/43.
167 *(exJ10 5675)* 30/11/46.
4183 *(exF2 7106)* 29/10/49.
22770 *(exN4 69236)* 26/7/52.

SHEDS:
Gorton 3/11/20.
Trafford Park 7/1/28.
Gorton 1/1/29.
Wrexham 21/1/31.
Chester 1/11/36.
Gorton 3/12/36.
Colwick 3/4/37.
Sheffield 17/11/37.
Barnsley 30/5/38.

RENUMBERED:
5943 13/11/26.
9367 26/8/46.
69367 21/8/48.

CONDEMNED: 4/11/55.
Cond. & cut up at Darlington.

5944

Beyer, Peacock 4251.

To traffic 2/1901.

REPAIRS:
Gor. 8/8—5/9/14.**G**.
Gor. 10/6—19/8/22.**G**.
New cylinders.
Gor. 7/3—25/4/25.**G**.
Gor. 12/11—17/12/27.**G**.
Gor. 25/1—15/2/30.**G**.
Altered to LNE gauge.
Gor. 13—27/5/33.**G**.
Gor. 6—20/6/36.**G**.
Gor. 16/12/39—6/1/40.**G**.
Heating app. both ends.
Gor. 14—29/5/43.**G**.
Gor. 9—23/2/46.**G**.
Gor. 4—25/9/48.**G**.
Gor. 17/11—8/12/51.**G**.
Gor. 6/6—11/7/53.**C/H**.
New cylinders.

BOILERS:
744.
574 *(new)* 5/9/14.
1689 *(exN4 5613)* 17/12/27.
15 *(exN4 5608)* 15/2/30.
1197 *(ex 5051)* 27/5/33.
304 *(ex 5914)* 20/6/36.
105 *(ex 5750)* 6/1/40.
4253 *(ex 5907)* 29/5/43.
951 *(ex 5519)* 23/2/46.
4221 *(ex 9267)* 25/9/48.
22722 *(new reno. from 4339)* 8/12/51.

SHEDS:
Wrexham 17/3/22.
Chester *by* 26/10/23.
Wrexham 20/12/29.
Gorton 9/1/30.
Barnsley 23/1/34.

RENUMBERED:
5944 25/4/25.
9368 12/1/47.
69368 25/9/48.

CONDEMNED: 2/5/55.
Cut up at Gorton 2/7/55.

5945

Beyer, Peacock 4252.

To traffic 3/1901.

REPAIRS:
Gor. 19/6—31/7/09.**G**.
YECo. 9/4—28/6/21.**G**.
Gor. 8/11—13/12/24.**G**.
Gor. 3/11—8/12/28.**G**.
Gor. 26/9—17/10/31.**G**.
Altered to LNE gauge.
Gor. 7—21/3/36.**G**.
Gor. 3/2—2/3/40.**G**.
Heating app. both ends.
Gor. 28/6—10/7/43.**G**.
Gor. 8/11—6/12/47.**G**.
Gor. 9—23/12/50.**G**.
Gor. 17—31/10/53.**G**.

BOILERS:
657.
604 31/7/09.
1065 *(ex 762)* 28/6/21.
1797 *(exJ10 5829)* 17/10/31.
196 *(ex 5767)* 21/3/36.
378 *(exN4 5629)* 10/7/43.
4245 *(exJ10 5191)* 6/12/47.
22675 *(exN4 69227)* 23/12/50.
22654 *(ex 69365)* 31/10/53.

SHEDS:
Gorton 19/1/17.
Neasden *by* 17/8/24.
Woodford 24/1/29.
Neasden 27/1/32.
Sheffield 12/12/54.
Boston 30/10/55.
Immingham 11/3/56.

RENUMBERED:
5945 13/12/24.
9369 5/1/47.
69369 23/12/50.

CONDEMNED: 2/2/57.
Cut up at Darlington.

5946

Beyer, Peacock 4253.

To traffic 3/1901.

REPAIRS:
Gor. 21/7/17—16/2/18.**G**.
Gor. 28/2—16/10/20.**G**.
New cylinders.
Gor. 17/5—28/6/24.**G**.
Gor. 26/2—9/4/27.**G**.
Gor. 10—31/8/29.**G**.
Gor. 12—31/12/31.**G**.
Altered to LNE gauge.
Gor. 28/7—11/8/34.**G**.
Gor. 19—31/12/36.**G**.
Gor. 6—20/1/40.**G**.
Heating app. both ends.
Gor. 16—30/1/43.**G**.
Gor. 23/6—7/7/45.**G**.
Gor. 17/1—14/2/48.**G**.
Gor. 4—25/3/50.**G**.
Gor. 2—23/6/51.**G**.
New cylinders.
Gor. 28/6—5/7/52.**C/L**.
After collision.
Gor. 14/11—5/12/53.**G**.
Gor. 25/8—29/9/56.**G**.

BOILERS:
634.
1716 *(new)* 16/2/18.
190 *(exJ12 505B)* 16/10/20.
1896 *(exJ13 5573)* 31/12/31.
727 *(ex 5894)* 11/8/34.
401 *(ex 5528)* 31/12/36.
357 *(ex 5173)* 20/1/40.
4223 *(exN4 5622)* 30/1/43.
510 *(exJ10 5792)* 7/7/45.
4193 *(ex 9310)* 14/2/48.
4301 *(exN4 9231)* 25/3/50.
22699 *(ex??)* 23/6/51.
22830 *(exJ10 65163)* 5/12/53.
22807 *(ex 69359)* 29/9/56.

SHEDS:
Gorton 3/11/20.
Wrexham 4/1/28.
Bidston 7/3/28.
Wrexham 31/10/28.
Gorton 31/7/29.
Trafford Park 9/2/40.
Wrexham 28/10/45.
Trafford Park 18/11/45.
Sheffield 27/4/58.
Barnsley 22/6/58.
Mexborough 3/1/60.

RENUMBERED:
5946 28/6/24.
9370 24/11/46.
E9370 14/2/48.
69370 29/1/49.

CONDEMNED: 10/9/60.
Cut up at Doncaster.

The earliest noted with correct Gill sans 6 and 9 on the plate was No.69330, ex works 24th September 1949, one of the very few with correct figures and BRITISH RAILWAYS on the tanks.

It is not known whether No.69274 has been altered to 89274 by mistake or by some misguided enthusiast. Note that it is in service and carrying lamps at both ends, also that the maker's plate is still on the cab side.

Ex works on 6th November 1915, No.771 had not long been fitted with a superheater but also with long tanks, new cab and extended bunker which permitted an extra 640 gallons of water and one ton of coal to be carried. The purpose was to work the shuttle service between Chester and Shotton, there being no water column at Shotton. It worked fourteen months on that service but then reverted almost entirely to goods duties. In March 1916 an Intensifore lubricator was put on.

The LNER brought it within the 13ft 0in. loading gauge from 9th June 1928 and at its next repair – 20th September to 25th October 1930 – changed its boiler to non-superheated type but the long tanks and extended smokebox were retained.

Further small changes were replacement (from 17th February 1934) of the Intensifore lubricator by Wakefield sight feed type, and removal of the safety valve casing.

During the 1939-45 war a pair of bar iron footsteps were added at the front end. Ex works 27th April 1946, the NE carried from 11th March 1944 became LNER in 12 inch letters and its number became 9311. From then on, safety valves were Ross 'pop' type.

This engine had only one further repair. When ex works 28th August 1948 it was 69311 with the number moved to the bunker but with correct Gill sans 6 and 9 included. The plate on the smokebox door had been cast with modified version. Note upper lamp iron has been moved on to the door and a second handle had replaced the wheel for fastening.

Apart from details, this odd engine substantially retained the same appearance from its November 1915 rebuilding to 4th February 1952 withdrawal. It was the only N5 so altered.

Ten further engines, Nos.19 to 28, and built by Kitson & Co. for the LD&ECR from July 1899, were taken over by the GCR on 1st January 1907 and then renumbered 1159 to 1168 but in 1920 Nos.1164 to 1168 became GCR Nos.40 to 43 and 66. From 1903 all had their fireboxes changed to the Belpaire type. Note taper shank buffers, smokebox door with hinge straps, and two handles for fastening, also wing plates with lamp irons on them, and built-up chimney, all of which changed later. The lamp iron on the chimney was temporary for this special September 1906 Royal train working.

From 1907, Gorton built the replacement boilers, and the washout plugs were on the shoulders of the firebox and the safety valves had direct mounting, but never had the GCR type casing, and after Grouping, few had the circular cover around their base.

CLASS N 6

1145B/6414

Kitson 3605.

To traffic 9/1895.

REPAIRS:
Tux. ?/?—6/3/11.**G**.
Tux. 14/5—23/6/15.**G**.
Tux. 10/4—16/5/18.**G**.
Tux. 14/10—18/11/20.**G**.
Tux. 25/4—22/6/23.**G**.
Tux. 12/3—1/5/25.**G**.
Don. 16/10—10/12/27.**G**.
Don. 25/3—27/4/29.**G**.
Gor. 5—31/12/31.**G**.
Gor. 1—29/9/34.**G**.
Gor. 25/10/38. *Not repaired.*

BOILERS:
1109 *(new)* 6/3/11.
540 *(new)* 23/6/15.
1730 *(new)* 16/5/18.
1914 *(new)* 18/11/20.
461 *(new)* 22/6/23.
256 *(ex6156)* 1/5/25.
258 *(ex5043)* 10/12/27.
1730 *(ex5043)* 27/4/29.
1728 *(ex6156)* 31/12/31.
116 *(new)* 29/9/34.

SHEDS:
Langwith Junction.
Tuxford 12/9/35.

RENUMBERED:
1
1145B 1907.
6414 1/5/25.

CONDEMNED: 25/10/38.
Sent to Don. Cut up 21/1/39.

1146B/6413

Kitson 3606.

To traffic 9/1895.

REPAIRS:
Tux. 1/4—14/5/15.**G**.
Tux. 22/11—20/12/17.**G**.
Tux. 29/8—31/12/19.**G**.
Tux. 18/7—13/10/21.**G**.
Tux. 25/7—3/9/23.**G**.
Tux. 25/6—17/8/25.**G**.
Don. 19/11—29/12/28.**G**.
Don. 2/2—7/3/31.**G**.

BOILERS:
1363 *(ex41)* 14/5/15.
144 *(ex43)* 20/12/17.
569 *(ex1147B)* 31/12/19.
635 *(ex1155)* 3/9/23.
1728 *(ex6155)* 17/8/25.
1914 *(ex6159)* 29/12/28.

SHED:
Tuxford.

RENUMBERED:
2
1146B 1907.
6413 17/8/25.

CONDEMNED: 13/2/34.
Into Gorton 17/2/34.
Cut up at Doncaster 28/4/34.

1147B/6412

Kitson 3607.

To traffic 11/1895.

REPAIRS:
Tux. ?/?—14/2/14.**G**.
Tux. 28/1—15/3/16.**G**.
Tux. 25/5—3/7/17.**G**.
Tux. 12/4—30/5/19.**G**.
Tux. 7/1—15/3/21.**G**.
Tux. 29/11/22—2/2/23.**G**.
Tux. 19/8—2/10/24.**G**.
Tux. 15/1—26/2/27.**G**.
Don. 11/5—1/9/28.**G**.
Gor. 6/6—11/7/31.**G**.
Gor. 30/12/33—27/1/34.**G**.

BOILERS:
753 14/2/14.
143 *(new)* 15/3/16.
569 *(ex1162)* 3/7/17.
969 *(ex1160)* 30/5/19.
1728 *(ex1160)* 15/3/21.
1730 *(ex1163)* 2/2/23.
210 *(ex5041)* 2/10/24.
569 *(ex5041)* 26/2/27.
259 *(ex6158)* 1/9/28.
143 *(ex6162)* 11/7/31.
8217 *(ex6155)* 27/1/34.

SHEDS:
Langwith Junction.
Leicester 1/1/35.
Langwith Junction 12/1/35.

RENUMBERED:
3
1147B 1907.
6412 2/10/24.

CONDEMNED: 22/6/36.
Into Gorton 27/6/36.
Cut up at Doncaster 23/1/37.

6154

Kitson 3608.

To traffic 10/1895.

REPAIRS:
Tux. 3—30/9/08.**G**.
Tux. 9—24/2/10.**G**.
Belpaire boiler fitted.
Tux. 10/4—6/5/11.**G**.
Tux. 3/2—13/3/13.**G**.
Tux. 18—30/4/14.**L**.
Tux. 23/7—4/9/14.**G**.
Tux. 12/4—17/5/16.**G**.
Tux. 23/3—2/5/17.**G**.
Tux. 11/6—22/7/18.**G**.
Tux. 17/12/19—27/2/20.**G**.
Tux. 16/12/21—22/2/22.**G**.
Tux. 5/11—5/12/23.**G**.
Tux. 4/6—3/7/25.**G**.
Tux. 22/1—26/2/27.**G**.
Don. 9/4—4/5/29.**G**.
Gor. 25/7—29/8/31.**G**.

BOILERS:
146 24/2/10.
726 *(ex1158)* 6/5/11.
967 *(ex1159)* 13/3/13.
216 *(ex1156)* 4/9/14.
1380 *(ex66)* 2/5/17.
567 *(ex1157)* 22/7/18.
143 *(ex1156)* 22/2/22.
1380 *(ex1157)* 5/12/23.
1109 *(ex6162)* 3/7/25.
1291 *(ex6156)* 26/2/27.
569 *(ex6412)* 4/5/29.
461 *(ex6157)* 29/8/31.

SHED:
Langwith Junction.

RENUMBERED:
4
1154 1907.
6154 3/7/25.

CONDEMNED: 2/8/34.
Into Gorton 4/8/34.
Cut up at Doncaster 13/10/34.

6155

Kitson 3609.

To traffic 11/1895.

REPAIRS:
Tux. 31/7—31/8/08.**G**.
Tux. 6—29/7/10.**G**.
Tux. 9/8—5/9/12.**G**.
Tux. 3/4—7/5/14.**G**.
Tux. 16/11/16—9/1/17.**G**.
Tux. 7—28/10/18.**G**.
Tux. 11/8—15/9/20.**G**.
Tux. 13/2—25/3/23.**G**.
Tux. 26/9—7/11/24.**G**.
Tux. 3/2—29/3/26.**G**.
Don. 23/7—1/10/27.**G**.
Don. 23/10—16/11/29.**G**.
Gor. 18/2—18/3/33.**G**.
Gor. 21/3/36. *Not repaired.*

BOILERS:
985 *(ex1163)* 29/7/10.
107 *(ex ?)* 5/9/12.
146 *(ex1154)* 7/5/14.
753 *(ex1147B)* 9/1/17.
540 *(ex1145B)* 28/10/18.
635 *(ex41)* 15/9/20.
1728 *(ex1147B)* 25/3/23.
1906 *(ex6160)* 7/11/24.
635 *(ex6413)* 29/3/26.
567 *(ex6162)* 1/10/27.
8217 *(new)* 16/11/29.
114 *(new)* 18/3/33.

SHEDS:
Langwith Junction.
Tuxford *in* 1932.
Langwith Junction *by* 1/1/35.

RENUMBERED:
5
1155 1907.
6155 7/11/24.

WORKS CODES:- Cow - Cowlairs. Dar - Darlington. Don - Doncaster. Gor - Gorton. RSH - Robert, Stephenson & Hawthorn. Str - Stratford. Tux - Tuxford. YECo - Yorkshire Engine Co.
REPAIR CODES:- **C/H** - Casual Heavy. **C/L** - Casual Light. **G** - General. **H**- Heavy. **H/I** - Heavy Intermediate. **L** - Light. **L/I** - Light Intermediate. **N/C** - Non-Classified.

By Grouping, all had lost smokebox wing plates and lamp irons were in the usual position above the buffer beam.

When given the GCR numbers, the original rectangular plate on the bunker was replaced by the oval Robinson type plate.

All the boilers built and used until 1929 were fitted with open safety valves of the Ramsbottom type.

During June and July 1929 Doncaster built three boilers for renewals and they were fitted with Ross 'pop' valves. The engines which carried them were Nos.6155 (November 1929 to February 1933); 6157 (February 1933 to August 1935); 6158 (December 1929 to October 1932); 6160 (July 1932 to August 1935); 6162 (October 1929 to March 1932); 6412 (January 1934 to June 1936).

Two more renewal boilers were built in January/February 1933 but at Gorton and they also had Ross 'pops'; they were used on Nos.6155 (March 1933 to March 1936) and 6414 (September 1934 to October 1938).

By the LNER takeover, hinge straps on the smokebox door had all but disappeared. No.1146B, here seen on 14th April 1923, was probably the last to have them – until it went for repair on 25th July 1923. From 1924/25, Nos.1147B, 1146B, and 1145B were renumbered 6412, 6413 and 6414 respectively.

6155 cont./
CONDEMNED: 21/3/36.
Cut up at Doncaster 23/5/36.

6156

Kitson 3610.

To traffic 11/1895.

REPAIRS:
Tux. 31/3—28/5/09.**G.**
Tux. 25/4—15/6/10.**G.**
Belpaire boiler and new cylinders fitted.
Tux. 21/6—2/8/12.**G.**
Tux. 24/4—11/6/14.**G.**
Tux. 4/4—2/5/16.**G.**
Tux. 2/1—28/2/18.**G.**
Tux. 13/10—26/11/19.**G.**
Tux. 6/7—17/8/21.**G.**
Tux. 23/2—13/4/23.**G.**
Tux. 11/12/24—29/1/25.**G.**
Tux. 23/4—7/7/26.**G.**
Don. 24/11/27—14/1/28.**G.**
Don. 11/5—15/6/29.**G.**
Gor. 5/9—10/10/31.**G.**
Gor. 15/9/34. *Not repaired.*

BOILERS:
1363 *(new)* 15/6/10.
216 *(ex1162)* 2/8/12.
1291 *(ex1157)* 11/6/14.
971 *(ex1158)* 2/5/16.
143 *(ex1157)* 26/11/19.
529 *(ex42)* 17/8/21.
256 *(new)* 13/4/23.
1291 *(ex6159)* 29/1/25.
1380 *(ex6154)* 7/7/26.
210 *(ex6412)* 14/1/28.
1728 *(ex6413)* 15/6/29.
569 *(ex6154)* 10/10/31.

SHED:
Langwith Junction.

RENUMBERED:
6
1156 1907.
6156 29/1/25.

CONDEMNED: 17/9/34.
Cut up at Doncaster 27/10/34.

6157

Kitson 3611.

To traffic 12/1895.

REPAIRS:
Tux. 23/8—19/9/10.**G.**
Tux. 28/9—21/10/12.**G.**
Tux. 14/3—3/4/14.**G.**
Tux. 22/11/15—18/1/16.**G.**
Tux. 8/8—9/10/17.**G.**
Tux. 4/7—29/9/19.**G.**
Tux. 2/11—13/12/21.**G.**
Tux. 22/6—27/7/23.**G.**
Tux. 29/1—11/3/25.**G.**
Don. 27/4—9/6/28.**G.**
Don. 7/7—2/8/30.**G.**
Gor. 14/1—4/2/33.**G.**

BOILERS:
416 19/9/10.
1291 *(ex43)* 21/10/12.
635 *(ex43)* 3/4/14.
567 *(ex1160)* 18/1/16.
143 *(ex1147B)* 9/10/17.
210 *(ex42)* 29/9/19.
1380 *(ex1159)* 13/12/21.
529 *(ex1156)* 27/7/23.
1907 *(ex6163)* 11/3/25.
461 *(ex5040)* 9/6/28.
464 *(ex6158)* 2/8/30.
8218 *(ex6158)* 4/2/33.

SHED:
Tuxford.

RENUMBERED:
7
1157 1907.
6157 11/3/25.

CONDEMNED: 7/8/35.
Into Gorton 10/8/35.
Cut up at Doncaster 28/9/35.

6158

Kitson 3612.

To traffic 12/1895.

REPAIRS:
Tux. 9—28/1/09.**G.**
Tux. 16/3—15/4/10.**G.**
Tux. 19/7—19/8/12.**G.**
Tux. 7/2—20/3/14.**G.**
Tux. 24/8—22/9/15.**G.**
Tux. 30/6—2/8/17.**G.**
Tux. 17/5—30/6/19.**G.**
Tux. 14/12/21—22/5/22.**G.**
Tux. 30/4—5/6/24.**G.**
Don. 24/6—20/8/27.**G.**
Don. 11/11—7/12/29.**G.**
Gor. 22/10—19/11/32.**G.**

BOILERS:
726 28/1/09.
1290 *(ex42)* 19/8/12.
971 *(ex42)* 20/3/14.
1109 *(ex1145B)* 22/9/15.
1353 *(ex1163)* 2/8/17.
1731 *(new)* 30/6/19.
259 *(ex5040)* 5/6/24.
464 *(ex6160)* 20/8/27.
8218 *(new)* 7/12/29.
258 *(ex6160)* 19/11/32.

SHEDS:
Tuxford.
Langwith Junction 8/3/30.

RENUMBERED:
8
1158 1907.
6158 5/6/24.

CONDEMNED: 14/11/35.
Into Gorton 16/11/35.
Cut up at Doncaster 7/3/36.

6159

Kitson 3903.

To traffic 7/1899.

REPAIRS:
Tux. 27/4—23/5/08.**G.**
Tux. 30/3—5/5/09.**G.**
Tux. 18/11—22/12/10.**G.**
Tux. 19/12/12—30/1/13.**G.**
Tux. 30/1—1/4/15.**G.**
Tux. 5/10—3/11/16.**G.**
Tux. 1—16/2/18.**G.**
Tux. 25/1—4/5/19.**G.**
Tux. 19/3—23/5/21.**G.**
Tux. 28/9—6/11/23.**G.**
Tux. 8/7—11/9/25.**G.**
Don. 11/4—23/6/28.**G.**
Don. 6/8—6/9/30.**G.**
Gor. 11/3—8/4/33.**G.**

BOILERS:
967 22/12/10.
996 *(ex1161)* 30/1/13.
706 *(ex40)* 1/4/15.
996 *(ex spare)* 3/11/16.
1380 *(ex1154)* 4/5/19.
1291 *(ex1163)* 23/5/21.
969 *(ex66)* 6/11/23.
1914 *(ex5043)* 11/9/25.
1109 *(ex6154)* 23/6/28.
464 *(ex6157)* 8/4/33.

SHEDS:
Langwith Junction.

RENUMBERED:
19
1159 1907.
6159 11/9/25.

CONDEMNED: 19/9/35.
Into Gorton 21/9/35.
Cut up at Doncaster 26/10/35.

6160

Kitson 3904.

To traffic 8/1899.

REPAIRS:
Tux. 4—20/5/09.**G.**
Tux. 1/4—10/5/11.**G.**
Tux. 13/9—22/10/13.**G.**
Tux. 20/6—21/7/15.**G.**
Tux. 10/10—6/11/17.**G.**
Tux. 3/12/18—17/1/19.**G.**
Tux. 25/8—13/10/20.**G.**
Tux. 27/11/22—22/1/23.**G.**
Tux. 12/7—18/8/24.**G.**
Tux. 10/10—17/12/26.**G.**
Don. 29/6—3/8/29.**G.**
Gor. 28/5—2/7/32.**G.**

BOILERS:
1025 20/5/09.
1380 *(new)* 10/5/11.
567 *(ex1163)* 22/10/13.
416 *(ex1161)* 21/7/15.
969 *(ex1161)* 6/11/17.
1728 *(new)* 17/1/19.
1732 *(ex1161)* 13/10/20.
1906 *(ex1161)* 22/1/23.
464 *(new)* 18/8/24.
1906 *(ex6155)* 17/12/26.
258 *(ex6414)* 3/8/29.
8219 *(ex6162)* 2/7/32.

SHED:
Tuxford.

RENUMBERED:
20
1160 1907.
6160 18/8/24.

CONDEMNED: 27/8/35.
Into Gorton 14/9/35.
Cut up at Doncaster 28/9/35.

6161

Kitson 3909.

To traffic 8/1899.

REPAIRS:
Tux. 6—24/12/09.**G.**
Tux. 12/5—29/6/11.**G.**
Tux. 9/11—18/12/12.**G.**
Tux. 1/12/14—7/1/15.**G.**
Tux. 18/8—13/11/16.**G.**
Tux. 5—19/9/17.**G.**
Tux. 20/8—13/9/18.**G.**
Tux. 7/6—9/8/20.**G.**
Tux. 22/5—23/10/22.**G.**
Tux. 26/3—12/5/24.**G.**
Tux. 2/7—15/9/26.**G.**

After the GC absorbed the LD&ECR the Kitson built-up chimney was soon replaced by this Robinson tapered casting, all being so fitted at Grouping and until maintenance passed from Doncaster to Gorton in September 1931. Nos.6160, 6161, 6163 and 6413 kept this type to withdrawal.

Although heights from rail, even with Robinson chimney, were all below 13ft 0in., from 1931 at least half the class had their chimney changed by Gorton to the 'plantpot' type.

Although No.6160, in July 1932, got a boiler with 'pop' safety valves, this did not involve change of chimney, as shown here on 21st July 1935 and it was withdrawn 27th August 1935.

Before Grouping all the original taper shank buffers had been replaced by parallel shank type with hollow spindle, and no further change of type was seen or recorded.

From new, a re-railing jack was carried on the right hand running plate as standard equipment but they were removed by the LNER. After Grouping they were only seen on Nos.1145B and 43 in 1923. But No.6157 was still so fitted in this 25th March 1931 photograph.

The original fitting of two open coal rails was not altered, and no plating was ever fitted to them.

6161 cont./
Don. 7/6—13/7/29.**G.**
Gor. 5/12/31—23/1/32.**G.**

BOILERS:
996 24/12/09.
416 *(ex1157)* 18/12/12.
210 *(ex66)* 7/1/15.
969 *(ex42)* 13/11/16.
529 *(ex42)* 19/9/17.
1732 *(new)* 13/9/18.
1906 *(new)* 9/8/20.
216 *(ex40)* 23/10/22.
143 *(ex6154)* 12/5/24.
1732 *(ex5066)* 15/9/26.
529 *(ex6162)* 13/7/29.

SHED:
Tuxford.

RENUMBERED:
21
1161 1907.
6161 12/5/24.

CONDEMNED: 29/5/35.
Into Gorton 1/6/35.
Cut up at Doncaster 20/7/35.

6162

Kitson 3910.

To traffic 9/1899.

REPAIRS:
Tux. 4/10—16/11/09.**G.**
Tux. 29/4—22/5/11.**G.**
Tux. 1/8—29/9/13.**G.**
Tux. 20/2—18/3/15.**G.**
Tux. 9—29/11/16.**G.**
Tux. 1—23/2/18.**G.**
Tux. 3/1—3/3/20.**G.**
Tux. 26/9—12/12/22.**G.**
Tux. 4/6—2/7/24.**G.**
Tux. 29/3—11/6/26.**G.**
Don. 24/11/27—28/1/28.**G.**
Don. 6/9—5/10/29.**G.**
Gor. 12/3—2/4/32.**G.**

BOILERS:
216 *(new)* 16/11/09.
1289 *(ex41)* 22/5/11.
1363 *(ex?)* 29/9/13.
569 *(new)* 18/3/15.
635 *(ex1157)* 29/11/16.
1109 *(ex1158)* 23/2/18.
985 *(ex66)* 3/3/20.
1109 *(ex41)* 12/12/22.
567 *(ex5043)* 2/7/24.
529 *(ex6157)* 11/6/26.
143 *(ex6161)* 28/1/28.
8219 *(new)* 5/10/29.
1730 *(ex6414)* 2/4/32.

SHED:
Langwith Junction.

RENUMBERED:
22
1162 1907.
6162 2/7/24.

CONDEMNED: 18/10/35.
Into Gorton 19/10/35.
Cut up at Doncaster 30/11/35.

6163

Kitson 3911.

To traffic 9/1899.

REPAIRS:
Tux. 19/2—16/3/09.**G.**
Tux. 15—24/5/10.**G.**
Tux. 4—30/8/11.**G.**
Tux. 16/5—15/7/13.**G.**
Tux. 18/12/14—6/2/15.**G.**
Tux. 18—24/3/16.**L.**
Tux. 15/3—23/4/17.**G.**
Tux. 15/3—15/4/19.**G.**
Tux. 4/2—15/3/21.**G.**
Tux. 28/8—9/11/22.**G.**
Tux. 20/6—25/7/24.**G.**
Tux. 10/6—1/10/26.**G.**
Don. 14/12/28—12/1/29.**G.**
Don. 10/3—4/4/31.**G.**
Gor. 8/9/33. *Not repaired.*

BOILERS:
985 16/3/09.
971 *(ex43)* 24/5/10.
567 *(ex66)* 30/8/11.
144 *(ex42)* 15/7/13.
1353 *(ex41)* 6/2/15.
1290 *(ex41)* 23/4/17.
1291 *(ex41)* 15/4/19.
1730 *(ex1145B)* 15/3/21.
1907 *(ex43)* 9/11/22.
466 *(new)* 25/7/24.
1907 *(ex6157)* 12/1/29.
1906 *(ex6160)* 4/4/31.

SHED:
Tuxford.

RENUMBERED:
23
1163 1907.
6163 25/7/24.

CONDEMNED: 8/9/33.
Cut up at Doncaster 30/12/33.

1164/5040

Kitson 3919.

To traffic 11/1900.

REPAIRS:
Tux. ?/?—4/4/13.**G.**
Tux. 18/7—14/8/14.**G.**
Tux. 12/5—17/6/16.**G.**
Tux. 6/3—19/4/18.**G.**
Tux. 23/1—31/3/20.**G.**
Tux. 31/3—15/6/22.**G.**
Tux. 7/12/23—18/1/24.**G.**
Tux. 20/10—20/11/25.**G.**
Don. 13/2—31/3/28.**G.**
Don. 11/12/29—14/1/30.**G.**
Gor. 11—25/2/33.**G.**

BOILERS:
706 4/4/13.
107 *(ex1155)* 14/8/14.
1289 *(ex43)* 17/6/16.
216 *(ex1154)* 19/4/18.
259 *(new)* 15/6/22.
540 *(ex5042)* 18/1/24.
461 *(ex6414)* 20/11/25.
1731 *(ex5066)* 31/3/28.
1732 *(ex6161)* 14/1/30.
466 *(ex5042)* 25/2/33.

SHED:
Langwith Junction.

RENUMBERED:
24
1164 1907.
40 19/6/20.
5040 20/11/25.

CONDEMNED: 19/9/35.
Into Gorton 21/9/35.
Cut up at Doncaster 26/10/35.

1165/5041

Kitson 3920.

To traffic 11/1900.

REPAIRS:
Tux. 30/1—19/2/09.**G.**
Tux. 12/12/10—14/1/11.**G.**
Tux. 31/1—19/2/13.**G.**
Tux. 9/6—1/7/14.**G.**
Tux. 31/8—25/9/16.**G.**
Tux. 8/5—7/6/18.**G.**
Tux. 20/2—2/7/20.**G.**
Tux. 11/5—8/9/22.**G.**
Tux. 28/2—14/4/24.**G.**
Tux. 5/2—23/4/26.**G.**
Don. 16/8—13/10/28.**G.**
Don. 28/8—19/9/30.**G.**
Gor. 25/11—16/12/33.**G.**

BOILERS:
1289 *(new)* 19/2/09.
1353 *(new)* 14/1/11.
1363 *(ex1156)* 19/2/13.
1290 *(ex1158)* 1/7/14.
1291 *(ex1156)* 25/9/16.
635 *(ex1162)* 7/6/18.
1109 *(ex1162)* 2/7/20.
210 *(ex1157)* 8/9/22.
569 *(ex6413)* 14/4/24.
540 *(ex5040)* 23/4/26.
1731 *(ex5040)* 19/9/30.
1732 *(ex5040)* 16/12/33.

SHEDS:
Tuxford.
Langwith Junction 18/12/30.

RENUMBERED:
25
1165 1907.
41 24/7/20.
5041 14/4/24.

CONDEMNED: 13/2/36.
Into Gorton 22/2/36.
Cut up at Doncaster 4/4/36.

1166/5042

Kitson 3921.

To traffic 11/1900.

REPAIRS:
Tux. 25/8—16/9/08.**G.**
Tux. 23/2—15/3/10.**G.**
Tux. 30/8—25/10/11.**G.**
Tux. 4/12/13—20/1/14.**G.**
Tux. 24/9—28/10/15.**G.**
Tux. 5/5—7/6/17.**G.**
Tux. 20/2—25/3/19.**G.**
Tux. 24/11/20—5/1/21.**G.**
Tux. 29/12/22—10/2/23.**G.**
Tux. 24/11—22/12/24.**G.**
Tux. 17/12/25—11/2/26.**G.**
Don. 16/2—9/4/27.**H.**
Don. 30/5—22/6/29.**G.**
Gor. 13/6—25/7/31.**G.**
Gor. 12/3—16/4/32.**L.**
Gor. 26/5—16/6/34.**G.**
Gor. 20/1/38. *Not repaired.*

BOILERS:
1290 *(new)* 16/9/08.
144 *(new)* 15/3/10.
971 *(ex1163)* 25/10/11.
969 *(ex66)* 20/1/14.
529 *(new)* 28/10/15.
210 *(ex1161)* 7/6/17.
529 *(ex1161)* 25/3/19.
540 *(ex1155)* 5/1/21.
258 *(new)* 10/2/23.
1730 *(ex6412)* 22/12/24.

Begun in late GCR years, sliding shutters to reduce the size of the cab opening continued to be fitted by the LNER.

Fitted originally with screw adjustable couplings so that they could work passenger trains, most had changed to 3-link loose type, but Nos.6157 and 6163 still had screw type as late as May 1931. Note load class 2 collar on the standpipe.

On all the renewal boilers built from 1907 the vacuum ejector exhaust pipe was through the boiler, even on those built in 1933 – *see* page 85, middle.

The fastening of the smokebox door began with two handles and at least No.6157 – *see* page 94, bottom – kept that type. But all did change to the GCR type plate hinge.

Some of the class were fitted with a more dished door and a wheel replaced the second fastening handle.

(below) **Those receiving LNER painting to September 1923 kept their GCR numbering even retaining duplicate letter B. No.1145B was ex Tuxford works so painted on 22nd June 1923.**

5042 cont./
969 *(ex6159)* 11/2/26.
466 *(ex6163)* 22/6/29.
1907 *(ex6163)* 25/7/31.
1731 *(ex5041)* 16/6/34.

SHEDS:
Langwith Junction *at* 8/21.
Tuxford *at* 1/1/28.

RENUMBERED:
26
1166 1907.
42 28/8/20.
5042 22/12/24.

CONDEMNED: 20/1/38.
Cut up at Doncaster 12/3/38.

1167/5043

Kitson 3922.

To traffic 11/1900.

REPAIRS:
Tux. ?/?—29/2/08.**G**.
Tux. 24/9—30/10/09.**G**.
Tux. 15/6—14/7/11.**G**.
Tux. 31/10—8/12/13.**G**.
Tux. 17/7—17/9/15.**G**.
Tux. 13/7—29/8/17.**G**.
Tux. 18/10—28/11/18.**G**.
Tux. 12/3—26/7/20.**G**.
Tux. 3/5—20/7/22.**G**.
Tux. 14/8—1/10/23.**G**.
Tux. 12/3—3/4/25.**G**.
Don. 1/4—14/5/27.**G**.
Don. 2/6—13/10/28.**G**.
Don. 7/4—2/5/31.**G**.
Gor. 21/7—11/8/34.**G**.

BOILERS:
971 *(new)* 29/2/08.
1291 *(new)* 30/10/09.
635 *(new)* 14/7/11.
1289 *(ex1162)* 8/12/13.
144 *(ex1163)* 17/9/15.
706 *(ex1159)* 29/8/17.
1289 *(ex40)* 28/11/18.
1907 *(new)* 26/7/20.
567 *(ex1154)* 20/7/22.
1914 *(ex1145B)* 1/10/23.
258 *(ex5042)* 3/4/25.
1730 *(ex5042)* 14/5/27.
256 *(ex6414)* 13/10/28.
1906 *(ex6163)* 11/8/34.

SHED:
Langwith Junction.

RENUMBERED:
27
1167 1907.
43 25/9/20.
5043 3/4/25.

CONDEMNED: 7/1/37.
Into Gorton 9/1/37.
Cut up at Doncaster 20/2/37.

1168/5066

Kitson 3923.

To traffic 11/1900.

REPAIRS:
Tux. ?/?—27/8/09.**G**.
Tux. 21/1—6/3/11.**G**.
Tux. 2/5—11/6/13.**G**.
Tux. 9/5—25/6/14.**G**.
Tux. 17/6—19/7/16.**G**.
Tux. 11/11—7/12/17.**G**.
Tux. 12/8—9/10/18.**L**.
Tux. 12/7—3/9/19.**G**.
Tux. 24/6—30/7/21.**G**.
Tux. 11—30/4/23.**G**.
Tux. 9/2—23/3/25.**G**.
Don. 9/12/26—15/1/27.**G**.
Don. 22/2—6/4/29.**G**.
Gor. 23/1—13/2/32.**G**.

BOILERS:
567 *(new)* 27/8/09.
969 *(new)* 6/3/11.
210 *(new)* 11/6/13.
1380 *(ex1160)* 25/6/14.
985 *(ex1155)* 19/7/16.
996 *(ex1159)* 3/9/19.
969 *(ex1147B)* 30/7/21.
1732 *(ex1160)* 30/4/23.
1731 *(ex6158)* 23/3/25.
216 *(ex6161)* 15/1/27.
259 *(ex6412)* 13/2/32.

SHED:
Tuxford.

RENUMBERED:
28
1168 1907.
66 23/10/20.
5066 23/3/25.

CONDEMNED: 2/11/34.
Into Gorton 3/11/34.
Cut up at Doncaster 15/12/34.

(below) **No.43, ex Tuxford on 1st October 1923 had single red lining on its black paint but most were treated as goods engines and only had plain black. Tuxford did not use either the ampersand, full points or area suffix C from evidence so far discovered.**

Early in 1924, those with capital list numbers were allocated the normal 5000 addition, and the large GC plate on the bunker was replaced by the smaller LNER type.

The three which had duplicate list numbers were cleared by making them Nos.6412, 6413 and 6414.

Tuxford works closed at the end of February 1927, Nos.6154 and 6412 being the last N6s repaired there, out on 26th February 1927, and in plain black.

All that were shopped at Doncaster and Gorton got unlined black, but late changes still took place. No.6157, ex Gorton 4th February 1933, lost its screw coupling – *see* page 91, top – and joined the others with 3-link type. This class was extinct when No.6414 was withdrawn on 25th October 1938, curiously the first of the class to be built.